AIMR Conference Proceedings
Improving the Investment Process through Risk Management

Proceedings of the AIMR seminar "Risk Management 2003: Quality Control of the Investment Process"

17–18 June 2003
Chicago

Leo J. de Bever
Damian Handzy
Peter S. Jarvis, CFA, *moderator*
Elizabeth MacElwee Jones
Michael J. O'Leary, Jr., CFA
Kent H. Osband
Bluford H. Putnam

Leslie Rahl
Jeffrey A. Rosenberg, CFA
Timothy J. Rudderow
Ronald J. Ryan, CFA
M. Barton Waring
D. Sykes Wilford

Association for Investment Management and Research

Dedicated to the Highest Standards of Ethics, Education, and Professional Practice in Investment Management and Research.

This proceedings qualifies for credit under the guidelines of the Professional Development Program. Using Reference Time, this proceedings qualifies for 4.5 credit hours. The self-test for this proceedings can be found at www.aimr.org/pdprogram/self-tests_list.html. For more information on the PD Program (including how to use Clock Time and the Standard Documentation in lieu of the self-test), go to www.aimr.org/pdprogram.

CFA®, Chartered Financial Analyst®, AIMR-PPS®, GIPS®, and Financial Analysts Journal® are just a few of the trademarks owned by the Association for Investment Management and Research®. To view a list of the Association for Investment Management and Research's trademarks and the Guide for Use of AIMR's Marks, please visit our website at www.aimr.org.

©2003, Association for Investment Management and Research

All rights reserved. No part of this publication may be reproduced, stored in a retrieval system, or transmitted, in any form or by any means, electronic, mechanical, photocopying, recording, or otherwise, without prior written permission of the copyright holder.

AIMR CONFERENCE PROCEEDINGS
(USPS 013-739 ISSN 1535-0207) 2003

Is published seven times a year in February, March, April, July, July, September, and November, by the Association for Investment Management and Research at 560 Ray C. Hunt Drive, Charlottesville, VA. **Periodical postage paid at Charlottesville, Virginia, and additional mailing offices.**

This publication is designed to provide accurate and authoritative information with regard to the subject matter covered. It is sold with the understanding that the publisher is not engaged in rendering legal, accounting, or other professional services. If legal advice or other expert assistance is required, the services of a competent professional should be sought.

Copies are mailed as a benefit of membership to CFA® charterholders. Subscriptions also are available at $100.00 USA. For one year. Address all circulation communications to AIMR Conference Proceedings, 560 Ray C. Hunt Drive, Charlottesville, Virginia 22903, USA; Phone 434-951-5499; Fax 434-951-5262. For change of address. Send mailing label and new address six weeks in advance.

Postmaster: Please send address changes to AIMR Conference Proceedings, Association for Investment Management and Research, P.O. Box 3668, Charlottesville, Virginia 22903.

ISBN 1-932495-05-3
Printed in the United States of America
November 14, 2003

Editorial Staff
Rodney N. Sullivan, CFA
Editor

Maryann Dupes
Book Editor

Rebecca L. Bowman
Assistant Editor

Roger Mitchell
Book Editor

Kara H. Morris
Production Manager

Sophia E. Battaglia
Assistant Editor

Kelly T. Bruton/Lois A. Carrier
Composition and Production

Contents

Authors.	v
Overview . . . . Peter S. Jarvis, CFA	1
Disaster Risk and Investment Guidelines . . . . Bluford H. Putnam	4
Risk Measurement versus Risk Management . . . . D. Sykes Wilford	17
The Dimensions of Active Management . . . . M. Barton Waring	22
Portfolio Risk Assessment Tools for Hedge Fund Managers. . . . . Timothy J. Rudderow	32
Risk Management for Alternative Investment Strategies. . . . . Leslie Rahl	41
Pension Fund Management: Addressing the Problem of Asset/Liability Mismatch. . . . . Ronald J. Ryan, CFA	52
Developing and Implementing a Risk-Budgeting System . . . . Leo J. de Bever	62
Techniques for Controlling Embedded Short Option Risk in Credit Securities . . . . Jeffrey A. Rosenberg, CFA	73
A Simplified Alternative to Monte Carlo Simulation . . . . Damian Handzy	86

Focus on Equity, Fixed Income, and Hedge Funds

www.aimr.org/featuring/ed_central/

Following is a sample of the wealth of information on Equity, Fixed Income, and Hedge Funds found in the Education Central area of AIMR's website.

Featured AIMR Publications
www.aimrpubs.org

Equity Portfolio Construction
(AIMR Conference Proceedings, 2002)

Hedge Fund Management
(AIMR Conference Proceedings, 2002)

Fixed-Income Management
(AIMR Conference Proceedings, 2003)

"The Mismeasurement of Risk"
Mark Kritzman and Don Rich
(*Financial Analysts Journal*, May/June 2002)

"Budgeting and Monitoring Pension Fund Risk"
William F. Sharpe
(*Financial Analysts Journal*, September/October 2002)

Featured Webcasts
www.aimrdirect.org

A Portfolio of Investment Challenges
Marc Faber, Kent H. Osband, Bryan Boudreau, CFA, and Fabio P. Savoldelli (July 2002)

Equity Topics: Highlights from the 2003 AIMR Annual Conference
Michael J. Brennan, Bruce A. Gulliver, CFA, Mark P. Kritzman, CFA, Terrance Odean, Lawrence S. Speidell, CFA, and David A. Zion, CFA (May 2003)

Hedge Fund Management Conference Highlights
Robert E. Kiernan III, Christianna Wood, CFA, Todd E. Petzel, Richard M. Ennis, CFA, George D. Oberhofer, Clifford S. Asness, Leslie Rahl, and Gene A. Gohlke (February 2003)

Fixed-Income Management 2002—Innovation Continues Conference Highlights
Kenneth R. Meyer, Stephen Kealhofer, Kathleen M. Shanley, CFA, Scott E. Grannis, Marc P. Seidner, Guy Davidson, Robin L. Diamonte, and Kurt D. Winkelmann (September 2002)

Hedge Fund Benchmarks: A Risk-Factor-Based Approach
David A. Hsieh (May 2003)

Featured AIMR Conferences
www.aimr.org/conferences

Equity Research and Valuation Techniques
2–3 December 2003
Philadelphia, PA, USA

Points of Inflection—New Directions in Portfolio Management
30–31 March 2004
New York, NY, USA

Hedge Fund Management
25–26 February 2004
Philadelphia, PA, USA

Authors

We would like to thank Peter Jarvis for serving as moderator at this conference and for writing the overview and Ann Logue, CFA, for serving as guest content editor. We also wish to express our sincere gratitude to the authors listed below for their contributions to both the conference and this proceedings:

Leo J. de Bever is a senior vice president at the Ontario Teachers' Pension Plan Board, where he oversees the fund's risk management, tactical asset allocation, and economic research. Previously, he worked in the field of asset management at Crown Life and Nomura Securities and started an economic consulting firm for Chase Bank in Toronto. Dr. de Bever holds a PhD in economics from the University of Wisconsin at Madison.

Damian Handzy is co-founder, chairman, and managing director of Investor Analytics LLC. Previously, he worked with Deloitte Consulting's information technology practice as an advisor on technical and business issues in the financial services industry, including risk management, Internet-based customer reporting, and data management. Dr. Handzy's research has been published in many financial and scientific journals, most recently in *Global Investor*. He holds a BA from the University of Pennsylvania and a PhD in nuclear physics from Michigan State University.

Peter S. Jarvis, CFA, is a vice president at the Ontario Municipal Employees Retirement Board, where he is responsible for the management of all fixed-income programs, cash management, and the development and implementation of the alternative strategies program. Previously, he was a vice president at TAL Investment Counsel, Scotia McLeod, and Nesbitt Thomson. Mr. Jarvis is a past president of the Toronto Society of Financial Analysts and a fellow of the Canadian Securities Institute. He holds a BA in economics from the University of British Columbia.

Bluford H. Putnam is president of Bayesian Edge Technology and Solutions, Ltd. His primary responsibilities include risk management and financial market research. Previously, he was president of CDC Investments and chief investment officer (equities) at Bankers Trust. Dr. Putnam is chairman of the investment committee at St. Mary's College and a fellow of the Investor Analytics Institute. He has published numerous articles and books and writes a monthly column for *Global Investor*. Dr. Putnam holds a PhD from Tulane University.

Leslie Rahl is founder and president of Capital Market Risk Advisors, Inc., a risk advisory firm that serves institutional clients. She is also partner of L^2 Alternative Asset Management, which provides institutional-quality funds of funds. Previously, she served as co-head of Citibanks's Derivatives Group in North America. Ms. Rahl was named among the top 50 women in finance by *Euromoney* in 1997 and has been profiled in *Risk Magazine* and *Fortune*. She is the author of *Hedge Fund Transparency: Unraveling the Complex and Controversial Debate*. Ms. Rahl chairs the Investor Risk Committee Steering Committee of the International Association of Financial Engineers. She holds an undergraduate degree from Massachusetts Institute of Technology and an MBA from MIT's Sloan School of Management.

Jeffrey A. Rosenberg, CFA, is managing director and head of the Fixed-Income Credit Strategy Research Group at Banc of America Securities (BAS). He is responsible for BAS credit strategy, both high grade and high yield, on a global basis. Previously, Mr. Rosenberg was a U.S. investment-grade strategist at Credit Suisse First Boston and worked on derivative pricing and risk management models at Bankers Trust. He holds a BA in business and mathematics and an MA in computational finance from Carnegie Mellon University.

Timothy J. Rudderow is co-founder and president of Mount Lucas Management Corporation, which provides hedge fund products and futures investment programs to institutional investors and high-net-worth individuals. He has more than 20 years of experience in all aspects of futures and options analysis and trading. He holds a BA in mathematics from Rutgers University and an MBA in management analysis from Drexel University.

Ronald J. Ryan, CFA, is founder and president of Ryan Labs, Inc. He was previously president of Ryan Financial Strategy Group and director of research and strategy at Lehman Brothers. Mr. Ryan holds a BBA and an MBA from Loyola University.

M. Barton Waring is managing director and head of the Client Advisory Group at Barclays Global Investors, where he advises institutional investors on total portfolio and total asset class investment concerns. Previously, he was head of Ibbotson Associates, regional practice leader at Towers Perrin Asset Consulting, and head of the defined-contribution business at Morgan Stanley Asset Management. Mr. Waring has written many articles on topical issues in finance and is a regular speaker at industry conferences. He holds a BS in economics from the University of Oregon, a JD from Lewis & Clark College, and an MBA in finance from Yale University.

D. Sykes Wilford is a founding partner of Hamilton Investment Partners and chairman of the advisory board of Beauchamp Financial Technology. Previously, he was chief investment officer at CDC Investment Management Corporation (CDC Investments) and Bankers Trust's Private Bank. Dr. Wilford also served as managing director at Chase Manhattan Bank, an economist at the Federal Reserve Bank of New York, and chief international fixed-income strategist at Drexel Burnham Lambert. He has been a faculty member at New York University, Pace University, L'Université de Saint-Louis, the University of New Orleans, and, most recently, the City University of London. Dr. Wilford is the author of numerous articles and books, including *Managing Financial Risk*. He holds a BS in economics from the University of Tennessee, an MS in economics from Vanderbilt University, and a PhD in economics from Tulane University.

Overview

Peter S. Jarvis, CFA
Ontario Municipal Employees Retirement Board

Recent market history and developments in technology have set the stage for dramatic developments in risk management. In the past several years, there has been an apparent increase in the incidence of financial disasters typically thought to be rare events—for example, the Asian currency crisis, the Russian government bond default, the historic credit default wave, and the recent U.S. equity market bubble and ensuing meltdown. These events, coupled with corporate accounting debacles and a mounting pension crisis, have caused investors to reconsider standard assumptions about risk and to seek new ways to measure and manage exposure to risk, both for individual securities and for total portfolios.

This conference brought together a notable assembly of thinkers and practitioners with diverse expertise in the area of financial risk to offer their diagnosis of the challenges in risk management and their prescriptions for ameliorating current ills and preventing future ones. The insights of the authors in this proceedings run the gamut from the theoretical considerations of risk modeling techniques to how best to reform investment guidelines to the specific concerns of dealing with risk in pension funds, corporate bond portfolios, and the many risk considerations surrounding alternative investment strategies. As a whole, they provide a kind of snapshot of a field in flux, a picture that shows the details of the main features in the foreground and traces the broad landscape on the horizon.

Measurement, Management, and True Alpha

Financial disasters that were supposed to be extremely rare seem to occur every three or four years. Given such recent market history, Bluford Putnam observes, investors need to consider whether the current risk models and investment guidelines are sufficient to understanding investment risk. As an example, Putnam points out that value at risk (VAR), one of the most common risk measurement tools, is often misused. Although VAR is useful and can provide an effective estimate of the frequency with which returns should fall within a certain range, it cannot estimate the magnitude of returns beyond the normal range.

Putnam identifies three areas in which the challenges of risk management are greatest: embedded short options, correlation structures, and investment guidelines. Perhaps the primary problem with options is that, although mathematical models are good at pricing them, the same models are not good at estimating the risk of a disastrous outcome. Furthermore, despite being familiar with securities with embedded options, investors often overlook the options that are induced in markets by government policies, which often can be just as important, if not more so. Unstable correlation structures are of critical significance because they can lead to financial disasters, and Putnam identifies the two main sources of instability as flight to quality and monetary policy shifts. The problem is compounded by the fact that portfolio diversification strategies are based on correlations, meaning that managers will face extreme difficulty in managing portfolio risk if they do not possess the ability to short some securities for asset classes in which long positions are held.

In Putnam's view, the key to improving the ability to cope with the risks inherent in embedded short options and correlation structures lies in improving investment guidelines. The emphasis should change from asset allocation and credit risk to embedded short options and liquidity risk. Transparency and risk-reporting requirements should be mandatory and downside risk-bearing capacity should be analyzed for both short- and long-term scenarios, with only true long-term investors continuing to operate in a two-dimensional risk–return framework.

D. Sykes Wilford highlights the distinction between risk *measurement*, which gauges changes in portfolio value corresponding to different market conditions, and risk *management*, which involves identifying and controlling portfolio risks. Because investment management consists of decisions about balancing expected risk and return, risk measurement has long been an integral part of the portfolio management process and portfolio managers are adept at using risk metrics. But the role of risk measurement is changing. No longer an exclusive province of investment managers, sophisticated risk measurement tools are increasingly being used by clients, both institutional and individual. Accordingly, portfolio managers must adapt by learning to treat risk measurement not simply as an esoteric subject fit only for internal discussion but as an essential component of client service. Companies that fail to accommodate investor demands for more risk information will struggle to acquire and retain investors.

Presumably, if investors continue to develop a more nuanced understanding of risk, they will also improve their ability to evaluate active risk and active return, the key dimensions of active management, according to M. Barton Waring. Active managers, Waring argues, can enhance investor understanding of their ability to add value by distinguishing their performance presentation of true alpha, which is active return in excess of the market beta. Active return is achieved through the application of special skill, either in security selection or in market selection. From the perspective of investors, however, the ability of managers to deliver alpha is haphazard at best, and managers compound this perception by reporting "performance alpha," which is a muddle of beta and true alpha. Although some managers are indeed capable of generating positive expected alphas, a service that is worth substantial fees, they often fail to differentiate their alphas in their performance reporting. Waring shows how both investors and managers can use the information coefficient, or IC, to quantify the degree of skill or value added in active management.

Risk and Alternative Investments

Applying traditional risk measurement and management techniques to hedge funds and other alternative investments is complicated by the atypical characteristics inherent in such strategies. According to Timothy Rudderow, the challenge is made even more complex by the changing environment for hedge funds, particularly as a result of institutional investors' growing interest in hedge funds and the move from directional strategies toward arbitrage strategies. Risk assessment tools that can handle such complexity are available. The most common tool is VAR, but not all VAR models are uniformly applicable. Rudderow uses a simple matrix to illustrate the suitability of different VAR models for particular types of hedge funds.

Leslie Rahl advocates a holistic approach to risk management for alternative investment strategies, arguing that risk cannot be reduced to a purely mathematical concept to be mapped on a theoretical framework. In her view, investment risk should be thought of as the possibility of any bad outcome, whether a failed investment or a damaged reputation. Although establishing a solid quantitative risk management framework is critical, expanding the due diligence process to consider the qualitative attributes of investment risk is particularly important for alternative strategies because standard risk metrics used for traditional approaches are not as effective when applied to alternative strategies. Rahl describes how her firm's approach focuses on allocating risks rather than assets and uses a detailed screening process incorporating quantitative as well as qualitative factors to evaluate potential fund managers' risk characteristics.

Risk and Pension Funds

The year 2002 was the worst year in pension history, Ronald Ryan informs us, and the pension crisis in the United States also threatens the solvency of corporations, cities, states, and possibly even the federal government. The problem stems primarily from pension accounting practices, particularly ambitious return on asset assumptions. After examining the nature, business and political circumstances, and accounting issues of pension funds, Ryan advocates three main solutions to solve the looming pension crisis: First, pension plans should create a customized liability index that matches their assets with their liabilities. Although this first step will not create a plan surplus, it ensures liability coverage. Second, with a liability index, a liability index fund would become the logical choice. Plan sponsors seek to fund liabilities at the lowest cost and lowest risk, and an index fund that matches the objective is most likely to satisfy this need. Finally, pension funds should switch from a focus on managing assets to provide alpha above some arbitrary benchmark (to meet the often misdirected goal of generating a plan surplus) to a focus on simply matching plan assets to liabilities, which is a much easier goal to achieve.

The biggest risk in any pension fund, according to Leo de Bever, is sponsor behavior. Sponsors generally have an inadequate grasp of volatility in financial markets—in fact, the typical active/passive risk management split is suboptimal—and they particularly need a better understanding of funding risk as it relates to the assumptions behind calculating any actuarial surplus. As a senior vice president of research and economics for the Ontario Teachers' Pension Plan, de Bever describes how OTPP is revising its pension management goals and policies after a decline in its funding position that resulted from sponsor decisions and market downturns.

Credit Risk

Credit risk is special, Jeffrey Rosenberg notes, because of its asymmetry, with limited upside and virtually unlimited downside. Rosenberg analyzes the causes of the recent historic increase in corporate bond default rates and the implications for modeling credit risk. After examining the nature of credit risk, he argues that understanding the average portfolio credit rating is no longer sufficient as a tool for measuring portfolio risk. An alternative approach incorporating equity market information leads to dramatic improvements in analyzing and understanding credit risk at the individual security level as well as at the total portfolio level. This credit modeling improvement, however, often leads to a misunderstanding of the asymmetric nature of credit risk. He calls this misunderstanding the "diversi*fiction*" problem—in which upside and downside risk are incorrectly assumed to be equal. Credit risk, as measured by historical equity price volatility, fails to fully account for this potential risk. This failure is significant because small changes in price volatility often lead to significant changes in a security's credit spread, a phenomena termed the "credit cliff." Rosenberg demonstrates how market-based credit models not only can provide early warning indicators about impending credit crises but also can offer a more effective way of quantifying portfolio-level risk.

An Alternative Modeling Technique

Monte Carlo simulation techniques provide a useful tool for the particular problem of modeling expected return distributions with fat tails. The inherent complexities of Monte Carlo methods, however, often lead to critical problems with implementation not only because they involve too many embedded assumptions but also because the underlying assumptions are usually known only to the creators of a given model and not the end users, resulting in a black box. Damian Handzy suggests an alternative analytical method that is easier to use yet still offers comparably robust results.

Using the example of a short put option, Handzy shows how nonlinear properties can render any model that assumes a normal distribution of expected returns worse than useless—indeed, such a model will produce results that may be disastrously misleading for investors. Monte Carlo techniques can handle the problem of nonlinearity, but given the complexities, Handzy recommends using a simplified, five-step approach that can consider all possible paths. Moreover, whereas Monte Carlo approaches become vastly more complicated when applied to a multiple-instrument portfolio, with Handzy's alternative method, a theoretical solution is easily generated for an entire portfolio.

Conclusion

We are pleased to bring you this proceedings and hope you find the presentations of practical value. The goal of the conference was to stimulate speakers' best insights across a broad spectrum of issues in risk management, and judging by the evidence offered in this proceedings, we believe it was a success.

Disaster Risk and Investment Guidelines

Bluford H. Putnam
President
Bayesian Edge Technology and Solutions, Ltd.
St. Inigoes, Maryland

> Traditional investment guidelines do not always work to reduce the risk of disaster. To better align investment guidelines with risk–return objectives, less emphasis should be placed on asset class allocations and credit risk constraints and more on liquidity concerns and managing the risks of embedded short option exposures. Transparency and risk-reporting requirements should no longer be optional, and downside risk-bearing capacity should be analyzed for both short- and long-term horizons. True long-term investors can still operate in a two-dimensional risk–return framework, and they can structure their guidelines to allow the portfolio to take advantage of liquidity risk (thus earning market premiums), complexity risk, and short option risk—risks that shorter-term investors with less risk-bearing capacity should avoid.

The supposedly rare events that investors think should happen in financial markets only once every 10,000 years seem to occur every third or fourth year in today's fast-changing world. As a result, some observers have wondered whether the current risk models and investment guidelines have important flaws. My task is to examine some of these potential challenges in risk analysis to see if anything can be learned from recent disasters. My perspective is that the potential for portfolio disasters is increasing, even as risk control systems give the appearance of greater sophistication.

My discussion will focus on three areas where the risk management challenges are greatest: embedded short options, correlation structures, and investment guidelines—all of which come into play when a significant market event occurs.

The embedded short option exposures in many securities are frequently mentioned in presentations on risk management for good reason. Embedded short option positions, hidden and explicit, are a critical source of portfolio disasters. Nothing is inherently wrong with selling options, but one must make sure the premiums received for short options are worth the considerable downside risk.

Correlation structures are another major source of problems for risk management. Correlation structures can often change more than commonly is expected, which can cause severe problems for the performance and risk measurement of seemingly diversified portfolios. Many investors who thought their portfolios were diversified have discovered that they were wrong. Paying attention to correlation structures and using scenario analysis can help prevent big disasters.

Finally, I will offer some ideas about investment guidelines. Modifying investment guidelines to better reflect desired portfolio risk characteristics can be an effective approach to controlling the risk of disaster. The key is to focus on the characteristics of securities that are closely related to the risk of disaster. These characteristics, such as short options exposures and liquidity risks, are not necessarily related to standard asset classifications or typical credit risk measures.

Value at Risk

Value at risk (VAR) is a common risk measurement tool that is often misused.[1] Many people attempt to use VAR in a way for which it was not designed, often because the user is assuming a normal distribution of expected returns and a stable correlation structure based on the recent past. Unfortunately, nonnormal distributions of returns are much more common than is generally appreciated, and correlation structures are much less stable than investors believe. Such non-normality in return distributions and instability in correlation structures mean that current investment guidelines, which are often predicated on normally

---
[1] For more discussion of the flaws in VAR, see Bluford H. Putnam, "Introduction to Risk Management," in *Risk Management: Principles and Practices* (Charlottesville, VA: AIMR, 1999):1–6.

distributed returns and stable correlation structures, are often constructed inappropriately and do not correspond to the true risk–return preferences of the underlying investors.

The good news about VAR is that it focuses attention on the degree of portfolio diversification for the recent past and can help answer questions about the typical range of profits and losses. VAR makes investors look at the impact of correlations and risks on portfolios, not just individual securities. Users of VAR can get an estimate of the degree of portfolio diversification during calm periods, and they can get a good estimate of the typical range of daily, weekly, or monthly returns. This analysis helps investors get closer to the efficient frontier for their investments, but it may not provide any information about the potential size of downside risks when disaster strikes.

That is, VAR shows what percentage of daily profits and losses will fall within a specified range. Given a normal distribution of returns, about 68 percent will be within plus/minus one standard deviation of the mean and 95 percent will be within plus/minus two standard deviations. Examining the profit/loss range graphically is easier than looking at raw numbers. For example, in **Figure 1**, the one-standard-deviation profit/loss range for an actual currency overlay portfolio is represented by the shaded area and the extreme, two-standard-deviation upside/downside events are in black. This sort of graph can help one get an intuitive feel for the return distribution and can be used to make sure portfolios are being managed within the expected or targeted risk range. If portfolios exceed the range too often, the risk models will need modification. In this particular case, the proportion of returns either too high or too low, in terms of what is expected by this distribution, is about right. Monte Carlo simulations can also be used, but as Damian Handzy notes, one must be careful of embedding assumptions of normal distributions of returns when options or other nonnormal return distributions are present in the portfolio.[2]

When the shape of the probability distribution is not known, one can use Chebyshev's inequality to generate a conservative estimate.[3] Chebyshev's inequality holds that for a given standard deviation, the actual distribution need not be known to determine the typical range of observations, but it also holds (although this point is generally neglected) that events outside the normal range could be anywhere. That is, Chebyshev is admitting complete ignorance of just how bad any disaster might be. Chebyshev's insight should be remembered for VAR because VAR provides a good indication of the typical range of returns but does not provide any guidance whatsoever about the magnitude of a disaster, only the probability of its occurrence.

---

[2] For more on using Monte Carlo techniques in risk assessment, see Damian Handzy's presentation in this proceedings.
[3] More information about Chebyshev's inequality can be accessed at www.btinternet.com/~se16/hgb/cheb.htm.

Figure 1. Profit/Loss Range for a Currency Overlay Model, September 2002–June 2003

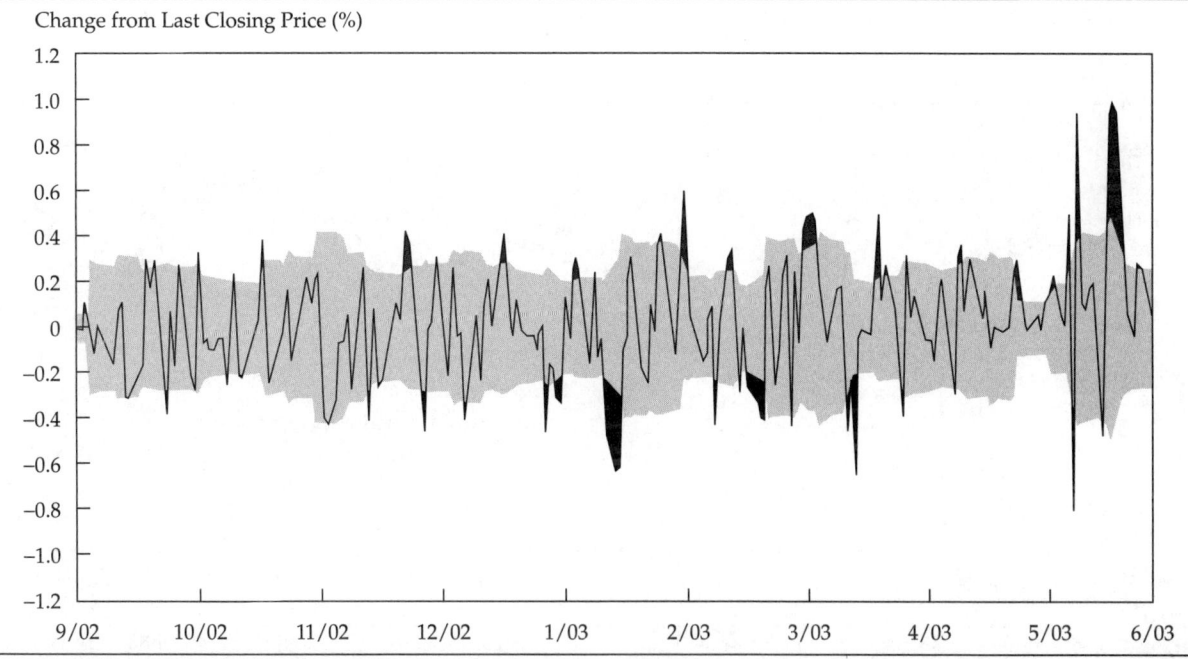

Note: Shaded area represents typical profit/loss range; extreme events are in black.

Consider the example of ImClone stock, which suffered a disaster at the end of 2001 and beginning of 2002. Panel A of **Figure 2** shows that monthly returns did not look too bad, but the actual price series, as shown in Panel B, indicates the real magnitude of the disaster. An unfavorable decision by the U.S. Food and Drug Administration regarding an ImClone drug drove the decline. In 2003, favorable regulatory decisions have driven the price back up. This sort of disaster risk should be a primary concern for risk managers because stocks with this type of business risk should never be assumed to have normally distributed return distributions.

So, just to drive home the point, VAR can provide a good estimate of the frequency with which returns should fall within a given range, but VAR cannot provide a good estimate of the magnitude of the next big portfolio disaster that will take returns outside the typical range. A 1-in-20 chance of losing at least $100 does not mean an investor can never lose more

Figure 2. Volatility of ImClone Stock: Monthly Return versus Actual Price Series, January 1998–April 2003

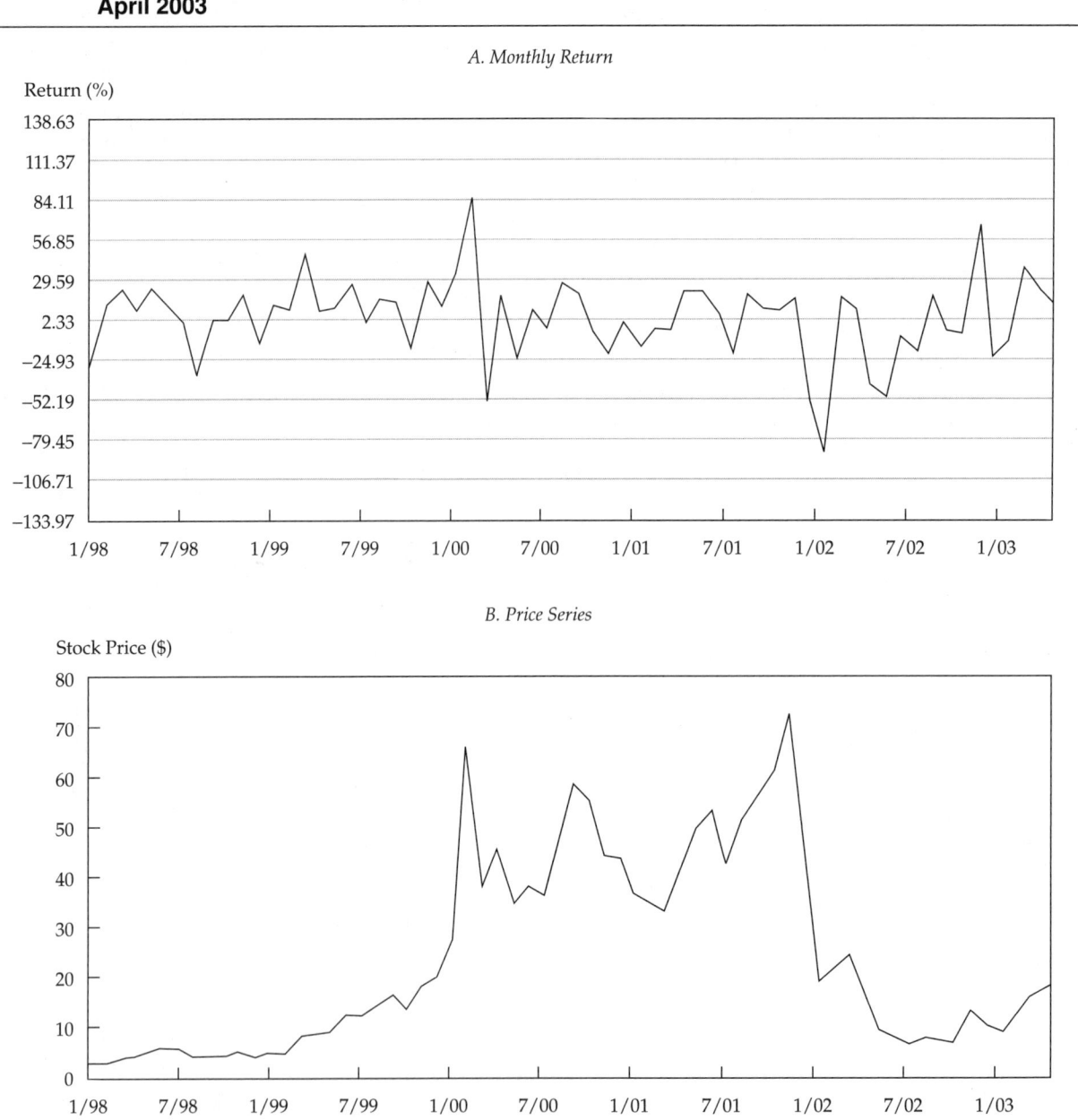

Note: Interval between gridlines in Panel A represents one standard deviation (i.e., mean = 2.33 percent, plus one standard deviation = 29.59 percent, minus one standard deviation = –24.93 percent, and so forth).

than $100. Once a disaster occurs, the loss could be much worse than $100. Thus, the rest of this presentation will focus on what investors should worry about when analyzing potential disasters.

What to Worry About

"The markets can remain irrational longer than you can remain solvent," John Maynard Keynes reportedly said. Unfortunately for the great Yale economist Irving Fisher, Keynes did not make this statement until the 1930s—after the market crash. Fisher did a lot of important work in economics between 1890 and the 1920s, with some particularly fine work on price indexes and interest rate theory. He knew all about correlation structures, and he knew all about portfolio diversification.[4] Fisher was also an investor. In the 1920s, Fisher inherited a big position in one stock. He borrowed some money and bought some more of that stock. Thus, in 1929, Fisher had a leveraged position in a single stock. When the market collapsed, he figured it had to turn around and recover soon. By 1933, Fisher was $1 million in debt. He had to borrow money from his sister and died a debtor.

One moral of Fisher's story is that when bad things happen, they can be *extremely* bad. Another moral is that great economists may not make good investors, as one large hedge fund with no less than two Nobel prize winners on its payroll learned in the summer of 1998. For risk managers, the lesson is that investors should investigate carefully the causes of fat tails in expected return distributions—the territory of extreme occurrences. The primary culprits are embedded short options and correlation shifts.

Embedded Short Options. There are two kinds of embedded options. Everyone knows about the first kind (options embedded in securities), but most people do not think about the second kind (options embedded in government policies), which I will discuss later.

At least five types of securities, in particular, are notable for containing embedded options:
- Mortgage-backed securities (MBS) have an embedded prepayment option, with no penalty for refinancing. Estimating the numbers of homeowners likely to refinance their mortgages during a period of bond market volatility can be enormously difficult and uncertain, and the result is illiquidity in the MBS market during times of interest rate uncertainty.
- Callable bonds obviously have the call option embedded in them.
- Convertible bonds have an option to convert to stock, which adds another level of volatility analysis to the equation.
- High-yield bonds have, in effect, about the same risk characteristics as being short a put option on the total assets of the company, so these bonds respond quickly to volatility in the equity markets.
- IPO stocks have highly uncertain future cash flows, so IPO investors are essentially long a call for which the assumed volatility is extremely hard to forecast.

Options are the focus here because to value an option, a volatility forecast, among other things, is needed. Because these five kinds of securities all involve option characteristics, they are the securities likely to cause problems whenever volatility itself becomes hard to forecast. Moreover, when investors do not know what something is worth, they are less likely to trade it, thereby reducing liquidity.

Complex securities will get killed in a liquidity crisis. For example, **Figure 3** shows how the stock prices of seven real estate investment trusts (REITs) specializing in mortgage securities were affected by the Long-Term Capital Management (LTCM) crisis. This special type of REIT, which invests mainly in MBS exposures, shows what can happen to a portfolio of complex securities in a liquidity crisis. Interestingly, these mortgage REITs usually own high-quality credits, such as AA and AAA mortgages. They tend not to be full of junk bonds or tranches of asset-backed securities with extremely low credit ratings. In the wake of the LTCM crisis in the summer of 1998, though, these REITs specializing in MBS became even more illiquid than some of the option-related securities in their portfolios, causing their prices to decline precipitously. Investors took their money out of the REITs, at least what was left. Consequently, these mortgage REITs never fully recovered, even though the MBS market did. If all of these REIT investors had stayed invested, the price would have come back in less than 18 months.

If you are invested in liquidity-challenged portfolios, you must take a long-term time horizon and not panic in a short-term liquidity crisis. Of course, if your fellow investors panic, even if you do not, then the fund in which your money is commingled with that of other investors will still get killed. When investing in portfolios with known liquidity issues, large pension funds and institutional investors should use their market clout to demand separate accounts and avoid commingled funds in which the time horizons and weak stomachs of other investors can cause problems for all investors in the fund.

---
[4] See Bluford H. Putnam and Donald Stabile, "Irving Fisher and Statistical Approaches to Risk," *Review of Financial Economics* (January 2002):191–203.

Figure 3. Effect of LTCM Crisis on Seven Mortgage REITs, January 1989–April 2003

Note: ANH = Anworth Mortgage Asset Corporation; CMM = Criimi Mae; CMO = Capstead Mortgage Corporation; HCM = Hanover Capital Mortgage Holdings; NLY = Annaly Mortgage Management; RWT = Redwood Trust; TMA = Thornburg Mortgage.

The mathematical systems that are good at pricing options may not be good at estimating their risk of disaster. The typical option analysis focuses on delta (the relationship of the option price to the price of the underlying security) and on gamma (the rate of change in delta or the second term in a Taylor expansion approximation method), which is a bad idea for estimating disaster scenarios: when embedded options are present, even if it is fine for price analysis in calm periods. Consider the example shown in **Figure 4**. A straight-line approximation for delta is drawn at the strike price. A large change in asset value results in a big estimation error. Now look at the gamma. The gamma is a parabola, and it is a slightly better measure than delta. Price behavior is approximated in the area around the strike price. Delta and gamma approximations are great for pricing options and for making arbitrage trades between the option and the underlying security, but they are not designed for risk management systems. If a big move

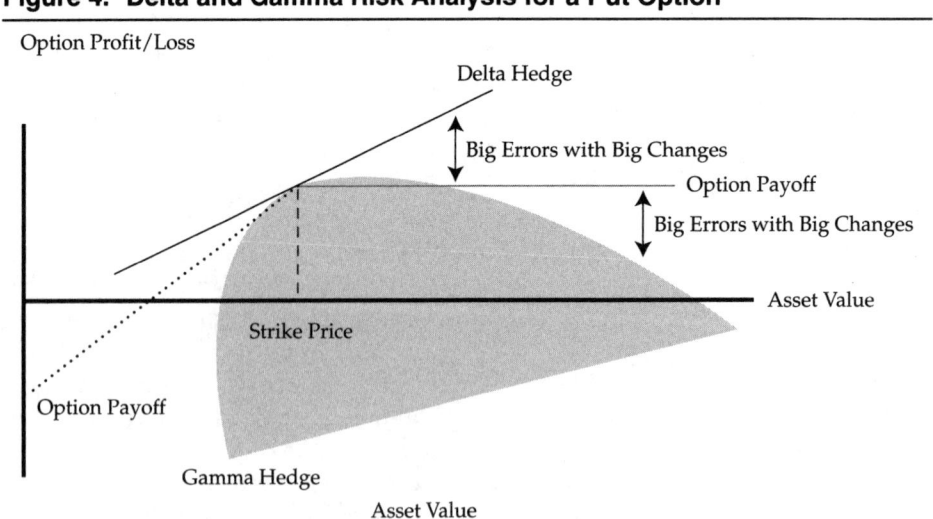

Figure 4. Delta and Gamma Risk Analysis for a Put Option

occurs in the underlying price, delta and gamma will not produce the information needed to manage large risks. In contrast, risk management systems are concerned with disasters, not with the effects of small price changes. Testing disasters requires, by definition, looking at big shocks, often with special scenario analysis. An option-pricing system based on delta and gamma will greatly underestimate disaster in the tough times.

Market-Induced Option Characteristics. Certain options may not be legally embedded or contained in securities but nonetheless may be present in the market for these securities because of government policies. Often, central banks can induce options in currency markets, interest rate markets, and other markets.

Consider two examples. In the wake of the October 1987 stock market crash, the Bank of England supported the price of British petroleum stock for a couple of months because the government was issuing it and wanted to let prospective buyers know that they need not fear further declines or another stock market crash. More recently, in the summer of 2003, the Bank of Japan indicated that it will buy the debt of Japanese companies under some circumstances, and with such a policy, it is supporting the stocks of the banks that lent money to risky Japanese companies. This stance makes investments in the Japanese stock market much less risky than before this policy was started. Whenever central banks become buyers of market securities, markets are affected.

In effect, the Bank of Japan has created implied options. Essentially, it has said it will be the buyer of last resort for certain types of debt, creating a floor on the price that resembles a call option. Any time a government picks a target, whether an exchange rate target or an interest rate target (or in the case of Japan, support for equities and debt markets), it should be treated as an option-related problem. As the market approaches the floor, the effect will be increasing volatility. In mathematics, these are boundary value problems, and in risk management, they are the cause of asymmetrical return distributions and render useless risk models based on embedded assumptions of normal return distributions.

Correlation Structures. Disasters can also come from unstable correlation structures. Two types of instability are notable: flight to quality and a shift in monetary policy.

Flight to quality merely means that as certain markets see prices crater, investors flee those markets with whatever is left of their capital and put it into an asset with little credit risk and plenty of liquidity—namely U.S. Treasury bonds. One example of the flight-to-quality effect occurred in the summer of 1998 during the LTCM meltdown. The flight to quality that occurred in the wake of the LTCM crisis had a significant impact. **Figure 5** shows that when the LTCM debacle happened in August 1998, one consequence was the widening of the spread between the average corporate bond yield and the 10-year U.S. T-bond yield as investors sold corporates and bought Treasuries. The embedded option in high-yield bonds made the pricing situation even more complex.

Take another example. Many people believe a significant correlation exists between the S&P 500 Index and 10-year Treasuries. **Figure 6** shows their performance from January 1982 through January 2003. In general, if bond yields are lower, equity valuations for a given cash flow will be higher. Certain situations, however, can interfere with this relationship, and these situations occurred with some frequency during this 20-year period. For example, during the October 1987 stock market crash, investors bought U.S. Treasury bonds as stocks fell. Investors also bought U.S. Treasury bonds heavily (so that bond yields declined) during the early 1990s savings and loan crisis when stock prices also fell and during the 2000–2002 "tech wreck" on Wall Street. So, the

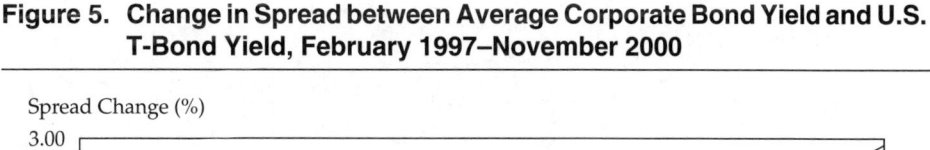

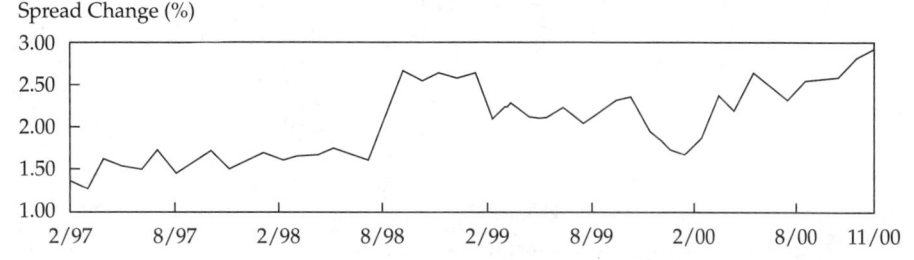

Figure 5. Change in Spread between Average Corporate Bond Yield and U.S. T-Bond Yield, February 1997–November 2000

Figure 6. S&P 500 versus 10-Year T-Bond Yield, January 1982–January 2003

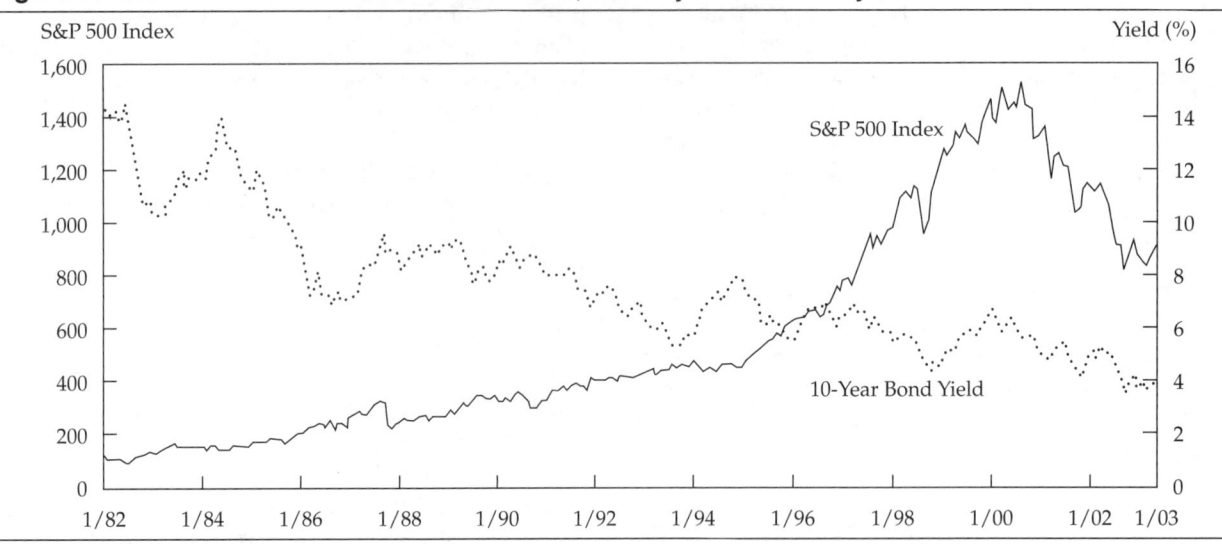

common case of a positive correlation between equity returns and bond returns may not be as stable as investors expect or as the embedded assumption in a risk model expects. As shown in **Figure 7**, which depicts the rolling 24-month correlation of the S&P 500 with 10-year Treasuries, risk models need to learn to cope with dynamic correlation structures.

Consider the effect of changes in monetary policy. **Figure 8** shows the 24-month rolling correlation of the yen and the euro (versus the U.S. dollar) from December 2000 to April 2003. The correlation started close to zero and actually went significantly negative in the last year of the sample because Japan's economy moved quite differently from that of the European Union.

An older, historical example perhaps makes the point even better. The euro is a new currency. But before the euro, one had to worry about the correlation of the German mark and French franc, both measured in terms of U.S. dollars. **Figure 9** shows the 24-month rolling correlation of the French franc with the German mark. In the mid-1970s, the German mark maintained a certain amount of strength versus the U.S. dollar, whereas the French franc fluctuated against the U.S. dollar, causing a low correlation. In the 1980s, the correlation rose and stabilized, reaching a very high correlation above 0.90 (1.0 is perfect)

Figure 7. Correlation of S&P 500 and 10-Year U.S. T-Bond, December 1983–December 2002
(24-month rolling return correlation)

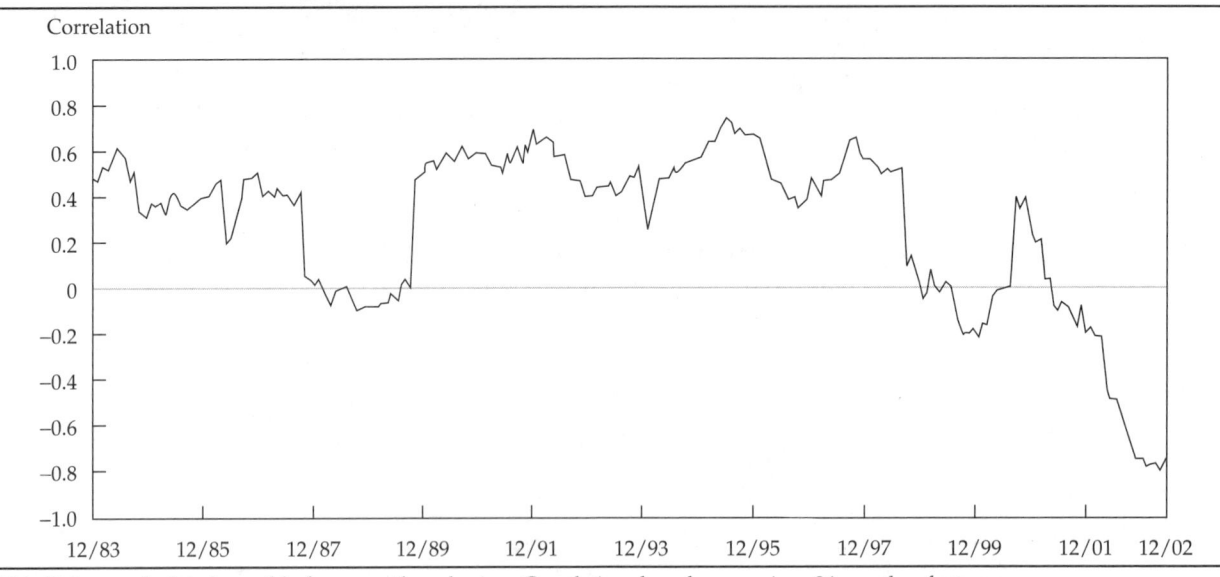

Note: Returns calculated monthly from month-end prices. Correlations based on previous 24 months of returns.

Figure 8. Correlation of Yen and Euro, December 2000–April 2003
(24-month rolling return correlation)

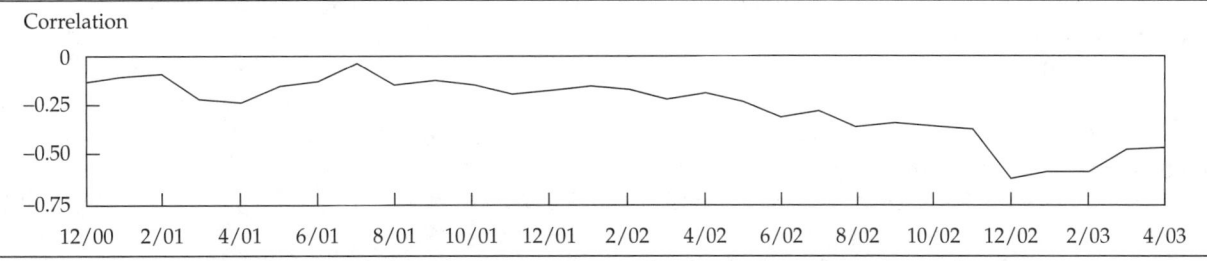

Note: Returns calculated monthly from month-end exchange rates. Correlations based on previous 24 months of returns.

Figure 9. Correlation of Franc and Mark, December 1973–December 2002
(24-month rolling return correlation)

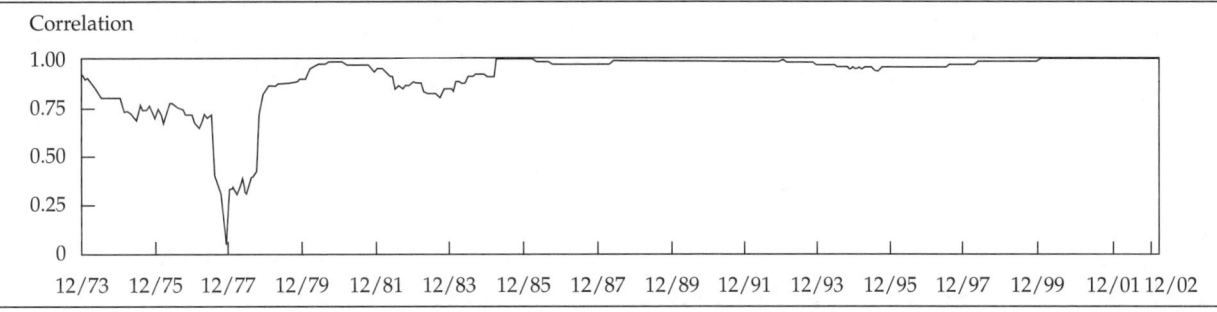

Note: Returns calculated monthly from month-end exchange rates. Correlations based on previous 24 months of returns.

in the late 1980s. In the mid- to late 1990s, with the advent of the euro, the correlation reached the perfection of 1.0 because after January 1999, the French franc and German mark literally did become the same currency—known as the euro.

Some statisticians will say that the more data, the better, and the larger the size of the sample data, the better. Anyone using a long-term sample for current financial forecasting or risk analysis and modeling securities affected by the franc–mark correlation structure, such as German bonds and French bonds, would need to increase the weight of more recent observations to avoid distortion from the 1970s and 1980s data, or they could use Bayesian statistical methods.[5] Clearly, correlation structures can change greatly if central banks alter their currency policies. Investors should keep this problem in mind as central bankers in England debate whether to join the European Monetary Union, those in Hong Kong debate whether to maintain the peg to the U.S. dollar or switch to the euro or a dollar-euro blend, and those in Japan decide at what ranges versus the U.S. dollar they want to encourage yen trading.

[5] See Jose Mario Quintana and Bluford H. Putnam, "Debating Currency Market Efficiency Using Dynamic Multiple-Factor Models," American Statistical Association, 1996 Proceedings of the Section on Bayesian Statistical Science.

More on the Importance of Examining Correlations. Portfolio diversification is based on managing correlations, but correlations can and do change. Thus, one needs to appreciate, even for simple cases, how correlations affect the degree of portfolio diversification and risk. For two uncorrelated assets (asset A, which has a 4 percent risk, and asset B, which has a 3 percent risk), an analysis using the Pythagorean theorem indicates that the total risk is 5 percent.[6]

But the situation changes if the assets are correlated. If the correlation is 1, asset B will be exactly the same as asset A. If the correlation is 0.75, the joint risk will be 7 percent risk. If the correlation is zero, asset B will be, in effect, a 75 percent hedge on asset A and the joint risk will be 1 percent.

Getting correlations as low as zero, or negative for that matter, is extremely hard without the ability of going short some of the securities in the same asset class in which long positions may be taken. Most long-only equity portfolios have correlations with an

[6] The Pythagorean theorem states that in a right triangle, the relationship between the distance of the sides is $a^2 + b^2 = c^2$, where c is the side opposite the right angle. For detailed applications to risk analysis, see Brian D. Singer, "Risk Analysis: A Geometric Approach," in *Risk Management: Principles and Practices* (Charlottesville, VA: AIMR, 1999):73–79.

appropriate benchmark or index of 0.6–0.8, and many of the core stocks in a large-cap equity portfolio may have a 0.80–0.95 correlation with a traditional equity index. In these long-only equity portfolios, adding additional securities usually does not decrease risk. Creating a portfolio with the powerful diversification effects of a zero or negative correlation with an index or benchmark requires a mix of assets that is totally different—say, gold and stocks—or it requires short trading.

In a market panic, correlations tend to rise between different securities within the critically affected asset class. So, stocks that normally have 0.5–0.6 correlations with each other will have 0.80–0.95 correlations in a crisis. Correlations between securities in different asset classes may not rise and may even diverge, which is symptomatic of the flight-to-quality problem. If an equity market crash occurs, investors will tend to sell stocks and buy government bonds, causing the normal (positive) correlation between bond and stock returns to invert.

Rising correlations within an asset class associated with a flight-to-quality effect usually increase the risk of long-only portfolio strategies. Because the typical diversification measures assume low correlations, if a crisis drives correlations higher, a long-only portfolio will have no offsets at times when they are most needed, magnifying portfolio risk. So, long-only portfolios are likely to perform much more poorly in disaster scenarios than a typical VAR estimate would suggest. In contrast, rising correlations within asset classes may work to decrease the overall portfolio risk for certain types of long–short portfolio strategies, but the effect depends critically on the nature of the relative exposures. That is, if all the long positions are in one asset class and the short positions in another, then it is not clear that the risk of this type of long–short portfolio will decline in a crisis. But if the short and long positions are in the same asset class, such as long U.S. equities and short international equities, then a very good chance exists that the correlation structure in this type of long–short portfolio will serve to decrease risks in an equity market crisis.

Correlation shifts caused by currency and interest rate policies can also increase portfolio risk. Currencies can be negatively correlated with bonds when the consumer price index growth rate is accelerating and when the interest rate policy is behind the curve of rising inflation pressures and expectations, but currencies can be positively correlated with bonds when the interest rate policy is aggressive enough to stabilize consumer prices. When a currency starts to weaken rapidly, high volatility is possible exactly because the currency movement may lead to a policy-induced interest rate movement.

For example, we can look at the life cycle of a weak currency. A weakening currency typically goes through three phases. The first phase is what I call "rhetoric." The government says, "The currency is weak. We do not want it to be weak. We have a policy of a strong currency." It is all talk and means absolutely nothing. The second phase is intervention, in which the central bank uses its reserves to buy the currency. The intervention, however, is intermittent and sterilized (meaning it does not affect domestic interest rates). Such intervention destabilizes the market, makes investors cautious, yet ultimately fails because the underlying cause of the currency weakness is not addressed. In the third phase, the central bank changes interest rates. When central banks begin to aggressively raise short-term interest rates to defend a weak currency, the currency experiences a lot of volatility, but this approach works to create currency strength where there was once weakness. For risk managers, though, the result is a regime change in the correlation structure.

In this year (2003), the United States is in Phase One of the weak dollar. The dollar is clearly weak, and the government, through the voice of Treasury Secretary John Snow, is saying it has a strong-dollar policy. Federal Reserve Board Chairman Alan Greenspan appears not to be concerned about dollar weakness, so the second and third phases of sterilized intervention and later short-term rate rises are a long way off, and in the case of the United States, where the usual currency policy is one of benign neglect, short-term rates may never be increased for exchange-rate-related reasons.

Since the latter part of the 1990s, Japan actually has desired a weak currency. In terms of currency management, Japan has been through all three phases. Japan, however, has other structural problems in its financial system that relate to currency determination. Perhaps I need a fourth phase for discussing structural issues and currency direction. But there are two key points to remember: Sterilized intervention usually raises volatility, and changes in short-term interest rate policies may also switch the correlation structure between exchange rates and domestic interest rates. Both of these central-bank-induced effects require special dynamic modeling in terms of risk analysis for currencies and the portfolios in which they are important, such as global equity or global bond portfolios.

In my opinion, the only way to understand the changing correlations and embedded options is to do scenario analysis. For instance, test a portfolio against an LTCM-type scenario using the correlation structure that existed in the summer of 1998. Another historical scenario that makes for a good test is the

Federal Reserve's tightening of monetary policy in the spring of 1994. This test would be good preparation for what may actually happen in 2004 or thereabouts. These and other analyses offer ways to calibrate a portfolio and understand its vulnerability to market disasters and government policy shifts that affect correlation structures.

Event Risk. Event risk is the hardest type of risk to deal with because it comes out of nowhere. Natural disasters, fraud, and regulatory changes are extremely difficult to predict. Weather forecasting has improved in the past 50 years but not enough to eliminate the risk of, say, hurricanes for insurance companies. Hurricanes are going to happen, even if they are tracked closely. Thus, insurance companies are good at diversifying their risk portfolio according to the probability of claims for certain events and diversifying geographically to offset one type of climate risk with another.

To my mind, no model can predict fraud. Historically, many analysts assumed that the U.S. equity market participants tended to believe that the reported corporate profit numbers were approximately accurate. Now, in the wake of recent scandals in the 2000–2003 period, investor confidence in financial reports is lower and more fragile, and if fraud is found at a company, its stock price will collapse even before the extent of the financial damage can be assessed.

Improving Investment Guidelines

Taking all these ideas about embedded options, dynamic correlation structures, and event risk and then thinking about financial disasters leaves investors (or should leave investors) grappling with the following questions:
- What is the risk exposure within a portfolio, both overall and for various sectors and classes?
- What is the short option exposure, explicit or embedded, and what is the magnitude? Particularly important is knowing how close the option is to the strike price because that amount could cause more nonlinearity.
- How are risks correlated within sectors of the same asset class and among different asset classes? This area is where flight to quality becomes a problem; when a disaster hits, correlations change.
- How does the risk change for various scenarios, such as flight to quality or an interest rate hike?

As one grapples with these questions, one can then turn to the related problem of how to construct investment guidelines that can control risks from these types of sources. When focusing on the sources of the risk of disaster, the inadequate nature of asset class restrictions and credit risk restrictions becomes blatantly obvious. Indeed, traditional investment guidelines have four main problems.

First, they force the primary focus to be on equities because equities constitute the high-return, high-risk asset class. Being typically long-only investments, however, equities are highly subject to the risk of disaster. Almost any time correlations change because of a crisis, risk increases in long-only equity portfolios as compared with previously estimated VAR measures of risk.

Second, within the fixed-income market, traditional guidelines place too much emphasis on credit ratings and not enough on liquidity and complexity, which is just another word for options. Traditional guidelines do not distinguish between liquid and illiquid investments within an asset class. They do not distinguish between complex securities with embedded options and vanilla securities in the same asset class.

Third, traditional guidelines have an overall bias against alternative assets and long–short strategies, even though the easiest way to effectively get zero and negative correlations in a portfolio is to include short positions. A truly diversified portfolio is difficult to achieve if the only possibility is to go long.

And fourth, traditional guidelines rely too heavily on one number (i.e., VAR) to represent risk and use simple asset allocation limits for risk control.

A method more sophisticated than asset class guidelines and credit risk guidelines is needed. To improve overall portfolio risk–return characteristics, guidelines should address the time horizon of investors (including the capacity to withstand downside shocks) and the ability to withstand liquidity crises.

Time Horizon. Thinking about portfolio risk–return characteristics is tantamount to thinking about time horizon because time horizon is the capacity to withstand downside risk. An investor with a lot of money may still lack risk-bearing capacity. For example, money managers that operate in the media spotlight, including mutual funds and government entities, often have to respond to a disaster rather than wait for prices to recover. Small mistakes can be blown out of proportion if reported in the press at the wrong time or in the wrong way. Likewise, managing a long-term portfolio for a board of directors that has a short fuse can be difficult. Managers often have to focus on the most sensitive constituency, not the overall risk–return characteristics of the portfolio.

Liquidity. Liquidity risk is closely related to time horizon. Liquidity is diminished in almost any kind of crisis, but VAR tends not to measure this risk. Many liquidity concerns disappear with long time horizons because the return distribution of securities with liquidity problems tends to become more normal as the return period is increased. The market will pay for long-term investors willing to bear the burden of short-term liquidity problems in otherwise high-quality credit securities. Investors with a short fuse cannot earn the market premium for illiquidity. Finally, certain types of embedded option issues relative to nonnormal return distributions are not necessarily dissipated by longer investor time horizons because they are inherent to the structure of the security and do not go away when the market crisis is over.

Next-Generation Guidelines. The next generation of investment guidelines will focus on embedded option exposures, the importance of time horizon for less-liquid securities, and transparency of risk reporting.

Most portfolios have credit risk guidelines, such as the requirement of owning only investment-grade securities. These securities, however, may have embedded short options that are not related to credit risk. For example, although many MBS often have AAA and AA credit ratings, they are loaded with embedded options, can have zero liquidity for short periods of time, and do not even trade by appointment in a crisis. Investors with shorter horizons need to make sure that their investment guidelines cover embedded options rather than simply credit risk.

I rank securities based on their likelihood of having a normal return distribution in a crisis, and this approach is related to the idea that securities that do not exhibit fat-tailed return distributions because of embedded options are less likely to have liquidity problems. Foreign exchange and government bonds are most likely to have normal distributions, but obvious exceptions exist, such as currencies of countries with commodity-based economies (for example, Australia).

The middle ground includes large-cap equities, investment-grade bonds, and commodity futures. Normality is not a bad assumption for the return distributions of securities in these asset classes, but they can have some problems in a crisis.

The riskiest category is securities with embedded options or option-like characteristics, which clearly have nonlinear expected return behavior. This category includes small-cap stocks, convertible bonds, MBS and asset-backed securities, and straight options and warrants. Investors who buy securities with nonlinear return profiles need a longer time horizon because of the lack of liquidity in a crisis. In exchange, investors earn a premium over time for complex securities with high-quality credit ratings. These types of securities have little place in a portfolio without a long time horizon, but they can earn nice premiums for truly long-term investors with a demonstrated capability of avoiding panic while every one else is running for cover.

Finally, investment guidelines should require that managers report frequently on the risk they are taking. Without frequent, consistent reporting, no risk management system can work. Reports must also involve more than just limits on asset classes, especially when the investment guidelines call for investment in an inherently volatile asset, such as equities. This topic obviously follows from my discussion of the risk of disaster, embedded options, dynamic correlation structures, and event risk, but I will leave the full discussion of transparency issues to others.[7]

Conclusion

In the future, investment guidelines should differ in significant ways from the traditional approach. The focus should shift from asset allocation and credit risk to embedded short options and liquidity, which should be addressed explicitly. Transparency and risk-reporting requirements should no longer be optional, and downside risk-bearing capacity should be analyzed in both short- and long-term scenarios. Fiduciaries, boards of pension funds and endowments, and others responsible for overseeing investments need to take a long hard look at their capacity to bear downside risk and not panic. Again, the amount of money involved is not a good indicator of risk-bearing capacity.

For short- and medium-horizon investors, setting guidelines should no longer be done simply as a two-dimensional trade-off between risk and return because of the greater threat from crisis events and liquidity concerns. They should also set exposure limits for embedded short options and complex securities with known liquidity problems. Exposure limits can be increased for strategies that do not use options and less-liquid securities, even if they are alternative strategies involving long–short positions or leverage.

True long-term investors can reasonably continue to operate in a two-dimensional risk–return framework. They should structure their guidelines to allow the portfolio to take advantage of liquidity risk (thus earning market premiums), complexity risk, and short option risk, where appropriate. Being a true long-term investor opens up possibilities for earning returns and risk premiums; short-term investors are only too happy to pay to get rid of those time-horizon risks.

---

[7]For a detailed discussion of the importance of risk transparency, see D. Sykes Wilford's presentation in this proceedings.

All in all, risk management has come a long way in the past two decades. The fact that some type of VAR measure is now calculated for almost all portfolios is a sign of real improvement in risk management. As I have noted, VAR, however, has severe limits when it comes to analyzing disaster scenarios. The more difficult problems of embedded options and dynamic correlation structures are not well handled by most VAR approaches. So, despite the impressive evidence of rapid improvement in investors' risk management sophistication, much work is yet to be done in risk management practices and in making critical adjustments to investment guidelines to reflect the lessons learned.[8] Making progress in these areas may be more important than many people realize because whether investors like it or not, a good case can be made that financial disasters will come more often than they once did, and investors will need all of the risk management sophistication they can acquire and implement.

---

[8] A comprehensive guide to some common traps in risk management practices can be found in Bluford H. Putnam, "Managing Firm Risk," in *Ethical Issues for Today's Firm* (Charlottesville, VA: AIMR, 2000):51–61.

Question and Answer Session

Bluford H. Putnam

Question: Short-term correlations are relatively unstable, particularly during periods of stress, but what about medium- and longer-term correlations?

Bluford: In many cases, longer-term correlations are just as unstable as short-term correlations. The problem is that almost every economic event is caused by a combination of three or more causes. With only one cause, a correlation can be stable. That is, a definite, direct, and simple link exists between cause and effect. But with multiple causes, many permutations are possible. Such complexity will produce unstable correlation structures. It will matter for correlation structures of security returns if A is caused by B or by C or by a dynamic combination of B and C.

In the long term for some asset classes or securities, change is the typical case for correlation structures, primarily because government policies change. In the 1970s, monetary policy focused on inflation and currency volatility. In the 1980s, the sole focus was on beating inflation. The 1990s saw a great run on stocks, with low inflation and stable and convergent monetary policies around the world. In the current decade, I do not see convergence in global economic policies. I see policies starting to diverge, with unstable correlations likely in both the short run and the long run, especially in currency markets and bond markets.

Question: How should the risk of Fannie Mae and Freddie Mac be assessed when they represent a cumulative 11 percent of the fixed-income markets and are the largest participants in the mortgage and swaps markets?

Bluford: Most people believe Freddie Mac, Fannie Mae, and Ginnie Mae are too big to fail. They are government-created agencies, so the risk is essentially political. Consequently, these investors assume that these agencies are not highly risky. The hypothesis about how much the government is willing to get involved in the business affairs of a mortgage agency may be tested because of accounting issues at Freddie Mac. I do not pretend to know what those issues are because I know only what I have seen in the paper, and it is clear that the reporters writing about it do not have a clue what a mortgage is or how to hedge mortgage-related risks. Note, however, that the housing market in the United States is about as politically "apple pie" as possible. I am betting that if we ever had a real crisis in the mortgage market (not like the current accounting scandals) that the government will live up to its guarantee, although it may happen through a very big rate cut on the part of the Federal Reserve Bank rather than through a congressional bailout. Volatility would increase in the share prices of the mortgage agencies, but long-term investors would be rewarded for not going into panic mode and selling at the bottom.

Risk Measurement versus Risk Management

D. Sykes Wilford
Chairman, Advisory Board, Beauchamp Financial Technology
Partner, Hamilton Investment Partners
Greenwich, Connecticut

> Risk management garners much attention in the investment management industry, but it differs from risk measurement. Portfolio managers, consultants, and clients each require different portfolio-related information. Managing the information derived from risk measurement is central to the portfolio management process. Portfolio managers must balance expected returns against the risk accepted to earn those returns. For them, risk measurement information has always been an integral part of the portfolio management process. But as the industry evolves, others are becoming interested in the structure of the portfolio risks taken. Firms not providing sufficient information will miss opportunities to acquire and retain clients.

Risk measurement and risk management are both integral to the portfolio management process, but the two are very different. Risk measurement gauges changes in portfolio value corresponding to different market conditions. It is a risk management tool. Risk management focuses on identifying and controlling portfolio risks. Management entails action to make the measurement activity useful. Measuring systems used for portfolio creation are also not the same as those used to manage portfolio risk. Confusing the two can lead to the underestimation of risk, as can be argued in the Long-Term Capital Management (LTCM) crisis case. Risk measurement information is based on *ex post* analytics applied to existing portfolios, which can have wide use by many different constituents.

Another issue looming on the horizon relates to interpreting the inherent complexities of such *ex post* risk measurement information. Portfolio managers may understand complicated statistical analysis, but they are not the only users of risk measurement data. My goal, therefore, is to discuss risk measurement in a nontechnical, client-friendly way and to encourage others to do the same. The institutionalization of hedge funds and the increasing number of parties that require risk measurement information necessitate a major change in the industry in this regard.

From Data to Useful Information

Many investors assume that portfolio managers are able to forecast a particular stock's future performance. Portfolios exist, however, because no one knows what is going to happen in the future. Thanks to the work of Harry Markowitz and modern portfolio theory, portfolio managers know they are trying to manage risk and return in the aggregate, not for individual stocks. If portfolio managers are not managing portfolio risk, they are not managing portfolios.

To help clients understand that portfolios are primarily a means to manage uncertainty, portfolio managers must convert risk measurement data into useful information that will help clients understand the information derived from their risk systems, such as value at risk (VAR) analysis. Portfolio managers are dealing with *ex ante* forecast risk, not *ex post* measured risk. But for risk management purposes, they are interested in the market-driven measurement of risk. Clients must be able to use this information and apply it to their investment decision-making process. Portfolio theory, risk measurement, and risk management must be integrated practically if the maximum value of the work is to be obtained by managers and clients as well.

Constituents. Risk measurement provides the information. With it, the portfolio manager or another interested party can take action in the form of risk management. Many firms now have risk managers charged with measuring risk and developing strategies to handle it. Web access for the risk measurement data is vital so that portfolio managers can get to it easily, wherever they happen to be. The data should be user-friendly, not obscure. To make efficient decisions, portfolio managers also need data that can be viewed in multiple forms.

Many other constituents need risk measurement data. Chief investment officers need the data to ensure proper management of their areas of responsibility. CEOs, investment committee members, and the board also need to conduct risk analyses. Clients are increasingly interested in knowing what the data mean and how to use it to make better financial decisions, so client service and marketing teams need to know how to deal with risk measurement data as well. Portfolio managers, therefore, cannot continue to simply engage in esoteric discussions of risk analysis among themselves. Making data useful to a wider audience is critical.

Need for Conversion. The development of risk measurement "toolkits" driven from a single data source is important in meeting the informational needs of different user groups. Portfolio managers have particular data needs in order to make decisions. For instance, they may prefer to see complicated equations that look at Greek letter variables derived from an option theoretic approach to portfolio analysis. The client service team, however, might not need to see complex mathematics, but it definitely needs to understand its implications.

Board members need information about risk to make sure they are meeting their fiduciary obligations. They cannot simply put this burden on their consultants. In the current market, clients have been requesting risk measurement data, especially as they consider alternatives to stocks and bonds. Furthermore, many clients perceive the existence of less regulatory oversight in such alternative investment classes as hedge funds and funds of funds than in more traditional asset classes. With these alternative investment classes come new types of oversight and investment committees, each with different informational needs.

The New Institutional Investor

Hedge funds were once the domain of wealthy individuals, but they are now attracting institutional investors. Because institutional clients care about risk management issues, the risk management topic has become even more important. Unfortunately, many people in the industry still respond to questions about risk measurement data simply by saying, "Leave it to me; I will manage risk. Trust me." Such an attitude will no longer suffice.

Traditional Investors. Traditionally, long-only institutional clients focused on the trade-off between stocks and bonds. Most of the major indexes were constructed accordingly, as were the methodological approaches to risk. Long-only clients focused on return history and tended to remain with managers for a long time. Periodic reporting was sufficient, and the desire for privacy outweighed any need for better information.[1] Furthermore, risk guidelines were not critical and often did not even exist, as evidenced by the LTCM crisis. Risk mattered, but risk management was not common practice. Correlation with other investments was important, but less so than today. Index tracking was more important for long-only clients than it is now.

Hedge Funds. The institutionalization of hedge funds has underscored the need for formal risk management. Committee decisions, which were never part of the decision-making process of wealthy individuals, are more prevalent. Committee decisions imply the involvement of economic agents who usually have fiduciary responsibilities and a different attitude toward risk than an individual might have. These agents view the risk–return trade-off differently and care about correlations with other investments in their portfolios. As a result, those hedge funds that wish to attract institutional clients need to explain average historical risk, crisis risk and correlations, and portfolio risk and cross-correlations.

Transparency and Risk Measurement: The New Constituency

To satisfy the institutional market, the hedge fund industry must make a commitment to transparency. In fact, transparency of risk may be just as important as historical performance. I would not invest any money in a hedge fund unless it could show the amount of risk it was taking to achieve its level of performance. Clients expect quick access to such information. Competition is driving firms to find ways to satisfy these new demands.

Marketing, Client Service, and Sales. The marketing department should be the largest user of

---

[1] Leo de Bever points out that fewer than 40 percent of hedge funds provide the level of transparency he would like to have in reporting. See Leo de Bever's presentation in this proceedings.

risk measurement information. As clients demand more information more quickly, marketing departments have become the real constituents for risk measurement, and they want the data fast, quick, and cheap. This desire for fast, quick, and cheap data is especially important because the marketing staff works in an increasingly competitive environment and needs to help institutional investors feel comfortable with the firm's investment process. High absolute future returns are unlikely in both the equity and fixed-income markets, so portfolio managers will have more difficultly concealing their mistakes. Volatility beyond a predetermined or preconceived boundary might be perceived as a portfolio manager mistake, which is not the same as a mistake in the legal sense. Portfolio managers simply must keep clients informed. They have the tools necessary to educate clients; now, they must provide their marketing departments with them.

The client service team should be equipped to provide the answers to clients' questions about return, risk, and correlations. Although portfolio managers use *expected* risk and returns in order to build portfolios, the client service team may need measurement tools based on *historical* information. The tools used to produce one set of data should be able to produce the other as well. Return data can be sliced in many ways and can be attributed to different sector and industry bets. Few firms do the same with risk and correlation data, which presents an opportunity to better serve clients.

Large firms should have the resources to provide these data. Because more and more clients now use risk measurement data, firms should strive to take advantage of the situation by marketing this information to them. If clients do not understand the usefulness of these data, firms can gain a competitive advantage by letting them know why they need the data.

Web Systems. Web-enabled services allow clients to see manager activity regarding risk–return analyses and correlations with other positions. Clients also need to have the ability to create sensitivity or crisis scenarios as well as to understand portfolio correlations with respective benchmarks.

Although expensive to implement, Web-based systems have benefits that should not be underestimated. I once managed a portfolio management team that managed investments for a Tokyo-based firm. The 12-hour time-zone difference wreaked havoc on their internal risk data. They spent considerable time on the phone with our trading desk. We eventually determined that the Japanese administrator was providing mismatched information to the risk managers because of the time-zone difference. A Web-based risk management system solved our problem. The calls from Tokyo, which used to occur once a day and take about three hours to resolve, ended. Needless to say, our client service representative was happy not to receive anymore irate phone calls from Tokyo, and we were able to make more efficient use of our time. An Internet-based risk analysis system for clients can save the managing firm money, time, and headaches and simultaneously keep the customer happy.

Providing the Tools

When providing services to clients, the data should be presented in a way that is meaningful to them. A screen full of numbers, for example, can be easily converted into a picture. Portfolio risk data should be divided into historical track record information and information on current portfolio positions. Historical information includes such items as return and risk statistics; examples include VAR standard deviation, skewness, and kurtosis. Portfolio position information includes VAR measures, shocks with crisis scenarios, and even Monte Carlo simulation with a bi-modal distribution of returns. The advantage of separating the data is that although portfolio managers are more interested in the current portfolio standing, clients are more interested in the historical information.

In deciding whether to purchase a particular investment, clients should be able to see the distribution in terms of skewness and kurtosis. These two simple measures convey a great deal of information about the amount of risk taken and have not traditionally been provided to clients.

Recall that skewness and kurtosis evaluate how a distribution of returns varies from normal. Skewness describes the asymmetry of a distribution to show where the risk is likely to be. A risk-averse investor would prefer that the skewness be positive. Kurtosis measures the size of the tails of the distribution. A risk-averse investor would like these to be as thin as possible because thin tails mean the returns generally fall closer to the mean. **Figure 1** depicts actual returns and a best-fit normal distribution for a typical asset-backed securities portfolio. It shows a little kurtosis and a little skewness. **Figure 2** shows the same portfolio's historical returns and distribution from January 1993 to July 1998. Back then, I would have wanted to invest with the manager of this portfolio because of its low risk and concentrated above-LIBOR returns, month after month, for five years. Institutional investors sought out these types of funds. A steady return of a couple hundred basis points a year in outperformance was deemed exactly what the doctor ordered. They would have loved this type of portfolio. Nonetheless, with the little bit of kurtosis in the middle, the distribution was not

Figure 1. Portfolio Returns Demonstrating Skewness and Kurtosis

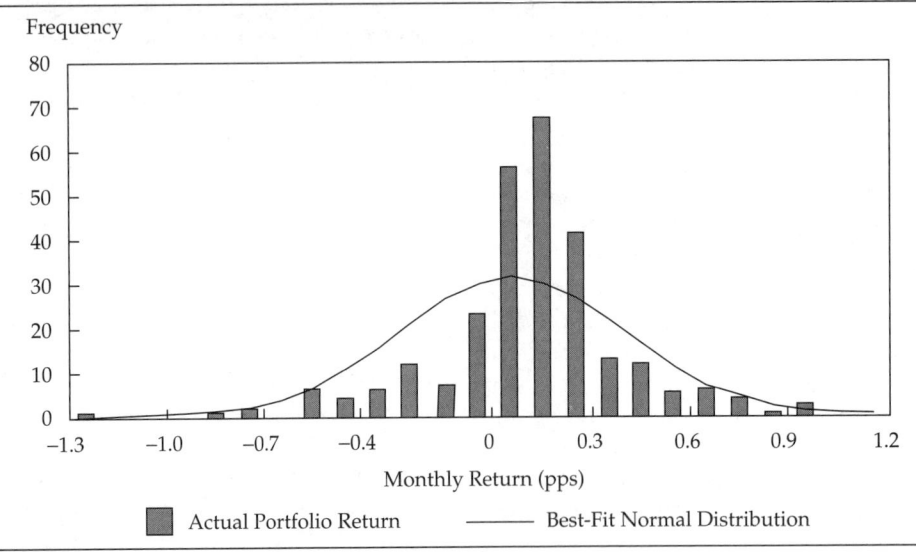

Source: Analytics by Investor Analytics, LLC.

Figure 2. Portfolio Returns, January 1993–July 1998

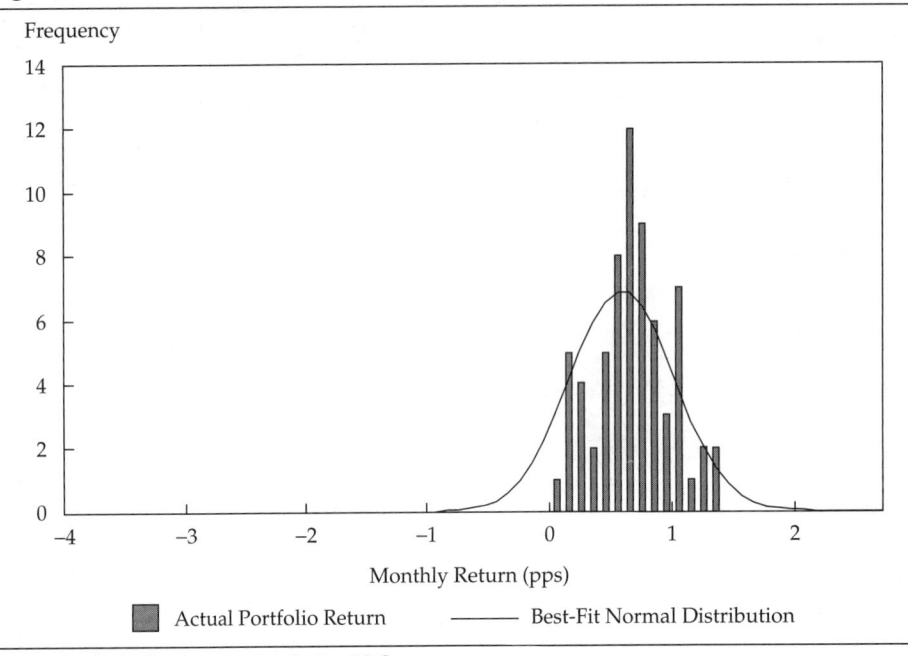

Source: Analytics by Investor Analytics, LLC.

normal. No fraud or fake accounting had occurred, but the distribution shows that the manager may have been taking on more risk than the client may have realized.

Figure 3 shows the portfolio's distribution through October 1998. Between July and October, the Russian government defaulted on its debt and LTCM failed. News and events affect the markets. In the long run, this distribution is more likely to occur than the five-year distribution with magnificent information ratios shown in Figure 2. Notice that the distribution in Figure 3 is more skewed to the left and has fatter tails (kurtosis). The investment style indicated that this portfolio would have unsurprisingly resulted in a distribution with more skewness and kurtosis after a market shock.

Figure 3. Portfolio Returns, January 1993–October 1998

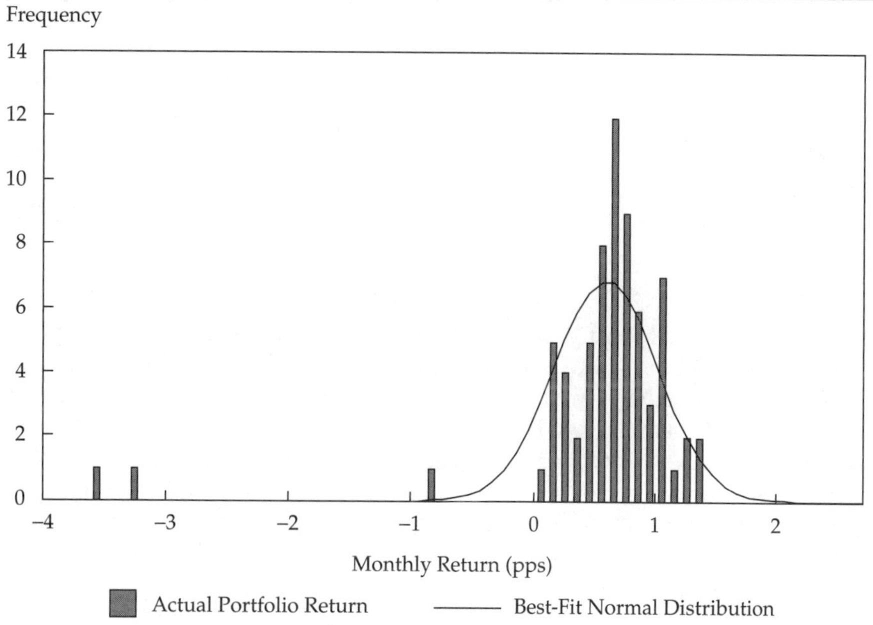

Source: Analytics by Investor Analytics, LLC.

Portfolio managers, of course, know how to look for skewness and kurtosis and manage the risks they signify. Conveying such information to clients may seem difficult at first, but it can be done through VAR measures and crisis scenarios. If a firm is unwilling to provide such information, an investor may question whether the portfolio manager is doing a good job.

Some portfolios have two planes of performance, one that reflects normal conditions and one that reflects a crisis. A variety of methodologies can be used to model these bimodal scenarios and provide appropriate information to an investor. The key is to give investors the information they need to assess portfolio risk. Most clients will want to see graphs with examples chosen for their needs. Some clients will want to know positions, but not all hedge fund firms will provide that information. Other clients will want different analyses of profit, loss, risk potential, distribution analyses, and so on.

The multiplicity of demands will be a challenge for fund managers. Tailoring each report and piece of information specifically to each individual's demands is a great deal of work. Traditionally, managers have simply chosen not to do it, instead giving everyone the same type of report. But now, improvements in information systems and presentation software make it easy to provide clients with all the information they want, in the way they want it, with the pictures they want. And they can receive it from the Internet according to their timetable, not the client service team's timetable. If managers do not deliver such information, their competition will.

Having a single-data source, or a single-portfolio platform, is a critical element in providing information in a useful form to the many user groups I have mentioned. The client service team has to make the data useful to the investor, and each individual need is an opportunity for the marketing team to explain the product. In taking the time to explain products to clients, managers improve their chances of client satisfaction and have the opportunity to steer clients toward the manager's products and away from the competition's products.

Conclusion

Now that *risk management* has become increasingly important in the investment management industry and many constituents need *risk measurement* information, people must be able to grasp the distinction between the two terms. The portfolio management process is about managing the information derived from measuring risk. For portfolio managers, who must balance expected returns against the risk accepted to earn those returns, risk measurement information has always been an integral part of the portfolio management process. But as the industry evolves, others are becoming interested not only in the accuracy of managers' forecasts but also in more sophisticated perspectives on risk as they try to understand how the value of their portfolios change as market factors change. Firms must consider their capacity to provide necessary investor information. If they do not, a competitor surely will. Firms not providing sufficient information will thus miss enormous opportunities to acquire and retain investors.

The Dimensions of Active Management

M. Barton Waring
Managing Director and Head of the Client Advisory Group
Barclays Global Investors
San Francisco

> Active management exposes investors to beta, or price volatility relative to the market, and to alpha, which is the value added by the active manager's luck or skill over and above the market. Most active managers do a poor job of separating their performance into the contributions of alpha and beta. But it is positive expected alpha that is valuable, and it is worthy of a substantial fee. Expected beta is, relatively speaking, much less fee worthy. Until managers communicate that their job is to add skill through active management and that clients should pay them for producing positive alpha rather than just for producing beta, investors will continue to undervalue the contributions of the investment management professional.

The past few years have been hard on active managers as well as on the investors, plan sponsors, foundations, and endowments that employ them. The markets, as well as active management returns, have been depressed. Many active management firms are reeling from several years of poor performance and have lost clients. They are experiencing weak revenues both from these client losses and from market-induced losses in their assets under management fee base, even for those firms that are considered to be "blue chip." Now is a good time to reconsider and redefine the nature of active management in the course of revitalizing our profession's value proposition.

In this presentation, which is based on an article I wrote with Laurence Siegel for the *Journal of Portfolio Management*,[1] I will begin by discussing the nature of markets, the types of risks and returns involved in market activity, and the nature of alpha. I will then identify and describe the two conditions that must be accepted if one is to believe in the value of active management. After that discussion, I will describe several equations that I have found valuable in modeling returns and risk in an active management scenario. Finally, I will demonstrate how the information coefficient (IC) can be used to quantify the degree of skill needed—by investors as well as managers—to find value in active management.

Bill Sharpe's Insight

An excellent way to start a discussion of active management is to reconsider an article about active versus passive management that Bill Sharpe wrote in 1991.[2] It was just a two-page article, and Sharpe could have thrown away the second page because the meat was all on the first page. The article makes a remarkably concise and powerful observation—in essence, that a market is composed simply of all participants in the market. Therefore, it has to be true that the average return of all participants in the market must be the same as the return of the market as a whole, before fees and costs (a zero-sum game), and below the return of the market after fees and costs are considered (a negative-sum game).

Consequently, the only way to beat the average, aside from luck, is to have special skill. A market participant has to be substantially better than all other market participants in order to win, especially when fees and costs are considered. And this "superior" investor then of necessity must take money out of somebody else's pocket if the macro average is to be maintained. The good active managers take away from the bad active managers; the smarter market participants take away from the slower market participants.

Bill Sharpe realized the importance of understanding the limitations imposed by a market's average return in thinking about the nature of active

---

[1] M. Barton Waring and Laurence B. Siegel, "The Dimensions of Active Management," *Journal of Portfolio Management* (Spring 2003):35–52.

[2] William F. Sharpe, "The Arithmetic of Active Management," *Financial Analysts Journal* (January/February 1991):7–9.

management. Unfortunately, not everyone perceives markets with such clear vision; from group to group, the clarity of vision varies tremendously. For example, typically when I conduct an audience response survey and ask plan sponsors what active return they really *expect* to get—not what they *want*, not what they are *targeting*, but what they really *expect*, that is, the middle of the distribution of possible returns—90 percent say they expect an active return of 1.5 percent to 2 percent. And they do so even after I have explained Sharpe's insight about the arithmetic of active management. Plan sponsors as a whole have a very ambitious attitude toward active management, but they cannot all be right in forming such ambitious expectations. It is like the problem of logic in Garrison Keillor's fictional town of Lake Wobegon, "where all the kids are above average." The return for every sponsor in a room full of plan sponsors cannot be above average.

Empirical data have been found that confirm Sharpe's theoretical insight. According to the studies of Gary Brinson, L. Randolph Hood, Gilbert Beebower, and Brian Singer, 90 percent of the *variance* of a typical portfolio's returns is attributable to the strategic asset allocation decision; only about 10 percent is attributable to active management.[3] According to the returns data reported in those studies, however, plan sponsors lose about 0.5 percent, or 50 bps, more or less, in their security selection efforts over time, which sounds like a good approximation of a zero alpha, less fees and costs. And thus investors do, on average, experience Sharpe's law of the arithmetic of active management. Yet despite this experience, they maintain their optimistic expectations.

Two Kinds of Risk, Two Kinds of Return

A good approach for developing clarity of thought on the concept of active management is to examine the old Evans–Archer diagram, as illustrated in **Figure 1**. This diagram is found in the beginning of nearly every finance textbook ever written, and it illustrates that as portfolios become increasingly diversified, portfolio risk is lowered and asymptotically reaches a minimum level that is shown in the figure as the horizontal line above the base line. Risk cannot be further reduced below this asymptotic level simply through more diversification. Consequently, the risk that remains at points below the

---
[3]Gary P. Brinson, L. Randolph Hood, Jr., and Gilbert L. Beebower, "Determinants of Portfolio Performance," *Financial Analysts Journal* (July/August 1986):39–44; and Gary P. Brinson, Brian D. Singer, and Gilbert L. Beebower, "Determinants of Portfolio Performance II: An Update," *Financial Analysts Journal* (May/June 1991):40–48.

Figure 1. Evans–Archer Diagram of Risk versus Diversification

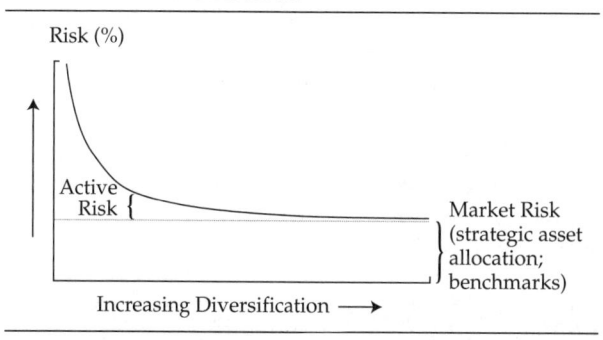

horizontal line is known as undiversifiable risk (or market risk, or systematic risk, or beta risk—all being equivalent terms).

When sponsors or other investors establish a strategic asset allocation policy, they are doing so across fully diversified asset classes by using benchmark indexes to represent each asset class. They are thinking in terms of the security market line, where there is an upward-sloping relationship between return and risk (risk being expressed in terms of beta). Market risk, or beta risk, is the risk component *below* the horizontal line in the Evans–Archer diagram. It is rewarded risk.

The risk component *above* the horizontal line is often called "diversifiable risk" (or "idiosyncratic risk" or "unsystematic risk" or "nonmarket risk"). In the context of this discussion, I call it "active risk" because it is the risk that confronts the active manager who holds securities in weights different from the total market benchmark in order to try to beat the market. Establishing the right mix of securities and their portfolio weights must be done with skill or the portfolio will lose value compared with the market. That is what active risk is: It is moving back up the curve to accept some amount of idiosyncratic risk over and above market risk in an effort to add value through active insights.

I mentioned that market-related risk is related to the upward sloping security market line and that it is rewarded risk. Market risk has to be rewarded, unconditionally, because it cannot be further reduced by simple diversification. Investors will not take it on if it is not rewarded. But through diversification, investors can shed active risk; therefore, active risk need only be rewarded expectationally through luck (but that is a mean zero expectation) or, more rarely, through sufficient special skill to make a positive, nonzero expectation. It has an *unconditional* expected return of zero and a *conditional* expected return proportional to skill, both observations being made prior to adjustment for fees and costs. This is an important conclusion and is consistent with what Sharpe observed.

If two types of risk exist, two types of return also exist. Active risk offers only a conditional expected return, the condition being the presence of skill, whereas market risk offers an unconditional expected return. Furthermore, market risk can be had at low cost (index funds are quite inexpensive). But active risk is expensive; active management requires effort, whether skillful or not. The investor would prefer to pay for active management only if it is skillful.

Does "Expected Alpha" Even Exist?

Is there such a thing as a nonzero "expected alpha"? I cannot help but think that this expression is oxymoronic, at least at first blush. After all, when finance professors teach the efficient market hypothesis, they explain that expected alpha must of necessity be zero if markets are efficient. They teach the unconditional expectation. Students are told, in essence, that the investor cannot beat the market. So, why am I discussing expected alpha, and why are so many managers and investors involved in active management? Why, then, are no significant plan sponsors 100 percent indexed, and why is active management still pursued universally to a greater or lesser degree?

The answer is that investors do not believe that markets are truly efficient. After all, investors cannot all be 100 percent indexed. So, how do investors and plan sponsors respond to the finance professors and their efficient market hypothesis? How do they adapt to the schizophrenic state of mind in which they are supposed to know that markets are efficient and yet they hire active managers? Based on their behavior, it is clear that investors implicitly understand the notion of conditionality with respect to positive expected alphas.

Two Conditions for Active Management

Two conditions (and their subconditions) must be accepted for an investor to decide to employ active managers. The investor must believe the following:
1. Some "good" managers really do exist, which, in turn, requires that
   - some inefficiency exists in the market and
   - differences in skill exist in the exploitation of those market inefficiencies such that some of the managers can be expected to beat the market through their use.
2. He or she has the skill to identify those good managers.

Can the first condition occur? Although finance professors have in the past taken strong views that markets are efficient, few today would argue that markets are *perfectly* efficient. After all, if markets were perfectly efficient, they could not and would not exist; there would be no need for markets. A market, therefore, may approach efficiency but will not be perfectly efficient.

Furthermore, differences exist in the ability of market participants to exploit these inefficiencies. Remember what inefficiency is: Inefficiency means that some information is not yet impounded into securities prices. If someone can find and appropriately process that information, that person will have an insight into the directionality of the market, a particular stock, a particular industry, or a particular asset class. With skill, the information can be exploited to beat the market.

Can there be any doubt that there are differences in skill among people? Since childhood, we have been observing that some people, based on their performance and the recognition they receive, are more skilled at certain activities than are others. So, the logical assumption is that different market participants, including different professional managers, will have different skills at exploiting inefficiencies. The more skilled a manager is at finding information and applying that information, the more likely that manager will outperform other managers. Of course, as I said earlier, any gains by that skillful manager must be experienced as losses by someone else.

Manager skill is customarily quantified as the information coefficient, or IC. It is simply the correlation coefficient between a manager's (or other participant's) forecasts and the actual realizations that follow them. As with any other correlation coefficient, it ranges from -1.0 to $+1.0$, with 0.0 representing no skill. I will use this coefficient later to demonstrate the level of skill needed to derive value from active management.

Once the first condition and its subconditions are accepted—that good managers exist and that they have the skill to exploit inefficiencies in the market—the second condition becomes paramount. Investors must have the skill to identify good managers. But it is this second condition that poses the real problem. Fortunately, both layers of skill—the manager's skill at exploiting market inefficiencies and the investor's skill at identifying skillful managers—are forecasting skills that can be measured and discussed using the IC.

Index Funds and Active Funds

Before discussing the IC, I want to review some of the significant differences between index funds and active funds. An index fund is a delivery mechanism only for market returns—it delivers pure beta, with no expected alpha—whereas an active fund is designed to offer a mixture of market returns and active returns. The unconditional expected return for an index fund is the market return less a small management fee (and, of course, a small tracking error). For an active fund, the unconditional expected return is the market return less a larger management fee and other costs. It has no unconditional expected active return, although the goal is for the manager to add positive alpha. This goal can only be expected conditional on skill. The manager may have a style, capitalization, or region bias, which simply means that the investor needs to define the beta exposure consistently with the manager's normal domain.

The risk for the index fund is the risk of the relevant market. The risk for an active fund is necessarily a bit higher than the market (if one assumes a beta of at least 1) because of the idiosyncratic risk involved in active management (think back to the Evans–Archer diagram). Costs for an index fund are low, whereas costs for an active fund are more substantial. As for the basis for outperformance, an index fund claims none, and that which is claimed for an active fund arises either from skill or luck. Active outperformance can come from only one or the other. The investor, therefore, can achieve the market return at quite a low cost, but simply to play the game of active management, the investor has to pay substantially more.

Every net long portfolio has a definable market exposure. In terms of simple benchmarks, an S&P 500 Index manager has S&P 500 market exposure. To the extent that a portfolio is actively managed, it will include some active risk exposure over and above the market exposure. If an investor hires an active manager but handles the hiring process unskillfully, thereby choosing a manager with no fair expectation that the manager is, in fact, skillful, the investor can expect, on average, to lose to another investor who has been more skillful in choosing a manager. It is like the old poker adage: If you do not know who the fool in the game is, it is you.

Modeling Returns and Risk

To model returns and risks, I will begin with a simple single-index model. Not surprisingly, such a model is internally consistent with the remainder of the theory I will discuss in this presentation, even though it comes independently from the field of regression in statistics:

$$r_p = \beta r_b + \alpha.$$

This equation models excess return, r_p, as beta, β, multiplied by the excess return of a benchmark, r_b, plus alpha, α. I use the phrase "return of the benchmark," but it can also be referred to as the "risk premium" because it is the excess return over the risk-free rate. Furthermore, I use the term "benchmark" rather than "market" because returns will be relative to the market in which the investor is participating.

The next equation models risk and follows from the first:

$$\sigma_p^2 = \beta^2 \sigma_b^2 + \omega^2.$$

In this equation, the variance of a portfolio, σ_p^2, equals beta squared multiplied by the variance of the benchmark, σ_b^2, plus omega squared, ω^2, which is the variance of the alpha. These two equations offer a clear and simple model of returns and risks based on a single index.

Style Boxes and Beta. Investors often categorize investment managers in terms of style boxes. For instance, they refer to managers (or portfolios) as being large-cap value or small-cap value, large-cap growth or small-cap growth. One approach to categorize manager structure is to force managers into one of these style boxes.

In reality, these boxes are just descriptors of betas for particular market segments. Investors can think about them as a multifactor set of betas that can be used to explain manager returns or portfolio returns, much like Sharpe's style analysis. In fact, a reread of Sharpe with this new organizational concept in mind shows that that is how he explained it first, using the word "weights" instead of "beta." He wanted a term that sounded less technical, but weights in style analysis are really just betas from a regression context.

Because few managers fit into a single style, using a multifactor beta set offers valid advantages, although it does cause the math to appear less elegant to those not accustomed to matrix algebra:

$$r_p = \begin{bmatrix} 1 \\ 1 \\ 1 \\ 1 \end{bmatrix}^T \begin{bmatrix} \beta_{LV} r_{LV} \\ \beta_{LG} r_{LG} \\ \beta_{SV} r_{SV} \\ \beta_{SG} r_{SG} \end{bmatrix} + \alpha,$$

where
LV = large-cap value,
LG = large-cap growth,
SV = small-cap value, and
SG = small-cap growth.

This approach provides a summation (through multiplication by the ones vector) across a vector of betas and returns that is more precise and complete than a single-beta model, although it is less easily communicated. It implies a comfortable ability to use complex benchmarks similar in form to the output of Sharpe style analysis.

Isolating Active Beta. A portfolio's beta relative to that of a benchmark can be further decomposed into two parts, its "active beta" and, for lack of a better term, its "neutral" beta. If neutral beta is 1, as it is in a single-beta analysis, subtract 1 from the portfolio's beta and the remainder is what I call "active beta." (In a multifactor analysis, the vector of neutral betas will be the percentages of each factor in the benchmark combination, adding up to a total of 1.) The active beta is just the difference between the portfolio's beta(s) and the neutral beta(s), and it can be positive or negative. The following series of equations show how the single-index model can be decomposed to isolate active beta, demonstrating that the excess return of a portfolio is equal to the excess return of the benchmark, r_b, plus an active beta component, β_a, and a true alpha component, α:

$$r_p = \beta_a r_b + \alpha$$
$$= (1 + \beta_a) r_b + \alpha$$
$$= r_b + (\beta_a r_b + \alpha).$$

(I will skip the multifactor matrix algebra version—the intuition is consistent.)

Why is this equation important to this discussion? In a typical performance measurement delivered today, it is the joint contribution of the active beta and the true alpha that is typically reported, not the true alpha in isolation. I call this "performance alpha" ($\beta_a r_b + \alpha$). Recognizing, again, that investors can adjust their beta exposure on their own, and for a relatively low cost, performance alpha does not do a very informative job of telling investors whether the manager has done well or not.

Consider a value manager who is working in an S&P 500 benchmark space—not an uncommon situation, even if it is not healthy, as this discussion will show. When value stocks are strong and the manager is able to improve on the benchmark's performance, the manager will claim to have active management skills. But the value, and thus the "skill," is derived merely from the market's return. In effect, one can think of S&P 500 value and S&P 500 growth as the market components, with neutral beta weights of 50 percent for each. Relative to the entire S&P 500 benchmark, a strict value manager has a beta to value of 1 (an active beta to value of +0.5 relative to an S&P 500 benchmark) and a beta to growth of 0 (an active beta to growth of –0.5).

So, the manager's performance alpha will be:

$$r_p = r_{S\&P\ 500} + \underbrace{[(0.5 \times r_{S\&P\ Value} - 0.5 \times r_{S\&P\ Growth}) + \alpha]}_{\text{Performance alpha}}.$$

One can easily see that alpha, true active return, can be zero or even negative but that the manager's performance alpha will look good when value stocks do better than growth stocks. So, regardless of whether the value manager has selected securities well against the value benchmark, this manager will present himself or herself to the client as if he or she were skillful. In fact, it is just the manager's beta exposures that have had a fortunate return, which is of little value to the investor because a value index fund could have been obtained at low cost and would have generated the same result. The lesson is that by separating the components of return into the market component and the active component, investors can better evaluate the true alpha earned by their managers. In this case, it might show up to be zero or worse.

Finding and Using Sources of Alpha. True alpha can be created in two ways—through security selection, the most common, and through market selection, which includes market timing or benchmark timing and which is another way of saying that the manager is varying the levels of active beta over time. Actively managing the active beta relative to the fixed betas of a benchmark is a perfectly legitimate way of adding value, of course conditional on skill at the task. Unfortunately, such skill seems to be rare. Investors should be wary of hiring active managers that are sector rotators or otherwise manage their active betas actively unless they are convinced that the managers have exceptionally high skill levels to get past the low-breadth problem inherent in market-timing approaches.

Choosing a Portfolio Manager. Choosing a portfolio of managers is no different from choosing a portfolio of securities. It is an optimization problem. The investor can optimize across expected alpha—which is active return against expected active risk. The best of the current scientific active managers all optimize expected alpha versus expected active risk at the individual security level. Similarly, the sponsor can optimize across the collections of securities that are represented by managers. It is a straightforward task. By controlling the betas of the managers, furthermore, the investor can make the portfolio of managers mirror the investor's overall benchmark.[4] And the alpha estimation problem is identically difficult for both portfolios.

Figure 2 shows how this process provides the investor with an efficient frontier in active

---
[4] For an accessible discussion of this topic, see Charles Castille, John Pirone, M. Barton Waring, and Duane Whitney, "Optimizing Manager Structure and Budgeting Manager Risk," *Journal of Portfolio Management* (Spring 2000):90–104.

management space. Any point on that efficient frontier represents the mix of managers that the investor is considering. On the lower-left side of the frontier, at the zero active risk budget position (where the benchmark is indicated), the investor would be 100 percent indexed. The index fund would sit atop that benchmark. On the upper-right end, the other extreme, the portfolio would consist of a single highly concentrated manager. Between those two extreme risk budget positions are many other mixes of potential active managers. At risk budgets toward the low-risk end of the frontier, the mix will include index funds (and low-risk active funds) as well as higher-risk traditional active funds.

Figure 2. Efficient Frontier of Expected Alpha versus Active Risk

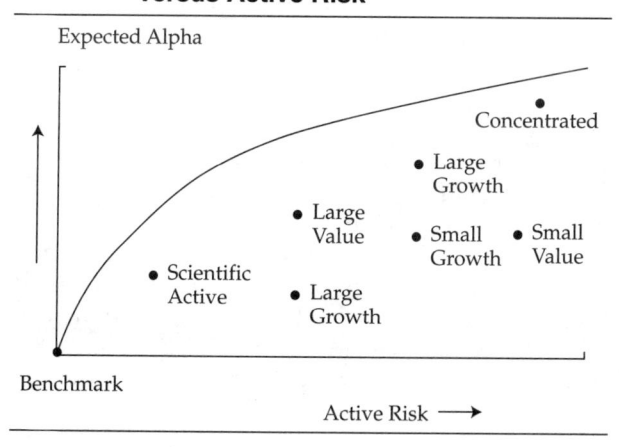

This figure helps the investor rethink core–satellite indexing, in which a portion of the fund is placed in indexed investments and the rest is allocated among different styles of active management. In this more complete view, the core is not necessarily a pure index fund but will likely include low-risk active funds as well.

If the betas are mathematically corrected as I discussed earlier, the investor can incorporate managers with growth betas, small-cap betas, large-cap betas, and value betas and come up with a portfolio that looks like the benchmark. The technology for this analysis exists and is in fairly wide use (see Castille, Pirone, Waring, and Whitney 2000, cited previously).

Points on the frontier demonstrate how active and passive management can be integrated as a means of risk control. The investor simply needs to determine how much active risk and how much active return each manager brings to the portfolio and then how much active risk and active return the investor wants to engage. These are the same quantitative tools that many of the most scientific of the active managers use to manage portfolios of securities. The technology is published and widely read.[5]

The next step is for the investor to determine how large a portion of the portfolio to give each manager. The short answer is that in the course of an optimization, those managers with the highest expected information ratio should generally get the largest mandates. More precisely, their allocation percentage, which I will call h, is a function of the ratio of expected alpha divided by variance of alpha, which can be shown mathematically as follows:

$$h = f\left(\frac{\alpha}{\omega^2}\right).$$

Those managers with a high ratio of expected alpha to variance should get the largest mandates. Because variance is standard deviation squared, a premium is placed on low active risk managers who have any reasonable level of expected alpha. This result may come as a surprise to those who embrace the notion that the best strategy is to buy an index fund and then add a few highly concentrated, higher-risk managers, those who just buy "a few really good stocks." But in an optimal world, an investor who is skilled at picking managers is better off picking lower-risk managers skillfully than higher-risk managers skillfully, manager skill held constant.

Investors should also favor managers that squeeze out uncompensated risks in their portfolios, those who use modern portfolio construction methods. Risks that are accidentally taken (i.e., risks that are not associated with an expected alpha) reduce the expected information ratio that the manager can be expected to provide (again for a constant level of skill). As a consequence, the expected alpha-to-omega-squared ratio will be lower than it could be.

Skills Needed for Successful Active Management

As I mentioned earlier, two types of skill are involved in active management—the manager's skill at forecasting and exploiting inefficiencies in the market and the investor's skill at choosing successful managers—both of which can be measured using the IC. But how much skill is needed? As it turns out, not much. Because of the implications of the efficient market hypothesis, many investors question whether active management is even feasible and whether value exists in trying to forecast alpha. But that concern may be overblown because only minimal skill is needed to make active management worth the effort.

---

[5]Richard C. Grinold and Ronald N. Kahn, *Active Portfolio Management* (New York: McGraw Hill, 2000).

For an active manager who is buying securities, it takes remarkably little skill to add value, and the costs are relatively low in that environment.

Consider the IC. If an IC of zero represents no skill, an IC as low as 0.02 to 0.10 will create a top-quartile performance record for picking securities. An IC of 0.04 means a manager will be right only 52 percent of the time; an IC of 0.10 suggests that the manager will be right only 55 percent of the time. It requires a bit more skill, however, for an investor to pick active managers—perhaps 0.25 to 0.40—to create enough alpha to pay for fees and costs and still add value to the portfolio. For example, at 0.25, the investor will pick the right manager 62.5 percent of the time. Depending on their alphas and their fees, this IC may be sufficient to pay for the fees and still leave some alpha for the investor to keep. As can be seen, skill is required, but it does not have to be overwhelming skill. The manager and the investor do not have to be prophets. (A prophet has an IC of 1.0.) They do not have to be accurate on every forecast. But if they are right slightly more often than they are wrong, they will add value to the portfolio.

Flaws in Using Historical Data as a Resource in Forecasting Expected Alpha. A typical means of forecasting is to use historical data to determine historical alphas. Two problems arise from this method. First, even though historical alphas are easy to use, they do not provide much information. Although they are "real numbers" that can be used to generate satisfying averages and other comparisons, their first problem is that they combine both beta and alpha in the "performance alpha" I discussed earlier. Therefore, they are not representative of true alpha. For example, consider international managers who have been underweight the market beta in Japan during the past 10 years. They look like stellar performers. But when the return associated with the underweight beta is compared with the return of the normal beta in Japan, little real alpha remains. On average, no group beats the benchmark; only some of the more skillful individual members of a group might do so.

The second problem is that the three- and five-year performance histories typically considered are seldom statistically significant. Using such performance histories is like cooking eggplant—slice it, spice it, bake it, and then throw it away, because eggplant is good for nothing! That is all anyone can do with manager alphas that are not statistically significant. They have absolutely no value as an input to a forecast of alpha. And even when they are statistically significant, they cannot necessarily be projected into the future, although in that case it is at least fair game to pay some attention to them.

An Alternative to Using Historical Data. My recommendation, therefore, is to (1) regress the data against the likely benchmark components; (2) check the t-statistics on the residuals, the alphas; (3) ignore the historical alpha if its t-statistic is not significant; and (4) even if the t-statistic is significant, use the alpha with care because any forecast of value requires some degree of judgment. A valuable forecast cannot be created from a recipe. If recipes provided good forecasts, they would be impounded into the market and they would stop being good forecasts. If judgment is not being used, investors have no chance except through luck.

That being said, I have found the following formula to be helpful in forecasting alpha, or at least in forecasting it on a more level playing field:

$$\alpha = (IC \times \omega \times z\text{-Score}) \times \text{Efficiency} - (\text{Fees and costs}).$$

The product in the parentheses, IC multiplied by risk multiplied by z-score, can be used as a way of normalizing a forecast of alpha (see Grinold and Kahn, cited previously). The key judgment-based input is the z-score. A normal distribution z-score indicates the number of standard deviations that a manager falls above and below the mean. In the formula, efficiency is the portion of alpha left over as a result of the long-only constraint, skill being held constant, while fees and costs are subtracted. Some rules of thumb applicable here are that concentrated managers are perhaps only 15–20 percent efficient, traditional active managers are 35–45 percent efficient, and low-risk, scientific, active managers are 55–70 percent efficient at harvesting their raw skill.

Many managers and investors will argue that assessing their own skill level—through the IC—is subjective, which it is. It requires judgment. But some judgment is required to take advantage of active management; otherwise, investors are simply randomizing their portfolios, accruing higher fees and higher risks.

Conclusion

Historical, or realized, alpha is a valuable measure of past performance, but investors are understandably jaded because they see inconsistent evidence that managers can really deliver alpha except randomly through luck. This suspicious attitude is not helped by the fact that the investment management profession routinely provides its clients only with "performance alpha," a muddled mixture of beta and true alpha.

And yet, some managers certainly can generate nonzero, positive, expected alphas. Such expected positive alpha is a valuable commodity, well worth a substantial fee. Unfortunately, most investment managers themselves do not know how to differentiate and qualify their alphas as positive, or in any other way. These simplest of technologies are lacking in a manner that almost suggests that the ignorance is intentional.

Managers need to recognize that the performance game is, in fact, hard to play and that it cannot be won without special skill. Nor can client confidence be improved until managers make it clear to their clients that they understand the game. Until managers recognize that no secret recipes to winning exist, that they must provide greater skill than the other smart players in the market do, and that they must organize that skill in order not to waste risk, they will not be able to add value except by luck, and luck will sooner or later run out. Luck is a poor foundation for a long-term business. Unless they do these things, managers will not persuade investors to put their confidence in the investment management profession. Therefore, discipline and clarity are needed—clarity about normal portfolios, clarity about beta exposures, clarity about the search for true alpha, or expected alpha, which, if produced, deserves not only the fees that are typically charged but also even higher fees. It is genuine value added. But based on the random alpha, the performance alpha, that managers deliver today, it is puzzling that clients pay any fees at all for performance that is, in reality, mostly just beta.

In summary, active return—that is, true alpha rather than performance alpha—and active risk are the key dimensions of active management. Forget style boxes; risk and return are the elements that matter. Style can be managed in such a way that the portfolio of managers is summed to have beta characteristics close to that of the benchmark. It is a secondary issue in manager structure, not a primary issue.

In finance, all roads lead to risk and return, and in active management, it is active risk and active return that matter. When active management is especially skillful, it is especially valuable.

Question and Answer Session

M. Barton Waring

Question: Does a combination of various investment management styles really offer a source of value added, or does it just result in a conglomeration of betas?

Waring: I'm not sure what the question is, but I'll try. Underlying that question seems to be a concern about benchmark-relative investing because, of course, betas represent benchmarks; they are close to equivalent terms. The concern usually comes as a plea, always from traditional active managers, "Don't constrain me with benchmarks that tie my hands. Benchmarks keep me from doing what I do best, which is picking stocks that go up in price. Don't constrain me from doing what you want me to do in the way I see best to do it!"

I hear that argument, and I want to believe it. At a visceral level, it sounds good. It just seems like it might be true that a manager should be unhampered.

But the reality is that betas are embedded in every portfolio, and they are measurable. Beta is measurable in a single-factor sense, and it is measurable in a multifactor sense. It is measurable using style factors. It is measurable using Barra factors. A dozen different good ways exist to measure the market risk exposures in a given manager's style of investing.

Furthermore, the market risk and return components can be separated from the active risk and return components. Certainly, there are statistical accuracy problems with understanding the "normal portfolio," another way of referring to the vector of betas, of an active manager who does a lot of factor timing. But aside from the statistical difficulty of discerning the normal portfolio, we know that there is one, that predictable beta exposures are there. We may not be able to say exactly what it is, but there is some set of normal parameters that represents the beta exposures for any long manager. And if we know what they are, we could, if we chose to, invest in those normals in an inexpensive way through index funds or some other equivalent passive form of investing.

It is only to the degree that the manager can beat that collection of benchmarks, that normal portfolio, that any value added is generated for the client. So, in reality, there is very little reason to be sympathetic to the plea from traditional managers to be freed of benchmark constraints. The plea itself reveals that they themselves don't understand what they are being paid to deliver.

Question: Is there a point at which a portfolio encompasses so many styles constrained by the benchmark that the mix has a negative impact on return-generating ability?

Waring: I do not think that a benchmark necessarily constrains managers or investors. A complex multifactor benchmark is no more constraining than a simple benchmark for all the reasons stated in the prior answer.

The question may be directed to active management across a large number of benchmark components—also known as market timing or style rotation. This is a legitimate active management activity, but it of course requires skill, and unfortunately, it tends to be low "breadth" in nature. To the extent that there is sufficient skill to add value in the face of low breadth, that skill should be applied. But low breadth implies low expected information ratios.

Fixed-income investing is another low-breadth game. Fixed income offers only a handful of sources of alpha. Managers can bet on interest rates. They can bet on credits. Nevertheless, a skillful active manager will add value across those factors, but probably not by concentrating on one factor. At such a low breadth, a manager has to be a pretty good forecaster, but it can be done.

Question: Can you relate your presentation to hedge fund active management?

Waring: Most hedge funds are not completely hedged out on all their market exposures. So, they too consist of a mixture of beta and alpha. Usually, they are net long in one or more beta dimensions. William Goetzmann and Stephen Brown published a wonderful paper in the *Journal of Portfolio Management*.[1] It is worthy of review by anybody interested in hedge funds because they investigated the amount of beta risk and the factors of beta risk represented in hedge funds and discuss how much of a hedge fund is "smoke and mirrors" and how much of it is true active risk.

A hedge fund is a mixture of betas and alpha that is being sold as if it were all alpha, and for this the investor pays a high price—a high base fee plus a high participation fee. But remember, the beta exposures could be purchased as index funds or as passive funds elsewhere for very low fees! If the investor does not have some clarity about the true alpha that is being generated relative to the net return from betas, then that investor should question whether the hedge fund is pursuing the right investment strategy. Because hedge funds seldom, if ever, offer

---

[1] Stephen J. Brown and William N. Goetzmann, "Hedge Funds with Style," *Journal of Portfolio Management* (Winter 2003):101–112.

the transparency necessary for that parsing, it is worthwhile being careful of them. I strongly support the new breed of market-neutral hedge funds, especially if they use a strong and detailed risk control model to keep all the betas at close to zero levels.

Question: Considering the nature of the index, does the indexing versus active management argument work for fixed income?

Waring: I am not sure how best to answer this—there are many facets. For one thing, many fixed-income securities are not represented in the benchmark indexes—all the non-exchange-traded securities, for example, the privately traded bonds. The published indexes, therefore, represent only about one-half of the fixed-income world and are probably not great benchmarks for the entire market, although some corrections can be made to strengthen their viability. So, on the one hand, for investors who are only buying exchange-traded fixed-income securities, the published indexes are relatively good benchmarks for active management. On the other hand, the published indexes may not be adequate for investors that work freely in private markets.

There is another issue with respect to the use of market indexes as benchmarks. Published index benchmarks do not represent the liability of most investing organizations, really not of hardly any organization. Any organization that invests its money to fund a liability will probably be gravitating to the use of custom fixed-income benchmarks in the coming years. The customization will be for the purpose of matching the market-related characteristics of their liability, particularly in terms of the dual durations, inflation duration, and real rate duration. It is a coming development.

Question: Are you suggesting that an active manager who cannot tell you his or her IC cannot create alpha except by luck?

Waring: No. What I am saying is that if an active manager has an IC of zero or does not have a determinable positive IC, then that manager is probably one who creates alpha only randomly.

The question points out that determining skill is hard. If a manager has an IC of 0.1, really quite low as correlation coefficients go, it is sufficient to put that manager in the top quartile. It doesn't take a lot of skill to make one stand out in the crowd.

Think about this result, however, that comes from thinking about the skill of this top-quartile hypothetical manager: The R^2 that is associated with that IC of 0.1 is $(0.1)^2$, or only 0.01. How do you interpret this? It means that only 1 percent of the alpha that is generated is based on signal (skill); the rest is random noise. (This is a bit of an exaggeration; see Waring and Siegel, 2003, cited previously.)

That is the problem we have in active management. Most of the measured alpha that is realized over time in a portfolio is just random noise, and that is why it is so hard to discern a true signal. This is a disheartening bit of information, but it is the reality with which we must work. So, assessing one's own IC is itself a judgment-based task.

Question: It does not seem that hard to find good managers, but it seems much harder to fire good managers before they become bad managers. Any comment?

Waring: It is certainly not hard to find managers that were good; I will agree with that. I do not know that it is so easy to find good managers prospectively. It takes a special skill, and not everybody can do it. It is like buying securities.

The firing discipline is difficult. In an ideal world, investors would be free to buy and sell managers quickly, even to short them in the same way that they short securities. But because of the frictions and costs of portfolios and because of institutional restraints, investors are not quick to sell managers. The transaction costs are high. But perhaps investors should try to have longer holding periods for manager positions. Even with the best modern transition management capabilities, significant costs are involved in moving portfolios from one manager to the next. It is nice to be able to avoid such transitions.

Question: How can an organization be proactive, in terms of hiring managers, to make itself more successful than others?

Waring: As I have been discussing, part of what makes an organization more successful than others in hiring managers is luck, and the other part is skill. If all the people in a room were to flip coins 100 times, some people would flip a lot of heads. Likewise, some organizations flip a lot of heads when hiring managers. That part is luck. The disciplines that I have talked about—clearly thinking about the true active return and the true active risk and optimizing and squeezing out unnecessary risk—will help an organization accentuate its skills. And at the end of the day, skill will generate alpha. An organization can have the best process, but if it doesn't have skill, it is not going to add any value. Bottom line advice: Focus your manager research less on past performance and more on a clear-eyed, but necessarily subjective, evaluation of whether you think the manager's people and processes can fairly be expected to generate alpha in the future.

Portfolio Risk Assessment Tools for Hedge Fund Managers

Timothy J. Rudderow
Co-Founder and President
Mount Lucas Management Corporation
Princeton, New Jersey

> Risk measurement in alternative portfolios, including hedge funds, is complex, and the challenges are further complicated by the fact that the hedge fund landscape is changing. Nevertheless, risk assessment tools are available that can handle the complexity and still be relatively simple to use. One such tool is value at risk (VAR), but depending on the type of portfolio being assessed, different models should be used for calculating VAR.

The hedge fund environment is fluid and dynamic. Conditions change quickly, and risk can be great. To operate in such an environment with any confidence of success, hedge fund managers (and their clients) need risk assessment tools that are appropriate to the environment's complexity but not so complex that they inhibit the decision-making process. These tools must encapsulate a simplicity that can be found only on the far side of complexity.

In this presentation, I will give an overview of the hedge fund environment (including the continued trend toward institutionalization and the heightened risk aversion by hedge fund managers); describe value at risk (VAR), the most common risk assessment technique; offer a simple matrix of the hedge fund trading space; and discuss which VAR models work best in the different quadrants of that matrix. I will then discuss two decision points—location and software—that managers and clients face once they decide to use VAR. And I will conclude with a brief discussion of the primary risk to risk information—risk avoidance.

Complex and Changing Landscape

Two main issues characterize the current hedge fund environment: (1) Risk measurement in alternative portfolios is complex, and (2) the hedge fund landscape is changing.

Complexity of the Environment. As an example of the hedge fund environment's complexity, consider my own firm, Mount Lucas Management Corporation. In our own global macro strategy, we use equities, futures, options, swaps, and many instruments with nonlinear payouts. Generally, the instruments we use are liquid, but many firms use nongeneric, illiquid instruments. Another consideration is the complexity inherent in global markets, such as exchanges that open and close at different times. Furthermore, the environment encourages the use of a great deal of leverage of various types—financial leverage, futures leverage, and embedded leverage.

For example, one of our clients asked our advice on a situation the client had with another manager. The manager had invested the client in a AAA rated mortgage-backed security (MBS) portfolio. But the securities in the portfolio were trading at 60 cents on the dollar because the portfolio manager had put them in an array of inverse floaters that had plummeted with rising interest rates. The structure of the inverse floaters was basically a three-times levered bet on LIBOR. As it turned out, the trade was a great one to hold at that particular point in time, but the client learned a meaningful lesson about embedded leverage.

Changing Landscape. The hedge fund landscape is changing dramatically, and one of the most important changes is that the business is becoming even more institutionalized. As institutions have become more interested in hedge funds, the demand for more uniform standards of reporting has increased and the role of risk has taken on greater importance. Institutions are looking to hedge funds to increase their returns, naturally, but they are concerned about risk and risk management as they enter this new investment space. Risk awareness can turn quickly into risk aversion, and risk aversion can turn quickly into lower returns, which is hardly the result that institutions are seeking. Nonetheless, as hedge funds have moved from vehicles for the high-net-worth individual to an institutional asset, the level of risk tolerance has fallen.

Another change is the serious shift from directional strategies to arbitrage strategies, as demonstrated in **Table 1** and **Table 2**. In 1990, 71.07 percent of assets in the hedge fund universe were in macro strategy portfolios and the rest (with the exception of emerging markets) were spread among a wide array of arbitrage strategies. As of 2002, only 10.82 percent of hedge fund assets were found in macro strategy portfolios and the other arbitrage strategies—such as equity hedge, distressed securities, convertible arbitrage, and merger arbitrage—constituted the majority of the assets invested in the hedge fund market.

Table 1. Estimated Strategy Composition by Assets under Management, 1990

Strategy	Portion of Total
Macro strategy	71.07%
Relative-value arbitrage	10.08
Equity hedge	5.28
Event driven	3.84
Fixed income (total)	3.24
Distressed securities	2.40
Equity market neutral	1.68
Equity nonhedge	0.60
Merger arbitrage	0.60
Convertible arbitrage	0.48
Emerging markets (total)	0.36
Sector (total)	0.24
Short selling	0.12

Source: Data from Hedge Fund Research.

Risk Assessment Tools

To assess portfolio risk, be it for a traditional portfolio or for a hedge fund, managers need tools.

Benchmarks. To deal with this complex and changing landscape, clients and managers need reliable tools to assess and manage risk. In traditional investment management, the analyst's most important tool is a market-based benchmark (such as the S&P 500 Index for equity managers). Given the diversity of hedge fund styles and the range of approaches within a style, market-based benchmarks are not feasible for hedge funds. More prevalent in the hedge fund world is the use of peer group or manager universe benchmarks. These benchmarks are essentially compilations of the results of managers with

Table 2. Estimated Strategy Composition by Assets under Management, 2002

Strategy	Portion of Total
Equity hedge	32.07%
Relative-value arbitrage	14.21
Event driven	12.05
Macro strategy	10.82
Distressed securities	3.68
Sector (total)	3.28
Equity nonhedge	2.95
Emerging markets (total)	2.85
Fixed-income arbitrage	2.82
Fixed-income MBS	2.68
Equity market neutral	2.46
Merger arbitrage	1.72
Fixed-income diversified	1.44
Market timing	0.53
Fixed-income high yield	0.31
Regulation D	0.12
Fixed-income convertible bonds	0.07
Convertible arbitrage	5.79
Short selling	0.15

Source: Data from Hedge Fund Research.

similar investment styles—global macro, convertible arbitrage, and so on. Although these benchmarks can provide a general overview of peer group performance, as a risk assessment tool, they lack the necessary precision. Peer group benchmarks do not offer transparency to positions, so there is no way to accurately attribute a manager's results to his or her peers.

Nevertheless, hedge fund managers need a simple way of expressing risk—a way that is relevant, robust, and reliable while at the same time easy for clients to understand and easy for fund managers to communicate. As Leo de Bever mentioned in his presentation, risk is the language managers use to communicate their investment strategy.[1]

Previous Risk Assessment Tools. Before describing current risk assessment tools for hedge funds, I want to discuss—very briefly—the foundation on which these tools were based. Therefore, I will begin by describing a few early tools and why they are now out of favor.

One such tool, known as Risk Points, was designed at Citibank by my partner Paul DeRosa and his staff. It was the precursor of VAR and followed a very simple methodology. It assigned points to a securities position based on the position's riskiness relative to a benchmark. For example, if a manager held a 10-year position, that position might be

---
[1]See Leo de Bever's presentation in this proceedings.

assigned five risk points, and if the manager held a 2-year position, that position might be assigned two risk points, assuming the benchmark was the 10-year Treasury. Furthermore, each manager was assigned a risk-point budget to which his or her portfolios had to adhere.

Another tool used was the margin-to-equity tool, which originated in the futures world and was based on an exchange's margin calculations. Managers began to use it to gauge the level of leverage in their portfolios by adding up all the margin positions in their portfolios. They could then maintain a specified margin-to-equity ratio.

Both of these tools have the advantage of requiring fairly simple calculations, but they work only with homogeneous portfolios, collections of like instruments. They are somewhat effective for gauging directional risk, but they are not effective in reflecting the risk being taken in the alternative investments portfolios of today. For example, Mount Lucas Management runs a global macro portfolio. We use about 120 different securities traded worldwide on different exchanges with different margin and funding requirements. We use junk bond swaps, soybean calls, euro/dollar futures, cash, U.S. Treasury bonds, yen options, gold futures, regular equities, equity indexes, and options on equity indexes. With such a complicated array of instruments, the old simple tools, such as risk points and margin to equity, cannot adequately gauge the risk of such a complex portfolio.

In trying to understand the risk level in the portfolios that Mount Lucas Management manages, clients and traditional managers often ask me, "How much leverage do you use?" This question is irrelevant because answering it would offer no insight into appropriate portfolio risk assessment. For example, if we buy Eurodollar futures with a notional value of $1 million, a margin deposit of only $500 is needed to hold the position. So, I can get huge leverage on that instrument and still not be in a particularly risky position. But with an equity position, we can get 2-to-1 leverage. How much risk is involved with that position? And how risky is the portfolio that holds both of these positions? Examining leverage alone is simply not helpful. Hedge fund managers need a different language to discuss risk assessment, and that language is VAR.

VAR—State of the Art. VAR is *the* state-of-the-art tool for assessing risk in hedge fund management, and several different models are available for determining VAR:

- variance/covariance model, which uses current data to construct a risk profile,
- Monte Carlo simulations, which use manufactured data, and
- historical simulations, which use data from actual past events.

Each methodology uses a variety of assumptions, distributions, correlations, and other "unrealities" to deal with data problems. And no particular model provides the best solution in all situations. Ultimately, the trading strategy should determine the actual risk assessment methodology used.

Trading Space Matrix. To apply some structure to the complex environment of hedge fund strategies, I have designed a simple two-by-two matrix, shown in **Exhibit 1**. It certainly oversimplifies the trading environment, but it offers a reasonable framework in which to understand the various strategies used in hedge fund portfolios and suggests the particular risk models that might be effective in specific circumstances.

Exhibit 1. Trading Space Matrix

	Convergence Strategy	Directional Strategy
Diverse investment	Statistical arbitrage Risk arbitrage	Global macro funds Managed futures funds
Similar investment	Mortgage arbitrage	Sector stock funds and currency funds

Moving horizontally across the matrix, the top two quadrants reflect funds that use portfolios of diverse investments in their strategies, whereas the bottom two quadrants include funds that use portfolios of more homogeneous investments. The left column of the matrix reflects funds that use a convergence strategy, and the right column includes funds that use a directional strategy. Where a fund fits in the trading space matrix indicates the risk concerns associated with the particular fund strategy and the risk assessment tools likely to be the most effective.

Before I discuss the risk assessment implications, however, I will offer a brief description of the types of hedge fund strategies that fit into the different quadrants.

In the upper-left quadrant are statistical arbitrage and risk arbitrage. Hedge funds that follow these strategies hold portfolios of diverse investments and pursue convergence strategies; that is, they hope to identify temporary, abnormal market relationships and profit from the return to normality. For example, a statistical arbitrage fund takes direct data feeds from the equity market. It then applies a model that examines current relationships based on these data and looks for anomalies to exploit. The theory behind statistical arbitrage is similar to traditional pairs trading, but it is carried out in a highly computerized environment. If a particular relationship has gotten out of line, out of its normal boundaries, the hedge fund will take a position from which it will benefit when the relationship returns to normal. A simple example would be Ford Motor Company and General Motors Corporation. Under normal conditions, they trade within a certain range of each other, but when conditions change, either General Motors or Ford can wander outside that normal range. When that happens, a statistical arbitrage trader would buy one and sell the other. Statistical arbitrage is a mean-reverting strategy.

Risk arbitrage funds rely on classic short option trades. For example, when PeopleSoft made an offer to buy J.D. Edwards & Company, and then Oracle Corporation made an offer to buy PeopleSoft, the risk arbitrage traders went short PeopleSoft. Basically, the risk arbitrage traders just want to take a little premium on each trade, and roughly 90 percent of the time they are successful. The other 10 percent of the time they run the risk of the deal breaking and thus suffering significant loss.

In the lower-left quadrant is mortgage arbitrage, which is also a convergence strategy, but it uses homogeneous investments—in this case, a basket of mortgages. The ultimate variable in mortgages, and thus the crux of the mortgage arbitrage strategy, is prepayments. In mortgage arbitrage, generally speaking, traders are marking their own book because in most cases they are dealing with nongeneric securities. This situation can raise concerns about transparency, valuation, and performance measurement.

In the upper-right quadrant of the matrix are the funds following a directional strategy and holding diverse investments in their portfolios. These strategies include global macro funds and managed futures funds. These funds speculate on the direction of the market—taking positions in many different investments moving in many different ways at many different times.

Sector stock funds and currency funds in the lower-right quadrant also speculate on the movement of investments, but they focus on specific areas of the market rather than covering a wide range of asset classes.

■ *Upper-right risk assessment.* In general, the funds in the upper-right quadrant are "long volatility"; that is, they enter positions with payouts like that of an option buyer. As such, they need movement in the market for their strategy to pay off. In periods of general market equilibrium, these types of strategies are prone to a prolonged series of unsuccessful trades—a drawdown. At an extreme, the upper-right trader can be seen as "throwing money out the window and seeing how much money blows back in." The success of this strategy depends a great deal on the fat tails of the distributions of the individual securities that such funds trade. A trader can set up, essentially, an option-replication strategy and capture those fat tails while constraining risk.

A simple parametric VAR does a good job of capturing the risk of a long volatility trader. As an example, **Figure 1** demonstrates how Mount Lucas Management used VAR to analyze our trading for a 100-day sample from December 2002 to May 2003. Dollars are shown on the Y axis, and time is shown on the X axis. Each bar on the chart represents the daily profit from the strategy. The continuous line below the zero-dollar line indicates the 95 percent VAR calculation.

During any 100-day period, our trading activities should show about five observations below the 95 percent line, and that is about what this sample shows. Furthermore, because this is a macro trading example, it is fairly volatile; the 95 percent VAR averages between 1.5 percent and 1.75 percent. If clients are not comfortable with that level of volatility, this strategy is not the one for them. Finally, this parametric VAR does not capture the serial correlation of the returns, either positively or negatively. Because we are measuring risk, we are not so concerned about a big positive return but rather a big negative "return." In that respect, the model does a reasonably good job of capturing the dynamics of the strategy.

■ *Lower-left risk assessment.* In contrast to the funds in the upper-right quadrant, funds in the lower-left quadrant are essentially short volatility. They have concentrated portfolios and have payouts similar to a short option. And also in contrast to funds in the upper-right quadrant, funds in the lower-left quadrant are concerned about "explosions" rather than drawdowns. Explosions follow an unforeseen change in the market or in the assumed relationship between two or more securities. Leslie Rahl gave an excellent example of the sort of risk faced by funds following a convergence strategy and holding investments of a similar nature.[2] Her example was the Long-Term Capital Management (LTCM) trade, in which LTCM was long the 30-year Treasury bond and short the 29-year Treasury bond at a 5 bp spread, hoping that the spread would narrow to 3 bps but instead it widened to 35 bps. LTCM's estimated upside on this trade was 2 bps, but the risk associated with the trade was much greater than the fund managers had ever imagined. Volatility is bad for funds

---
[2]See Leslie Rahl's presentation in this proceedings.

Figure 1. Back Testing 95 Percent VAR in the 100 Days from 19 December 2002 to 12 May 2003

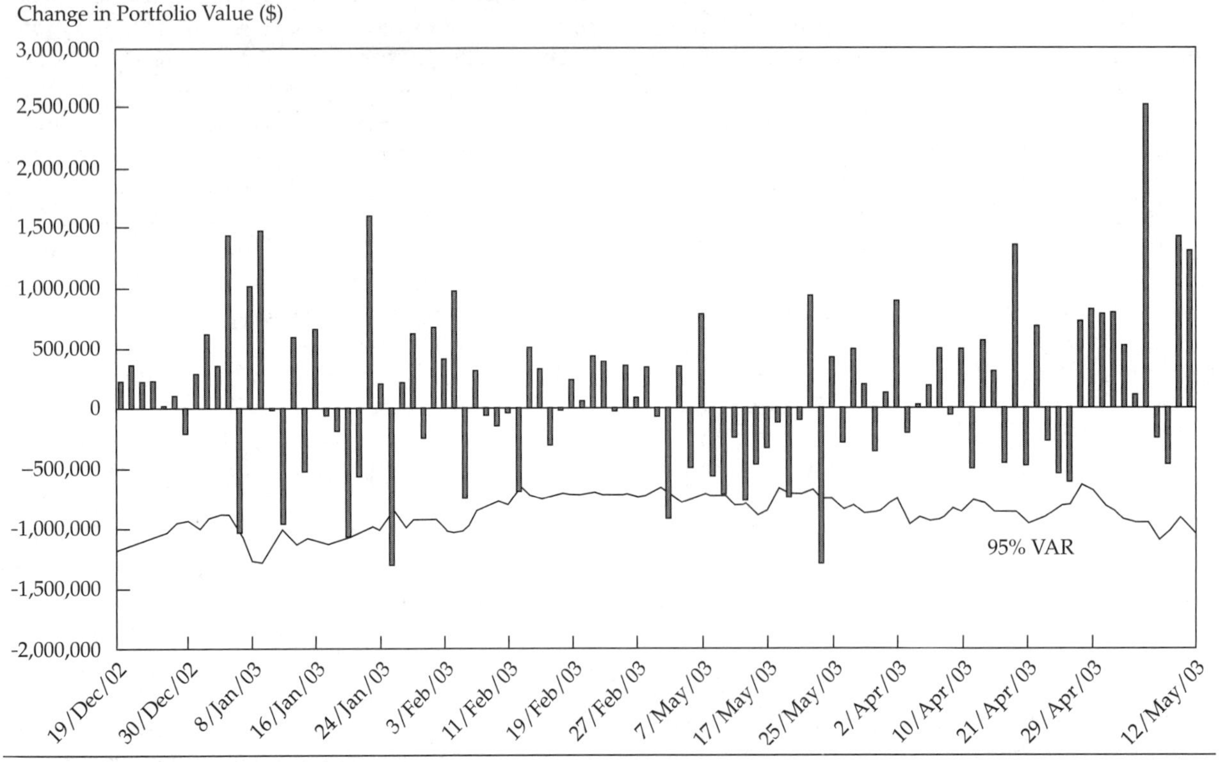

Note: Bars represent daily profit.

in the lower-left quadrant; they live constantly with the threat that a trade may explode, that the performance of a particular trade may fall into the left tail of the return distribution.

I characterize the strategy of these funds as "picking up dimes in front of steamrollers." It is a strategy that fits the profile of an options seller, and it provides investors with many ways to make small incremental profits with great regularity; however, it also exposes them to the risk of losing everything, and that risk is largely unseen and hard to predict. These are the traits of a convergence strategy.

For example, assume that a hedge fund manager is long Fannie Maes and short Treasuries. These securities are reasonably correlated. So, if the manager calculates the VAR for each position, the long position and the short position, the VAR of the two positions will be quite similar. But VAR in this case can be misleading because the spread between the two markets—depending on prepayments, convexity, and other such factors—can be volatile. This strategy, therefore, requires the risk manager to be something of an artist. Stressing the portfolio becomes vital. That is, testing a range of assumptions of possible conditions and asking all the appropriate what-if questions are important. It is also helpful to have lived through some of the crises that the hedge fund industry has faced and to have actually traded through them. But the reality is that not many hedge funds have that experience, which is another risk that hedge funds present. My understanding is that 55 percent of hedge funds operating today are less than five years old, and the percentage is much higher if gauged over a 10-year period. So, a lot of hedge fund managers have not risk-managed through some of the major crises of the last decade.

It is imperative that stress tests be done on portfolios in the lower-left quadrant, which requires having data from historical events. Examples of such events are as follows:
- U.S. Federal Reserve Board's surprise move in 1994 to raise interest rates,
- LTCM and Asian crises in 1998, and
- aftermath of the September 11 terrorist attacks.

Using data from each of these events, hedge fund managers can conduct sensitivity analysis on yield-curve swings, funding rates, and volatilities and thus determine the dangers to which a fund is most sensitive.

Ultimately, sensitivity analysis centers on correlations and on the manager's expectations of movement in the correlations. So, the manager has to begin with a premise about possible future risk events. For example, a manager might model a scenario in which

a crisis occurring on a weekend triggers a stock market fall of 20 percent at Monday's open. As a result, the portfolio manager's time to react is minimal. Such a scenario may have the following characteristics:
- the bond market goes up,
- short rates go down,
- the dollar gets crushed (assuming it is a U.S. phenomenon), and
- commodity prices fall.

If the portfolio is complex, the manager has to consider an intricate array of possibilities. And to each of those possibilities—and to the original crisis that led to the possibilities—the manager must assign round-number values. For instance, if short rates fall, the manager might estimate that decline to be around 50 bps. Once the round-numbered estimates are assigned, the manager must put distributions around each estimate and assign a standard deviation. Once that step is done, the manager can conduct a Monte Carlo simulation and see how bad the situation could be for the portfolio.

As an aside, a simple rule of thumb about risk that seems quite accurate is as follows: If a fund earns 15 percent, it should expect a 20 percent loss at some point, even if the sensitivity analysis does not indicate it. If a fund earns 20 percent, it should expect a 30 percent drawdown. If a fund earns 50 percent, it is risking ruin. There is no free lunch. If a manager wants to play the game, the risks involved have to be accepted; stress tests can prepare the manager to meet these risks. If a fund focuses on convergence strategies or is in a highly concentrated portfolio, stress testing is absolutely essential. As John Maynard Keynes said, "The market can remain irrational longer than you can remain solvent."

Decision Points for Risk Management

Once a firm realizes the value of appropriate risk assessment techniques, it has to decide two things: (1) where the assessment should occur and (2) what software should be used to perform the assessment.

Whether a firm outsources risk assessment or does it in-house typically depends on the degree to which parametric VAR fits the firm's trading style. If parametric VAR is not an appropriate risk measurement for the firm's trading style, then the firm will almost always keep the risk assessment function in-house. The advantage of in-house stress testing and risk assessment is that it allows more "art" into the process, a greater flexibility to test the range and the type of possible scenarios that could negatively affect the portfolio. The disadvantage, however, is that manipulation of the process is more likely to occur.

Objectivity is always in question when analysis is done in-house because every firm has a certain point of view, and the temptation is to keep working the data and the models until the firm gets the assessment it was hoping for. Our firm prefers to outsource its risk assessment. Outsourcing allows a firm to leverage the ability of another organization's experts, and it allows for better communication because a specialized firm has the infrastructure in place to report results efficiently. Admittedly, outside sources will tend to run the data through standardized, rather than customized, models, but that situation is improving.

If the decision is made to operate risk management in-house, the choice of software tools will depend on a firm's trading style—parametric or stress. For help in choosing the right vendor, firms should consider the compendium of software providers and their capabilities listed in *Hedge Fund Risk Transparency* by Leslie Rahl.[3]

There is one caveat to keep in mind: Beware of mapping. A vendor that uses mapping is declaring, in effect, "I am not going to keep a database of all your crazy positions. I am going to map your individual security into some generic security to make it much easier for me to compute your VAR and thus maintain my exorbitant gross margins." Mapping can mask serious portfolio risk and should be avoided. The hiring firm should require a database built around its own securities, not a generic portfolio.

Risk Management and Risk Aversion

Once the appropriate risk assessment tools are in place and the firm begins to examine its risk systematically, fear may take hold, especially among management. The firm may suddenly veer from risk management to risk aversion. This phenomenon is becoming more common, especially as the business becomes increasingly institutionalized. Consequently, firms begin avoiding risk, and returns suffer.

The question that arises is this: Will the institutionalization of the alternative investment world permanently lower returns? If so, then investors who are hoping that hedge funds will help their pensions achieve the desired return on assets must revise their return expectations. Investors are now reaching for yield by stretching their asset allocations to include more and more hedge funds. They foresee a 3.2 percent yield on the 10-year note and they need an investment to increase their annualized return. But as some of the factors that once helped fuel hedge

---
[3] Leslie Rahl, *Hedge Fund Risk Transparency* (London, U.K.: Risk Books, 2003).

fund returns—such as interest rates—offer fewer opportunities and as institutional hedge fund management becomes more risk averse, past returns are going to be difficult to duplicate. To get the return they want, investors and hedge fund managers must accept the risks involved, and by properly using the tools I have just described, they can assess and manage those risks.

Question and Answer Session

Timothy J. Rudderow

Question: What firm do you use when you outsource your risk assessment?

Rudderow: At Mount Lucas Management, we use Investor Analytics. They do an excellent job of delivering data in a useable form, and therein lies much of the value. Can you imagine me sitting at my computer each morning, trying to download our positions into a VAR program to calculate my portfolio's risk? It just isn't a viable option. So, outsourcing to a reputable firm facilitates our use of data.

Question: Does it make sense to use a customized Tremont Index to measure the performance of a fund-of-funds manager?

Rudderow: Yes, it probably does. Basically, you are paying a fund-of-funds manager to be a stock picker, and his or her "stocks" are these little information companies called hedge funds. The job of a fund-of-funds manager is to pick the ones that will outperform in their particular asset class. I would probably use more than one sector index to judge performance because big differences exist between asset-weighted indexes, such as the Credit Suisse First Boston Tremont Index, and equally-weighted indexes, such as the HFR (Hedge Fund Research) Index.

Question: How do you create long option positions without incurring normal cost?

Rudderow: When you say normal cost, I assume you mean time decay. We love time decay. Assume that I want to be long the stock market in a meaningful way, so I buy options on the Nasdaq 100 ETF (QQQ). By buying options, I am trying to match an idea of the world to a fairly valued position—that is, a value-price position. I am willing to eat the time decay to take a big position. That is the trade-off, and it reduces a lot of the catastrophe risk that I might have in an open-ended position.

If you look at the profile of our returns, the most frequently occurring return is between 0 and –1 percent on a monthly basis. So, it looks like we pay time decay. But our goal is to get the tail in the distribution. We are willing to pay the time decay to do it. Time decay is fine with us.

Question: Where multiple risk–return goals are incorporated into different buckets, are benchmarks for hedge funds useful? Would a benchmark of a floating rate over LIBOR be more useful as a way to measure performance?

Rudderow: Yes to the second question, if that is the performance target. But it does not address what a hedge fund manager is actually doing relative to a peer universe and the risks of the particular strategy. The purpose of a benchmark is really to address two different issues: the first is results and the second is goals.

Question: Recalling your comment on mapping, do you need the same precision in risk models as in pricing models?

Rudderow: The granularity in both cases is pretty similar. Daily pricing is about as granular as we get for both our risk and our pricing models. The real risk on the pricing side is when managers price their book based on models. This type of situation is most prevalent in the mortgage-backed and swap markets, in which complex, nongeneric transactions occur on a regular basis. Because it is a totally nongeneric market, managers price their book based on a model. In the mortgage-backed area, for example, the prepayment assumption drives price almost completely and is the primary determinant of the value of a particular position. Marking to model, as opposed to marking to market, is what scares me on the pricing side.

Question: A hedge fund investing solely in MBS claims to be market neutral based on its duration. How much do you buy the market-neutrality argument for derivatives-based MBS funds?

Rudderow: It seems to me that such a fund is quite susceptible to convexity risk. For example, in the space of one Fed move on interest rates, a 15-year bond that previously had a 2-year duration can morph into a bond with a 30-year duration. So, I do not understand how that duration can remain neutral without some sort of continuous hedging. As far as I am concerned, no stance is neutral. If it is neutral, it does not make money.

Question: What were your best and worst three-month periods and why?

Rudderow: Our worst three-month period occurred this past summer (2002). We were slightly ahead of the curve on the recovery theme (which we are still in), and we still owned a lot of junk bonds, or maybe I should call them high-yield bonds. Then, WorldCom had the poor manners to slip through the high-yield index like a bad meal, dropping from investment grade to high yield to bankrupt. We had put on a total-return swap in the high-yield market and assumed that we had isolated company risk and only faced generic risk. Unfortunately, WorldCom *became* the index for about two weeks. Unlike most fallen angels

(WorldCom must have been Lucifer himself), once WorldCom entered the high-yield index, its path accelerated downward as the investment-grade portfolios were forced to sell and dove toward the bottom of the pile. Eventually, fallen angels float back up from the bottom of the pond as the high-yield portfolios start to buy, and then they begin to recover. Unfortunately, because WorldCom had such a large amount of debt, it became the high-yield index and we got our clocks cleaned.

Because of our WorldCom experience, however, we learned something. We continue to have a total-return swap against the same index, but that position is now at about one-third of its original value. Instead, we have created a position of liquid instruments that mimics the high-yield return of the swap, which allows us to avoid doing the entire swap and thus avoid taking the direct high-yield risks associated with the full swap position. The result is that we have effectively recreated the full-sized position but as a hybrid of more liquid instruments with less company-specific risk.

Our best three-month period was probably the second quarter of 2003, although we have had other good three-month periods. We maintain a growth theme, and the markets seem to be coming around to our view.

Risk Management for Alternative Investment Strategies

Leslie Rahl
Founder and President, Capital Market Risk Advisors, Inc.
Partner, L² Alternative Asset Management
New York City

> A solid framework and an effective due diligence process are vital components of risk management for both traditional and alternative investments. Because many of the standard metrics used to manage traditional investments and measure risk do not work as well with alternative investments, managers must make many adjustments and be particularly cautious in choosing the proper analytical risk framework.

Although I have a strong quantitative background, I view risk as a real-world, not a mathematical, concept. Therefore, I will focus on risk and the issues associated with it, not equations. I define risk as the possibility of a bad outcome. For example, the most significant risk that pension fund managers face is probably reputational risk. No matter whether a pension plan sponsor, endowment, or foundation has done something brilliant or not so brilliant, that sponsor is most concerned about *not* seeing a front-page story in the *Wall Street Journal* about the fund's investment failures.

I will discuss how best to avoid risk through the establishment of a solid risk management framework. It is important, however, to remember that the goal is to maximize risk-adjusted returns, not to eliminate risk! I will then focus on the primary goals of managing risk and return and address the due diligence process and a few of the most significant risks posed by alternative asset strategies. Problems with valuation and the lack of transparency have become especially challenging and are requiring investors to increase their efforts to understand the risk practices of the funds in which they invest.

Risk Management Framework

Establishing appropriate policies and procedures, engaging in the requisite number crunching, and ensuring senior management oversight are all essential in building a solid risk management framework, but even more important is fostering a risk-conscious culture among investment professionals that internalizes the concept of the trade-off between risk and return. To better understand the underlying thinking of many of the large plan sponsors as to how they think about risk, I recommend that all investment managers read the Risk Standards Working Group's "Risk Standards for Institutional Investment Managers and Institutional Investors."[1] Although the report was written in 1996, it is still relevant and offers a good starting point for codifying the institutional investor's perspective on risk.

One of the problems that still pervades the investment management industry and inhibits the growth of a risk-conscious culture is confusion between the functions of compliance and risk management. They are both important functions, with some overlap, but just as a good compliance department cannot be equated with effective risk management, effective risk management does not mean compliance is necessarily satisfactory. Risk management and compliance are wholly different activities, and risk management should not be the compliance department's responsibility. Whereas compliance managers think in terms of checklists and simply want to ensure that they are doing what they said they would do, risk managers must seek to ensure that the entire investment management process is understood.

An effective risk management framework has many key components, only about one-third of which are quantitative in nature. The seemingly mundane separation of front- and back-office duties

---

[1]This publication can be accessed at www.cmra.com/html/the_risk_standards.html.

is critical, as are "Management 101" issues, such as independent risk oversight, education and knowledge, and clear organizational structure. Sometimes, a firm will claim it has "risk management" if it has acquired a fancy computer hardware/software system and hired a few quantitative analysts, but those steps are mere pieces of the puzzle.

Regarding written policies and guidelines, ambiguous language abounds across both traditional and alternative portfolios. The definitions of "low interest rate risk" and "high liquidity," for example, can vary. Or a fund may claim to have "no commodities" in its guidelines but, nevertheless, trade oil-linked notes. Some guidelines indicate that hedging is allowed, but speculation is not allowed. If I were to hedge a four-year Dutch guilder position with a five-year euro forward, is that hedging or speculation? The answer is in the eye of the beholder.

I strongly recommend avoiding broad statements in guidelines. Although no one cares about the language in documents when performance is solid, if the tide turns and pensioners or regulators become dissatisfied, loose definitions can cause problems. Tightening up the language so that all parties—both investors and managers—understand what they are agreeing to is important.

Managing Risk and Return

The goal of risk management is not to make risk disappear; after all, money cannot be made without taking risk. Rather, the goal of risk management is to achieve a reasonable balance between risk and return. To accomplish this task, risk managers must determine the level of risk management required, focus on the risk control, and choose appropriate tools.

Level of Risk Management. Today's investment manager can choose from a wide variety of financial market instruments. The types of instruments used will drive the level of risk management required. On one end of the spectrum are the highly liquid instruments with transparent pricing. On the other end of the spectrum are the illiquid, or less liquid, instruments that have to be priced based on a computer model, have optionality, or have uncertain cash flows. Mortgage-backed securities (MBS), for instance, have a lot of optionality and uncertain cash flows. Also, a manager who uses significant leverage or has large, concentrated positions requires a higher level of risk management.

Before structuring a risk management process, then, managers have to pinpoint where their portfolios fall on the scale between low- and high-intensity risk management needs. Someone who manages a portfolio of highly liquid instruments with transparent pricing can pay less attention to risk management than someone whose portfolio tilts toward the other end of the spectrum. Even instruments that are very transparent (e.g., micro-cap stocks) require a more intense risk management process if concentration reduces liquidity significantly. A manager may earn greater returns using the more complex instruments, but that manager has to realize that extra returns incur extra costs.

Level of Risk Control. Investment risk has been around for as long as financial markets have existed. Taking into consideration "old" risk controls that failed can be instructive. In the 1980s, for instance, the investment community was enamored with simple rules. As long as an instrument was AAA rated and had less than a two-year maturity, a manager could invest in almost anything. A month before Orange County's bankruptcy, I was asked to analyze the county's portfolio to determine the impact of the margin calls it was receiving on portfolio yield. Ninety-five percent of the portfolio had less than a 2-year final maturity, thus meeting the simple-rule criterion, but the portfolio included instruments with a 17-year duration! Capital Market Risk Advisors (CMRA) broke the news to the U.S. SEC that this portfolio probably needed some attention.

Given the complexities involved in risk management, the first goal of risk control is simply to recognize all the possible risks so as to be able to articulate them. Furthermore, because different firms, organizations, and pension plans have different risk tolerances, another goal is to clearly and specifically define those tolerances. Finally, the ultimate goal of controlling risk is to minimize unanticipated risks and uncompensated, or undercompensated, risks.

Another important aspect of the risk control portion of the risk management framework is taking into account that unexpected, or "once-in-a-lifetime," events seem to occur at least every three or four years. Between 1987 and 2001, for example, consider the impact of the 1987 stock market crash, 1990 Nikkei crash, 1992 European currency crisis, 1994–95 Mexican Peso and Latin American crises, 1997 Asian crisis, 1998 Russian crisis and Long-Term Capital Management debacle, 2000 technology meltdown, and the 11 September 2001 terrorist attacks. An effective risk management program should anticipate that such gyrations in the markets will occur and have a plan to adequately deal with them. Even though no one can predict the precise dimensions of a crisis, in a leverage situation, particularly with alternative investments, managers have to take extra precautions to ensure that they can withstand unexpected shocks.

Tools. In developing risk management strategies, plan sponsors and managers often make the mistake of becoming mesmerized by a single number, particularly through value at risk (VAR). VAR is a necessary and useful tool, but it is *not* sufficient. A single number cannot possibly relay enough information about the complexity of risk in a portfolio. Thus, unlike many in the industry, I do not think VAR is the answer, although it is one of the five or six tools that belongs in an effective risk management program, at least for all but the arbitrage type of strategies for which VAR does not work well.

When VAR is used, managers must consider it over time. VAR can be calculated many ways, and each way will yield a different number. One manager's "12" is not necessarily higher than somebody else's "11" because the result depends on the methodology used. So, as **Figure 1** shows, tracking VAR and the subsensitivities within VAR over time yields important information about a portfolio's risk exposure. Managers can see whether VAR is rising or falling and seek to explain why. This process uses risk attribution in the same manner performance attribution is used.

Stress testing is equally, if not more, important than VAR as a tool in risk management. Understanding how a portfolio might behave in certain adverse situations is extremely valuable, but surprisingly, stress testing is frequently neglected in the risk management process. To many portfolio managers, stress testing involves little more than considering the impact of a 100 bp increase or decrease in interest rates, or a 100 point rise or fall in the S&P 500 Index. But in my experience, the worst problems stem from changes in "relationships." What if correlations change? What if the shape of the volatility curve, the relationship between shorter-dated volatility and longer-dated volatility, changes dramatically? A robust stress-testing process should include complex scenarios to capture information about "relationships."

Exhibit 1 depicts several stress-test categories. Testing sensitivity to assumptions is as important as testing sensitivity to market moves, particularly for complex instruments. Risk managers must determine whether changing assumptions results in dramatically different answers. For example, when considering portfolio mix and markets, managers should analyze sensitivity to term-structure and yield-curve levels, volatility structure, assumed correlations, and so on. Managers should focus not only on parallel moves but also on the shapes, spreads, and basis relationships.

In developing the risk management framework, also keep in mind the value of studying market behavior. Crises, for example, have at least one thing in common: Bid–offer spreads tend to widen, and correlations tend to go to 1, as shown in **Figure 2**. Managers should thus consider the effect of expanding bid–ask spreads and strong, positive correlations on their portfolios.

The impact of the widening or narrowing of the spread on manager performance can depend on whether the manager marks to the midpoint or to the

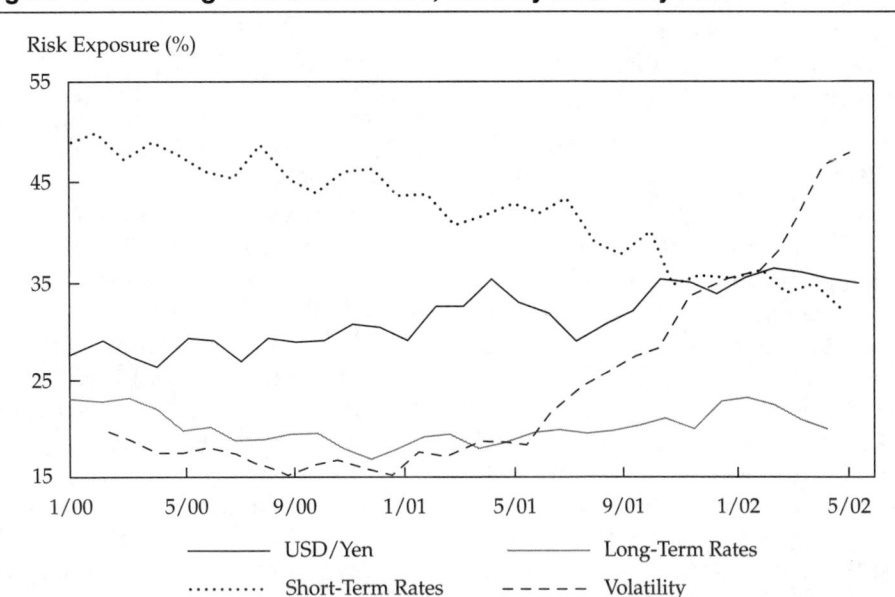

Figure 1. Trending VAR Sensitivities, January 2000–May 2002

Exhibit 1. Categories of Stress Tests

Portfolio Mix and Markets	Model Assumption	Product Complexity	Credit/Liquidity	Sea Change
Term structure and yield-curve levels and shapes	Yield curves building assumptions	Products with uncertain cash flows	Concentrations	Economic and Monetary Union
Term structure and relationship of volatility	Pricing models	Structured products and complex derivatives	Linkages	Y2K
Price shifts in equities, sectors, indexes	VAR and capital models	Emerging markets and difficult-to-handle risks	Credit components of securities	Changing competitive structure
Currency, commodities, price shifts	Asset/liability model		Volatility of credit spreads	
Spreads and basis relationships			Default assumptions	

bid and offer. Many traditional and alternative managers mark their portfolios to a midpoint, so a widening bid–ask spread will not affect their performance or the standard deviation of their returns. Many others mark their positions to the bid side if they are long the position or to the offer side if they are short. In these cases, portfolio valuation or the standard deviation of their returns will be sensitive to a widening or narrowing bid–offer spread. This concept must be understood in order to avoid reaching the wrong conclusion about which manager is doing a better job.

Bid–offer spreads often behave unusually, as shown in **Figure 3**, and the relationship between spreads is not stable. **Figure 4** illustrates how the returns of a convertible arbitrage (CARB) strategy might correlate with a credit-spread change between AAA and BBB industrials. A strong correlation is not evident because CARB strategies are really three strategies in one: CARB players who are playing the cash flow, those who are playing the volatility in the embedded option, and those who are playing the credit spread. For alternative strategies to be more understandable and better adopted by the pension fund community, better nomenclature will probably be required. Perhaps calling strategies by a name that conveys the risk factors (credit spreads, equity volatility, etc.) would help.

Due Diligence

An investment management firm's culture can usually be revealed through a thoughtful due diligence process. If a manager discusses only the fund's recent returns, for example, I begin to worry. No mention of risk measurement, whether qualitative or quantitative, means that I have no idea how big a bat that manager has to swing to achieve those results. My more than 30 years of experience with financial markets—particularly after running the derivatives business during most of the 1980s through the early 1990s for Citibank and inventing products that create risk—has shown that focusing only on how much money is being made is a recipe for disaster.

Due diligence is an extremely important part of the risk management process, especially for hedge funds. With hedge funds, the success of the fund often depends on an individual, or a small group of individuals, rather than an "institutionalized" process. Effective due diligence, therefore, requires eyeball-to-eyeball discussions at a very senior level on at least an annual basis. Junior staff members should not be the only ones involved in this vital due diligence process.

Effective due diligence requires a combination of both quantitative and qualitative analysis. In other words, it should include a thorough quantitative review of the fund's past performance and risks as well as in-depth qualitative discussions with managers regarding their style, strategy, successes, and failures. It also entails obtaining managers' perspectives on risk and risk limits, the use of leverage, and their views on past, current, and future market opportunities. Many plan sponsors, foundations, and endowments separate risk management due diligence from normal due diligence, but such a division is like sending your right arm to one doctor and your left arm to another doctor. To fully understand a manager's approach, investors should expect the investment process to manage both the rewards and the risk.

When engaging in a dialogue with a hedge fund manager, I avoid quantitative and checklist-type questions because they are too mechanical. I prefer more open-ended questions, such as the following:

- When you have a sleepless night, what about your fund keeps you awake?
- What have been your best and worst three months and why?
- If you were conducting due diligence on yourself, what would you ask?
- How do you ensure the separation of the front and back office?
- Who marks the book to market? (The SEC is certainly interested in the answer to this question.) Who reviews? Who has the authority to "override" those prices? Who receives the report on the overrides?

Figure 2. Driving Changes in Market Behavior

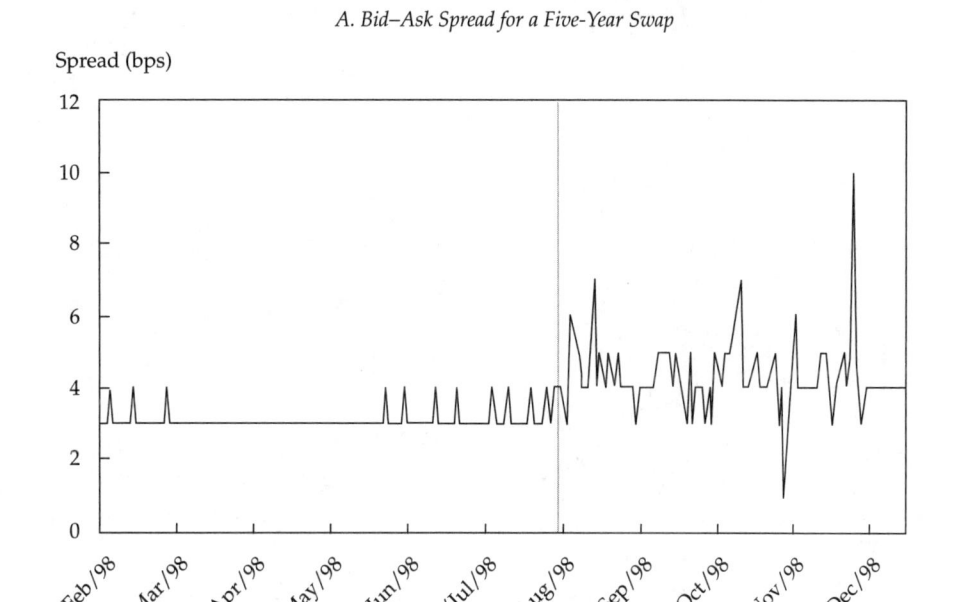

A. Bid–Ask Spread for a Five-Year Swap

B. One-Year U.S. Treasury and DJIA 60-Day Correlation

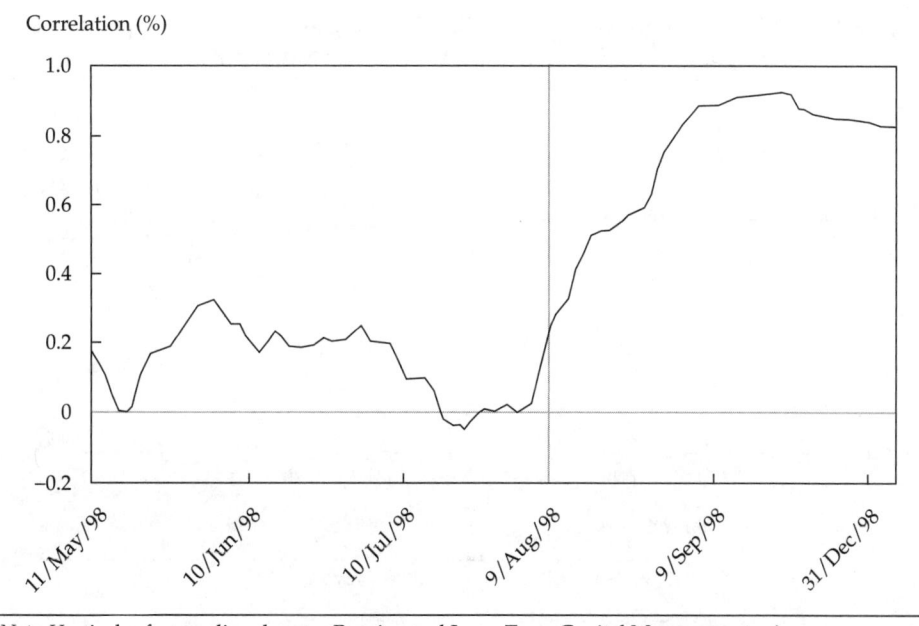

Note: Vertical reference line denotes Russian and Long-Term Capital Management crises.

- Do you have written policies and procedures? May I please see them? (Note that I do not bother to ask for a copy, but if no one can locate one, I wonder how effective the manager can be in guiding the policies.) How do you manage risk?
- Do you have a designated risk manager? What is his or her training? What else does he or she do?
- Do you include risk limits in your guidelines? If someone breaches his or her limits, what happens? (When I asked this question at an investment bank, the overwhelming response of each director was, "If they breach their limits and make money, I guess that is okay." Clearly, such an attitude is not conducive to a risk-conscious culture.)

Figure 3. Comparison of Bid–Ask Spreads for Russian and U.S. Government Bonds, July 2001–July 2002

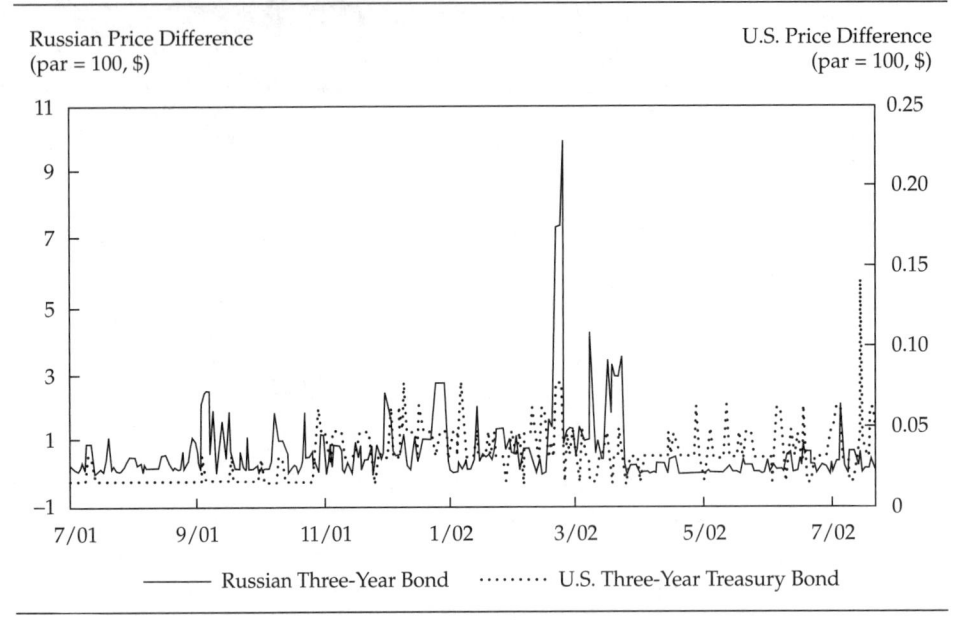

Source: Based on data from Bloomberg and CMRA analysis.

Figure 4. Comparison between a CARB Strategy and the Credit Spread of AAA–BBB Industrials, January 1997–December 2001

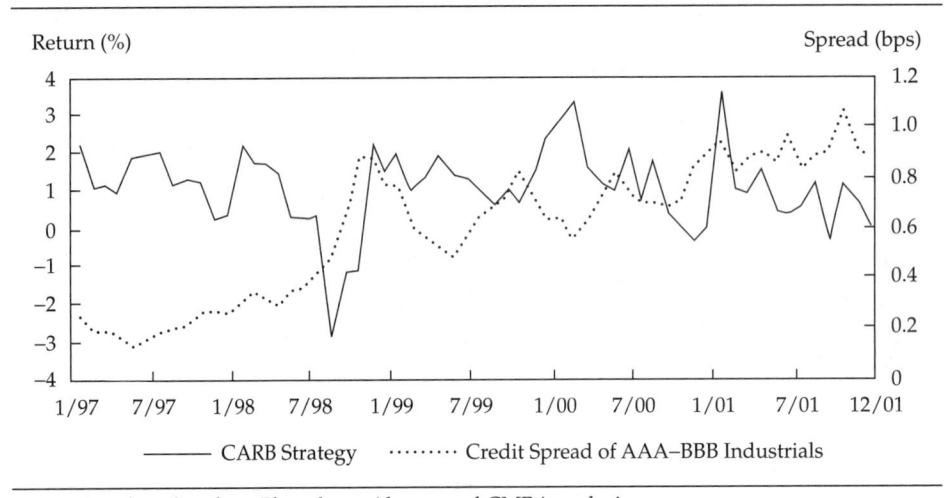

Source: Based on data from Bloomberg, Altvest, and CMRA analysis.

- What are your backup and recovery plans? Have they ever been tested? Where are the copies of the plans maintained?
- How do you define leverage? (For example, if a hedge fund manager did not realize the amount of leverage embedded in some of the fund's transactions, I would be concerned about the due diligence process.) What is the maximum leverage you are allowed? How often are you at or near the maximum? If you were maximum leveraged and your prime broker doubled your haircuts, how much would that cost the fund?
- What are your borrowing patterns, and to what degree are you financed on a term basis versus overnight? Short term? Long term? How has that changed over the past 12 months?
- Because you trade in multiple time zones, how do you calculate your net asset value (NAV)? What do you do when some markets close London time, others close Tokyo time, and still others

close New York time? Do you blend them all together and take the closes, or do you make some effort to adjust so that they are closed at the same time around the world?

I also find it very useful to benchmark both their performance and their risk characteristics against their peers and to go to a due diligence meeting with detailed questions about their risk sensitivities versus their peers as well as over time.

Additionally, the Alternative Investment Management Association (AIMA), headquartered in London, has produced a useful due diligence questionnaire.[2] CMRA has expanded this questionnaire for hedge funds by adding questions on transparency, leverage, risk management, limits, and so on.

Types of Risks

Risk is multidimensional, with many factors to consider. I will highlight just a few risks.

Concentration Risk. Highly concentrated positions are one of the risks that must be understood. One of my clients has a large controlled position in a biotech company, and I estimate that it would take at least seven years to unwind the position without being more than 50 percent of the open interest on any day. How does the client mark that to market? The stock trades and has a closing price. Through options theory and some other analyses (and with the approval of the client's accountant), the client haircuts the value of that investment by a reasonable 35 percent to reflect the illiquidity. Clearly, with large positions or a position that is difficult to unwind, the fact that it appears on the market monitor does not mean that that price reflects the correct way to mark the position in the portfolio.

Liquidity Risk. Liquidity, and the lack thereof, is probably the risk that has received the least attention but has inflicted the most damage to alternative investment portfolios. A hedge fund has multiple components of liquidity: One is the liquidity of the underlying instruments, another is the redemptions and liquidity lockups negotiated by the investor and the hedge fund, and a third is the liquidity of their funding arrangements. These components must be compatible. If a fund has illiquid instruments but allows frequent redemptions, it has embedded risks. Investors must understand the matching of interests between what a fund offers investors and the types of strategies it uses.

Liquidity, as reflected in bid–offer spreads, has a large potential impact on fund NAV. If a fund is marking its NAV to midpoint, an investor cannot assume the NAV reflects a fair value at which he or she can liquidate. Funds do not generally transact at midpoint. Funds frequently need to sell at the absolute worst time, when the bid–offer spreads are the widest. The firmness and stability of NAV is another facet of liquidity risk. Reasonable differences in opinion arise in portfolio valuation across these different facets. Estimation procedures must address position liquidity (as I mentioned earlier), borrowing arrangement sensitivities, and the timing of marking the positions.

An associated problem is that definitions of "illiquid" vary widely. The main responses to the question "What is an illiquid instrument?" in a 2002 CMRA survey were as follows: position represents greater than 10 percent ownership, zero or one market maker, no price change for five consecutive business days, inability to sell position in one week at one-third of the daily volume, inability to sell at the current value within seven days, and bid–offer spread greater than 1 percent. Except for the zero market maker response, these definitions are all reasonable. But if the investor and the fund have different definitions, problems can arise. For instance, if an investor invests in more than one fund and each fund has the same constraints and the same style but different liquidity definitions, the investor could be unwittingly investing in a fund that does not really match his or her objectives.

NAV Instability Risk. I mention NAV instability risk because of the extent to which it is on the regulators' radar screen. Complex instruments can be valued in many different ways, but investors are mostly interested in knowing how the fund is doing. In many cases, no right or wrong valuation method exists, but this risk is important because it could affect actual returns and is thus an important part of the due diligence process.

Following are some specific valuation-related issues for investors to investigate (these issues generally apply to both traditional and alternative investors):
- valuation methods and related processes and procedures (e.g., pricing sources, models, fair valuation, broker quotes, bid, offer, midpoint, discounts on publicly traded securities),
- estimate of proportion of portfolio NAV valued by each valuation method,
- proportion of portfolio valued using "stale" prices (i.e., not traded within 24 hours),
- the dollar value and number of securities valued at current prices that are greater than or equal to the average daily volume for those securities,
- percentage difference in NAV if prime broker marks for hedge funds were used exclusively,

---

[2] This questionnaire can be accessed at www.aima.org.

- percentage of NAV composed of positions with a bid–offer spread greater than or equal to the number of basis points for that position,
- overall NAV stability—for example, estimated maximum change in portfolio value if another valuation method is used, and
- pricing override policy, percentage of portfolio overridden, and policy on documentation of overrides.

Although CMRA conducts many surveys, I am never quite sure how respondents are interpreting our questions. In another survey conducted in 2002, we asked a variety of institutions whether they marked the midpoint, bid, or offer. Sixty-seven percent of fund-of-funds respondents said they marked to the midpoint. Funds of funds do not mark to anything, however, because they simply aggregate their underlying funds. In addition, 60 percent of hedge fund respondents said they marked to the midpoint (40 percent marked to some other measure), as did 38 percent of mutual fund respondents and 17 percent of traditional money manager respondents.

Investment managers often indicate that they use mark-to-market dealer quotes, particularly on products such as OTC derivatives. But when asked how those dealer quotes are used, 44 percent said that they average them, 27 percent said they make a "subjective judgment," 18 percent said they use the median, and 9 percent said they drop the high and low and average the rest. Other than using subjective judgment, each response represents a clearly acceptable method. Nonetheless, different valuation methods can, in the extreme, result in identical portfolios with a 40 percent difference in valuation. For the due diligence process, investors must clarify whether they are comparing apples with apples or apples with oranges when they compare one fund with another.

Figure 5 shows a time series for broker/dealer quotes on an MBS derivative from June 1999 to March 2001. The range of quotes across each month's observation is fairly wide for this exotic derivative. **Table 1** depicts returns, depending on the method used, for a portfolio that has only this derivative in it for the period between December 1999 and March 2000. Such a portfolio could yield a return ranging from 7.5 percent to 21.0 percent, depending merely on the methodology used. And what if two portfolios with just this one instrument existed? One could return 7.5 percent, and the other, 21.0 percent.

Table 1. Return Based on Mark Methodology, December 1999–March 2000

Methodology	Bid	Mid	Offer
Highest	12.9%	14.8%	15.0%
Lowest	18.6	21.0	12.5
Average	15.3	16.8	10.1
Drop high and low	15.1	16.3	7.5

Time-zone adjustments are also important to NAV stability. At CMRA, we examined how portfolio managers treat portfolios that trade in multiple time zones and received varied answers:
- adjust cross-exchange trades to the same time,
- adjust to the futures close in each local market,

Figure 5. Time Series for Broker/Dealer Quotes on an MBS Derivative, June 1999–March 2001

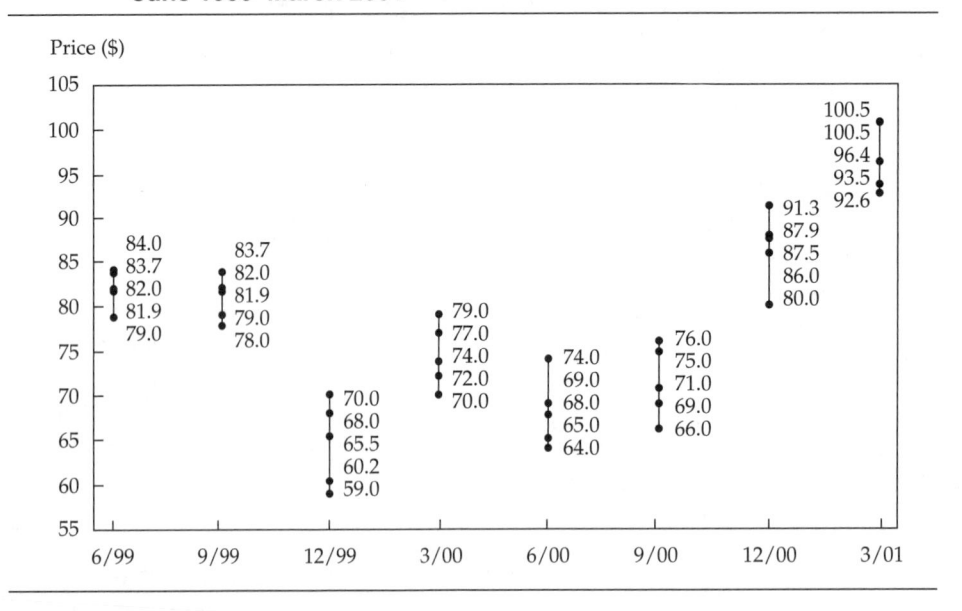

- use 4:00 p.m. New York time,
- use "fair-value pricing" adjustments,
- take all prices at 5:45 Paris time, and
- use closing prices the day before.

The different approaches probably produce similar results, except in times of turbulence. (This survey was conducted more than a year *before* the Spitzer investigation.)

"Overriding" prices is also an accepted practice because of the valid (and not-so-valid) reasons for doing so. Keeping track of the proportion of the portfolio that is being overridden, however, is an important part of the risk management process. A thorough due diligence review should examine controls and explore trends.

Reputational Risk. As I mentioned earlier, for pension plans, the most significant risk is probably reputational risk. If a fund makes promises it cannot deliver, its reputation will suffer. Rather than writing glowingly about the fund, managers should be honest about what they do and then do it. Such a strategy will prevent the fund from falling short of elusive aspirational goals. I always stress "say what you do" and "do what you say" with my clients.

Holistic Approach

At CMRA and L^2 Alternative Asset Management, we take a holistic approach to risk management for alternative strategies. Our approach focuses on allocating risks rather than assets. We have been working with a number of plan sponsors, endowments, and foundations that have selected a few hedge fund managers in addition to their traditional long-only managers. We study the overall portfolio from a risk point of view to identify which risk characteristics may be overlapping and, more important, which types of risks they are missing. We aim to construct a specialized portfolio that fills in those gaps.

In deciding which managers to visit as a preliminary screen (before we hire them), we construct a risk assessment based on NAV history. In this analysis, we group together funds of a given strategy and size that are, perhaps, in the first quartile in terms of both performance and Sharpe ratio and examine how they perform during crisis periods. Then, we consider drawdown and recovery patterns. Clearly, we want to see how quickly they recovered from any drawdowns. We continue this process by consecutively screening for the better and better funds.

Once this preliminary screening process is finished, we then consider liquidity and transparency. After writing a 700-page book on hedge fund transparency, I know that, without a doubt, transparency alone is not the answer.[3] Given the lack of full transparency for all funds (and that no one would probably know what to do with full transparency if it were available), we try to glean as much information as possible from publicly available sources as input to the due diligence process and the selection process.

We have created a series of risk factors derived from NAV trends that we use to examine funds' exposure to credit risk, slope of the yield curve, the level of interest rates, the level of volatility, and so on. We then compare these factors with fund performance and performance variability. This approach allows us to gather information about fund exposure and then use the information in constructing portfolios.

Building a risk profile based on the previous criteria allows for the creation of a targeted due diligence dialogue. For instance, if I say, "You seem to have a higher exposure to the slope of the yield curve than your competitors," much information can be garnered by whether the manager says, "Yes, that is true because . . ." or "I was not aware of that." Such a direct approach tends to elicit responses that are much more meaningful than the typical well-rehearsed platitudes.

Whether an investor should invest in an individual hedge fund or a fund of funds is a final important issue. Interestingly, when AIMA/CMRA asked a group of investors and a group of funds of funds what the advantages of funds of funds are, investors found risk management to be a significant advantage of investing through a fund of funds; funds of funds ranked it much lower. This discrepancy in the understanding of the importance of risk management indicates that investors may not be getting the excellence in risk management that they think they are.

Conclusion

Given the gap between investors and managers on many issues associated with risk management for alternative investments, I would like to see more investment professionals become involved in solving the problems we face. If our voices are not heard, Washington legislators and/or regulators will attempt to solve the problems for us, and I am certain that we can do a better job ourselves. To become involved in supporting an industrywide focus on risk management, I recommend becoming a member of the International Association of Financial Engineers, a not-for-profit organization based in New York City that consists of 300 institutional investors, funds of funds, hedge funds, and service providers. As a group, we are trying to tackle the transparency and valuation issues that I have outlined in this presentation.[4]

---

[3] Leslie Rahl, *Hedge Fund Risk Transparency: Unravelling the Complex and Controversial Debate* (London, U.K.: Risk Books, 2003).

[4] Visit www.IAFE.org for more information.

Question and Answer Session

Leslie Rahl

Question: Do you recommend that plan sponsors develop a risk-budgeting framework?

Rahl: Some form of risk budgeting makes sense, but detailed implementation is not necessarily the answer. For many plans, the implementation process of a detailed bottom-up approach is too overwhelming. Nonetheless, much can be done at the factor level by looking at allocating risks rather than assets. Leo de Bever has done fabulous work with the Ontario Teachers' Pension Plan.[1]

Not everyone has the stomach for risk budgeting or the patience to wait for proper implementation, but for those with the right staff and attitude, it is a worthy goal, and once it is done, the benefits are tremendous. But I often recommend shortcuts to clients that will garner them 80 percent or 90 percent of the benefits with a fraction of the work.

Question: Why is VAR unsuitable for relative-value managers?

Rahl: VAR does not fully reflect the subtleties of relative-value relationships. Say you did a VAR calculation on Long-Term Capital Management's portfolio. I believe it was long 30-year Treasuries and short 29-year Treasuries, but VAR will not capture the subtle difference there. VAR will focus on the term structure of U.S. Treasuries but not the nuances of a relationship. Stress testing, therefore, is critical.

Question: Are hedge funds a good risk–reward investment after fees?

Rahl: The fees are high, but the rewards can be significant and the fees are also high in other investments, depending on how they're structured. If you take the amount of mutual funds that are hugging the index and apply an index fee to that part, their fees on active management are quite high.

Question: How does performance attribution fit into risk management?

Rahl: You have to do performance attribution *and* risk attribution. Either one by itself is somewhat meaningless.

Question: Do you think that performance attribution is as much an art as it is a science?

Rahl: Yes, and risk management is also as much an art as it is a science.

Question: How do you select the risk factors for hedge funds?

Rahl: At L^2, we select risk factors based on our in-depth knowledge of the strategies and our previous experience as traders. Our approach involves saying, "Okay, I am familiar with these 20 convertible funds; let's go to a blackboard and figure out the main differences in the risk factors based on our own experiences." I don't know how one could academically select them without missing a lot of the realities of the market.

Question: Which strategies should you expect to have more transparency?

Rahl: Anyone playing in highly concentrated positions, as many strategies do, has a reason not to want to allow transparency. The algorithms of statistical arbitrage strategies, for example, can be easily replicated and, therefore, necessarily opaque.

If you want to push for getting position-level transparency, you better have the necessary tools and staff. The reports have to be carefully interpreted, and if you get information but don't do anything with it, you are reducing your ability to say to the manager, "You didn't tell me!" Moreover, you are taking on the fiduciary risk of someone saying, "If you had this information, why didn't you do something about it?"

Question: In the alternative asset space, Sharpe ratios are uniformly high, so are they a good measure of risk?

Rahl: Sharpe ratios are a lousy measure of risk because standard deviation doesn't measure the risks of an alternative portfolio or take into account illiquidity and valuation issues. Anytime you are short optionality, as with an MBS strategy, you will have a high Sharpe ratio for three or four years and then a disaster. That is why we have developed the L^2 ratio to address other forms of risk.

Question: What are the best risk management techniques for MBS and asset-backed security (ABS) portfolios?

Rahl: More and more emphasis is being placed on valuation in those areas, which is appropriate. One of the biggest risks in an MBS or ABS portfolio is the starting valuation. You can model different prepayments and so on, but future risk is often dwarfed by the potential difference in *today's* value based on your source and valuation method.

Question: Do plan sponsors generally do an adequate job in terms of risk management? Which plan sponsors are particularly good at it?

---
[1] See Leo de Bever's presentation in this proceedings.

Rahl: Because plan sponsors have such varying levels of expertise and staffing, I find it difficult to compare them. But some have made a stronger commitment to risk management than others. Clearly, Ontario Teachers' Pension Plan, California Public Employees' Retirement System, and General Motors Company have adopted a fairly rigorous approach, but many plans have yet to make a commitment. The primary risk management job of a plan sponsor is to ensure that the funds in which they invest are doing a good job of risk management.

Question: What are some things that a "nonquant" risk manager can do in a quant shop to ensure effective risk management?

Rahl: I recommend asking general questions, such as the ones I pose during the due diligence process. I would simply ask what can go wrong and see if the person has an articulate answer. Even if you don't have the quantitative skill to know whether they are giving you the right academic answer, you should be able to gauge someone's familiarity with the subject. And for a more quantitative strategy, you can always ask a "quant" risk manager to help you with your analysis or hire a consultant.

Question: Is there a regulatory hole that needs to be filled with respect to alternative assets?

Rahl: I don't think regulation is necessary, but I think it is likely to happen. I doubt it will be terribly onerous. I predict that hedge funds will have to register with the SEC, but regulators will basically want to see good valuation practices and disclosure of processes, not numbers. A large part of "best practice" should be self-imposed to minimize the impact of regulation.

Pension Fund Management: Addressing the Problem of Asset/Liability Mismatch

Ronald J. Ryan, CFA
President
Ryan Labs, Incorporated
New York City

> A crisis is upon the United States, and perhaps the world—a pension crisis. And the culprit is pension accounting, or more specifically companies' use (or misuse) of return on asset assumptions and discount rates. In turn, this creative accounting has led to a corporate earnings drag that will go beyond the short term. One solution to this crisis is to encourage companies to use a custom liability index and a liability index fund to match assets with liabilities. Without a custom liability index, all the asset side functions are in jeopardy: asset allocation, asset management, and performance measurement.

I am opening this presentation with bad news, but I will end with some possible solutions. The United States (and perhaps the world) is mired in a pension crisis that threatens the solvency of our corporations, our cities, our states, and even the federal government. Much of the problem stems from accounting issues, return on asset assumptions in particular. But before diving into the accounting issues, I want to review recent pension history.

Pension History

The year 2002 went down as the worst year in pension history. At Ryan Labs, we created a liability index in 1991 to conform to Financial Accounting Standards Board (FASB) Statement of Financial Accounting Standard (SFAS) No. 87. As **Table 1** shows, that generic liability index returned 19.47 percent in 2002. If in 2002 a plan had had an asset allocation of 5 percent cash, 30 percent bonds, 60 percent domestic equities, and 5 percent international equities, which is a good proxy for pension asset allocation, that asset allocation would have had a growth rate of –11.4 percent. So, the difference between the generic liability index return and the typical plan return was –30.89 percent.

Since the year 2000, that same static asset allocation has resulted in pension assets underperforming pension liabilities by nearly 68 percent, as shown in **Table 2**. When assets underperform liabilities by 68 percent, the result is corporate earnings drag, higher pension plan contributions, a Pension Benefit Guarantee Corporation (PBGC) insurance penalty, and solvency issues. In 2002, 144 companies went bankrupt because of underfunded pension plans. The two most notable were TWA and Bethlehem Steel.

Table 3 shows the asset/liability trend since 1989. The final column, "Assets – Liabilities," shows a great deal of undesirable volatility. In order to smooth out this undesirable volatility, companies make certain assumptions regarding future pension asset returns using a "magic pencil," discussed later. First, consider the following history of pension volatility. In 1994, the Lehman Aggregate had the first negative return in its history; the S&P 500 Index return was barely in positive territory. The press declared 1994 "a bad year." If one assumes that the Lehman Aggregate has a five-year duration, then if it has a negative return (as it did in 1994), pension liabilities, which behave like bonds with a 15-year duration, must perform three times worse, which actually makes 1994 a good year. That is, in 1994, liabilities had negative growth. A zero return on assets (ROA) would have won that year, which is basically what assets did. So, 1994 was a good year, but the press did not know it. Most people in this business did not know it either.

Now consider 1995, when the Lehman Aggregate returned 18.47 percent and the S&P 500 returned 37.57 percent. The members of the press could not wait for the year to be over. As early as December they said, "What a great year." The first week of

Table 1. Pension History for 2002

Index	Returns	Estimated Weights
Ryan Liability Index	19.47%	100%
Ryan cash	1.75	5
Lehman aggregate	10.25	30
S&P 500 Index	−22.08	60
MSCI EAFE	−15.64	5
Asset allocation model	−11.41	100
Assets − Liabilities	−30.89	

Table 2. Total Returns, 2000–2002

Measure	2000	2001	2002
Pension assets	−2.50%	−5.40%	−11.41%
Pension liabilities	25.96	3.08	19.47
Difference	−28.46	−8.48	−30.89
Cumulative		−36.94	−67.83

January, Ryan Labs declared 1995 the worst year in pension history. Someone from the press called me and asked why it was a bad year. I explained that if a 5-year duration Lehman Aggregate returned 18.5 percent, then a 15-year duration liability schedule potentially returned three times more. Thus, 1995 was a bad year; assets lost to liabilities. Then, the year 2000 rolled around, and it became the worst year in pension history. In 2000, the difference between the ROA and liability growth was −28 percent, more than double that of 1995. The year 2000 was followed by two more bad years, with 2002 being the worst year in pension history, so far.

Therefore, if a pension plan was fully funded in 1989, it would be 57 percent funded today if it had the asset allocation mix of 35 percent bonds and 65 percent equity, as shown in **Figure 1**. How, one might ask, did this dire situation happen? What is going on? The villain is accounting.

Figure 1. Funding Ratio, 1989–2002

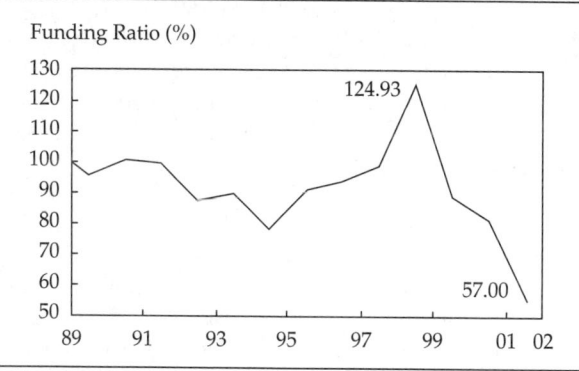

Note: Asset allocation is assumed to be 35 percent bonds and 65 percent equities.

Magic Pension Pencil

The pension crisis starts with the accounting assumption used for ROA. For corporations, pensions are an expense. The offset to this expense is the return on pension assets. Corporations can effectively calculate the pension expense a year in advance through actuarial analysis. But then corporations are allowed to *forecast* the return on pension assets a year in advance.

Table 3. Pension History, 1989–2002

Year	Ryan Labs Cash	Lehman Brothers Aggregate	S&P 500	MSCI EAFE	Assets	Ryan Lab Liabilities	Assets − Liabilities
1989	9.34%	14.53%	31.68%	10.80%	24.31%	25.40%	−1.09%
1990	8.73	8.96	−3.15	−23.32	0.16	3.23	−3.07
1991	7.42	16.00	30.45	12.48	24.13	19.26	4.87
1992	4.12	7.40	7.64	−11.85	6.44	7.87	−1.43
1993	3.51	9.75	10.07	32.95	10.79	22.46	−11.67
1994	3.94	−2.92	1.29	8.06	0.55	−12.60	13.15
1995	7.11	18.47	37.57	11.56	28.67	41.16	−12.49
1996	5.59	3.63	22.93	6.37	15.21	−3.70	18.91
1997	5.72	9.65	33.34	2.08	22.98	19.63	3.35
1998	5.48	8.69	28.55	20.24	21.37	16.23	5.14
1999	4.24	−0.82	21.03	27.32	13.69	−12.70	26.39
2000	6.49	11.63	−9.09	−13.87	−2.50	25.96	−28.46
2001	4.97	8.44	−11.86	−21.11	−5.40	3.08	−8.48
2002	1.75	10.25	−22.08	−15.64	−11.41	19.47	−30.89

Note: The asset allocation weights are the same as those specified in Table 1.

Does anybody know what the S&P 500 will do the rest of this year, much less 12 months from now? Well, the pension funds claim to know. And because they effectively know pension expense, they know what ROA is needed to completely offset that expense. And, therefore, many pension funds simply make their ROA assumption higher than their liability growth, thus making pension expense a negative number.

In this way, corporations make pensions a profit center. Indeed, doing so became a national trend; 10–15 percent of the S&P 500 earnings came from the magic pension pencil. In 2002, the average ROA assumption was 9.2 percent. And it has been at that level for several years. So, corporations continue to predict 9 percent growth on assets. The reality for the past three years, however, has been closer to –6 percent. Corporations never predict a negative ROA because pensions would be an expense and an earnings drag, which is undesirable. Remember, corporations do not want earnings volatility. The magic pencil says, "I will take the difference between the forecast and what actually happens and amortize it over the life of the pension, call it 15 years. I will then smooth these pension expenses, eliminating volatility in the financial statements." So, the corporation goes to sleep thinking, "All is well, and I can now make pensions a profit center." Any pension shortfall can be smoothed over time, thus having only a small effect on the earnings stream.

In the year 2000, the reality for ROA was about –2.5 percent. Corporations forecasted ROA at 9.2 percent, a difference of –11.7 percent. Corporations amortized that difference over 15 years, resulting in a –0.78 percent loss for the year. The same thing happened in 2001 and 2002. So for those three years, the cumulative amortized loss is –3.12 percent. As a result, in 2002, General Motors Company reported a 33 percent decline in earnings because of pension amortization and Northrop Grumman reported a 44 percent decline in earnings because of pension amortization. The companies conveniently omitted a clarification of whether that amount is the first of 15 or the third of 12 years to go.

I know of no security analyst who fully understands this phenomenon that this amortization deficit remains. I recently posed the following question to three analysts that I know well: "S&P has forecast that this amortization process will cost about 15 percent of earnings. Knowing S&P 500 earnings do not grow 15 percent a year, how are earnings going to grow?" Each analyst wrote back independently and said that he or she did not know. Consequently, I do not know why stocks are currently appreciating. The reason must be P/E multiple expansion. It is not from earnings growth, because earnings are in trouble, grabbed by this amortization problem. By smoothing pension expenses, corporations have made an annual problem into a 15-year problem. This problem is not going away soon.

The other side of the equation is liabilities. And sure enough, the magic pension pencil said, "I will take care of this one too." Later in this presentation, I will go through the accounting rules, but for now, suffice it to say that SFAS No. 87 states that corporations must price their liabilities using individual discount rates of high-quality bonds that match the maturity of the liability payment date. SFAS No. 106 states that if corporations do this matching correctly, they must use zero-coupon bonds. Most corporations attempt to find the highest yield because the higher the yield, the lower the present value of liabilities. So, they found the highest yield to price their liabilities—the Moody's AA long corporate rate. This instrument belongs in a museum, not on a financial statement. It was invented in 1929 and has more holes in it than Swiss cheese; for example, it lacks the inclusion of no finance-related bonds. The finance sector is now 50 percent of the corporate bond market. Back in 1929, it was nonexistent.

Public funds, in order to avoid an arbitrage situation, apply the not-so-brilliant idea of using a discount rate equal to the ROA assumption. The average ROA assumption is somewhere around 9 percent; the implications of this no-arbitrage decision are widespread. In 2002, a 10-year Treasury strip ended the year with a yield of 4.34 percent and a 15-year strip with 5.09 percent. One might think that the average pension fund liability has a 10- to 15-year duration, thus an average yield around 4.34–5.09 percent. This is not the case. Corporations use 6.50 percent; public funds use 9 percent. The result is that corporations underestimate their liabilities by 21–32 percent, and public funds are 46–70 percent too low. So, if a public fund thinks it is fully funded, it should subtract 70 percent.

For example, I met with the representatives of a pension fund for a major city. I knew they had problems, so I asked them what their funding ratio was—what was their assets-to-liability ratio? They said, "Fully funded, 100 percent." I said, "How did you come up with that calculation? What did you use as your discount rate?" They said, "By law, we have to use an ROA of 8.75 percent." I said, "The Treasury yield curve I am familiar with does not have 8 percent, does not have 7 percent, does not have 6 percent, but I can find 5 percent. You are 300–400 bps too high with that rate. I am assuming you have a duration of 10 years on your liability, so you are really 30–40 percent less funded than you think. You are not at 100 percent. You are at 60 percent or 70 percent." In further conversation, they said, "Because we thought we were fully funded, we increased benefits by 30 percent." I then said, "You are not at 60 percent or 70 percent funded; you are at 30 percent or 40 percent. You are going to have to borrow money." They said,

"We already did. We issued a pension obligation bond." I asked them where they put the proceeds, and their answer was 100 percent equities. And I thought they were in trouble before.

Political Manipulations

Public pension funds are often manipulated by politicians to serve something or someone other than the plan or plan beneficiaries. Governor Cuomo did not win re-election in the state of New York, and part of the reason was that he "stole" from the pension fund: He raided the pension fund for $3 billion to pad his operating budget. In an interview with a major reporter, he was asked about the pension fund. The reporter brought up the point that the courts had ruled that Cuomo and his staff raided the pension fund for $3 billion to balance the budget and that the money had to be paid back because it was an illegal raid of a pension fund. Cuomo first responded that the reporter was wrong; the courts said they could not take the money, so they did not; thus, nothing had to be paid back. When pressed by the reporter, Cuomo then reiterated that the courts said they could not take the money, but now he said that they were paying the money back. At this point, the reporter and the audience were confused. To clarify, Cuomo said that they "tried" to take the money but that the courts ruled that it was illegal, so the money was going to be paid back. He went on to say that the $3 billion that was taken was going to be amortized over 10 years—not paid back all at once, which is why he said the reporter was wrong.

That kind of manipulation happens in other states and at the federal government level. George W. Bush was elected partially on the grounds that he was going to put a lockbox on Social Security. But then he announced a major deficit and said he would pay part of it by raiding the Social Security pension fund. The Cato Institute is the watchdog for Social Security. Someone at the Cato Institute told me the Social Security liability is $21 trillion, the largest liability on the face of the earth. Where are the assets to fund this liability? Federal Insurance Contributions Act (FICA) tax is 12.4 percent of payroll, and it has been increased 37 times since it was enacted. U.S. citizens are now being told Social Security is bankrupt. So, where are FICA taxes going? U.S. citizens should revolt and protest this raiding of the pension fund. The politicians stole from the beneficiaries, and now the beneficiaries (U.S. citizens) have to pay it back. Texas has passed legislation that says if a state official manipulates the pension fund, the official has to pay; the citizens of Texas do *not* pay through higher taxes. Maybe such legislation should be considered at the federal level.

The Pension Game

Sports analogies might help one understand this asset/liability game. The objective of a pension fund is to fund the liabilities at the lowest cost and the lowest risk of the plan. Everybody seems to understand the main objective, although some secondary objectives do exist, especially for corporations that want to enhance their financial statements and their credit ratings. Pension funds have a lot of rules, just as sports do. And playing the game is hard without knowing the rules. If you wear a hockey uniform to play basketball, you will be ineffective; you ignored the rulebook. With pensions, the rules come from ERISA, FASB, Government Accounting Standards Board, U.S. IRS, PBGC, and the General Agreement on Tariffs and Trade. The pension teams are assets versus liabilities. The playing field is money, where money is defined as the present value of dollars. This game is not played in future value dollars. No one knows the future value of assets, which is why the discount rate is so important; to get the liabilities to the present value, a discount rate must be used, so out comes the magic pencil.

Most people seem to get the playing time wrong for this game. Pensions is not a long-term ballgame. It is an annual game. More precisely, it is a series of annual ballgames that may go into perpetuity. The reason it is an annual game is because that is how the calculations are made. The calculations are based on the present value of assets versus the present value of liabilities and are made annually. The size of the contribution, the size of the funding ratio, the size of the earnings per share drag, the size of the credit ratings—they are annual. And mistakes made in any year can cause problems that may bankrupt the company.

Pension Goals

Pension goals are relatively straightforward and begin with low cost—everybody wants low cost. No client wants high cost and high risk. Low cost is when a plan sponsor has to make a contribution, and high cost is when it has to make a big contribution. So, clients want low cost or preferably no cost (when the assets fully fund the liability and no contribution is needed).

How about risk? Academics tend to define risk as volatility, which is not correct. I had the pleasure of speaking with Bill Sharpe, the Nobel prize winner who is credited with defining risk. He defined risk as volatility and said that the lowest risk was the lowest volatility, namely the three-month T-bill. So, I posed two questions to him. I said, "I have two clients; the first one is a state lottery. It has to make liability payments every month going out for 27 years, but for this question just take the 10-year liability payment.

What is the lowest risk asset I can buy to match the 10-year liability payment with certainty?" Professor Sharpe's answer was the 10-year Treasury zero-coupon bond. I said, "So, a 10-year duration Treasury is less risky than a 3-month T-bill?" He said, "Of course. With that objective, the three-month T-bill would have 39 reinvestment moments, 39 moments of uncertainty. There is no way that the 3-month T-bill, reinvested, could match the 10-year liability payment with any certainty." Then, I posed my next question: "My second client is a mutual fund with the S&P 500 as its objective. What is the lowest risk asset I could buy to match that objective with certainty?" His answer was an S&P 500 index fund or an S&P 500 futures contract. I said, "So, equities are less risky than the three-month T-bill?" He said, "Of course. There is no way that the three-month T-bill, reinvested, could match the S&P 500 with any certainty, any consistency." My point was that a generic definition of risk is not helpful. The definition must be based on the client's objective. All pension liabilities, for example, are different. They are like snowflakes; no two liability schedules are ever alike.

Four months after this discussion, Bill Sharpe wrote a white paper suggesting the three-month T-bill is not the best risk-free rate. A better proxy for the risk-free rate would be to use the new Sharpe ratio, which is often called the information ratio: The numerator is the portfolio return versus the objective return, and the denominator is the portfolio volatility versus the objective volatility. He then wrote a second white paper criticizing Morningstar for using a three-month T-bill for all of its stars—its risk score and its reward score. This paper concludes with an interesting observation: It would be better for investors to use nothing than to use Morningstar. What he was saying was that Morningstar ratings will give poor guidance. So, until the liability is understood—its shape, its behavior, its growth, its volatility—how can the risk be understood? No risk occurs when the assets match the liabilities. Low risk is when the assets do not match but they behave similarly. High risk is when they do not match, they do not behave similarly, and they are not close. The result is surplus volatility, which corporate pension sponsors do not want and which led to the "invention" of the magic pencil.

Accounting Rules

Various accounting rules govern pension plans. SFAS No. 87 governs the financial statement for corporations. It says in Paragraph 199:[1]

[1] The full text of SFAS No. 87 can be accessed at www.fasb.org/pdf/fas87.pdf.

> Interest rates vary depending on the duration of the investments; for example, U.S. Treasury bills, 7-year bonds, and 30-year bonds have different interest rates.... The disclosures required by this Statement regarding components of pension benefit obligations will be more representationally faithful if individual discount rates applicable to various benefit deferral periods are selected.

Translation: Corporations must price the 1-year liability off the 1-year part of the curve, the 7-year liability off the 7-year part of the curve, and the 30-year liability off the 30-year part of the curve. Paragraph 44 states, "In making those estimates, employers may also look to rates of return on high-quality fixed-income investments currently available and expected to be available during the period to maturity of the pension benefits." Translation: Corporations have to use bonds that are high quality for life and noncallable for life. The only bonds that are high quality and noncallable are U.S. Treasuries.

The U.S. SEC became involved because corporations were not pricing their liabilities anywhere close to the Treasury yield curve. The difference was enormous. Naturally, the problem was that corporations priced them at too high a rate, creating too low a liability. The SEC then directed corporations to Paragraph 186 of SFAS No. 106 for guidance, which is interesting because SFAS No. 106 is for medical liabilities. The SEC is suggesting that whether the liabilities are medical or pensions, they should be priced the same way. The SEC also said that if corporations do not comply "The enforcement division could require restatement of the company's financial statements, as well as seek to impose civil or criminal penalties." Mispricing liabilities is a crime? Yes, it is fraud in the financial statements.

SFAS No. 106 (Paragraph 186) goes on to say that if companies price their liabilities correctly "the accumulated postretirement benefit obligation would equal the current market value of a portfolio of high-quality zero-coupon bonds whose maturity dates and amounts would be the same as the timing and amount of the expected future benefit payments." So, according to the FASB, the correct liability opponent is a bond portfolio, in particular a Treasury zero-coupon bond portfolio that matches the liability benefit payment schedule.

Custom Liability Index

The risk–reward history of assets versus liabilities is shown in **Figure 2**. The line shows liabilities as represented by the Treasury zero coupon's yield curve or strips. The dots show assets as represented by the major generic market indexes. The vertical lines separate short-term, from intermediate-term, from long-term, from very long-term liabilities. So, on the far left

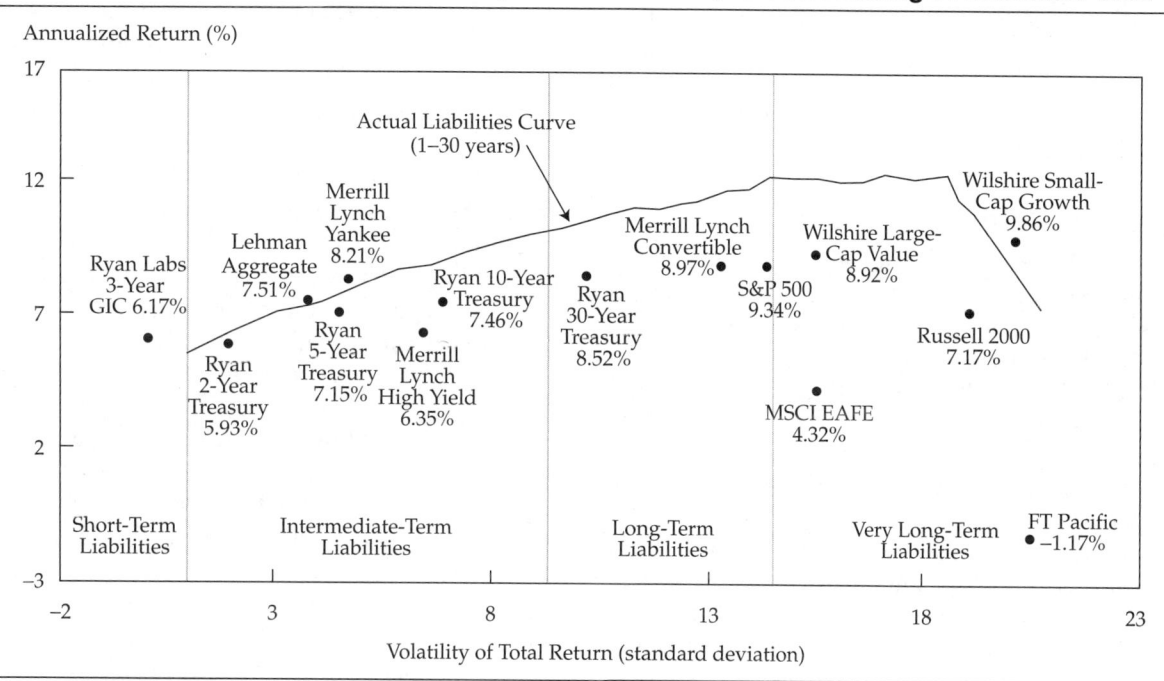

Figure 2. Annualized Return versus Volatility of Total Returns, 10 Years Ending 31 December 2002

are short-term liabilities. Thus, guaranteed investment contracts (GICs) behave like short-term liabilities. In the intermediate-term area are bonds. Because of their durations, these bond indexes behave like 1- to 10-year liabilities. In the long-term area are long bonds, convertibles, and the S&P 500. One might wonder about putting the S&P 500 in long-term liabilities. Well, think about the S&P 500 in asset allocation. It should not be used to fund short-term liabilities. Its volatility behavior does not look anything like those liabilities. Just as cash should not be used to fund long-term liabilities because the behavior does not match, the S&P 500 should not be used to fund short- or intermediate-term liabilities.

At this point, the models go astray. Asset allocation uses a mean–variance model, which excludes liabilities. The mean–variance models compare assets with assets. As a result, these models view the S&P 500 with a 10-year average return of 9.34 percent and the Lehman Aggregate with a 10-year return of 7.51 percent, leading to the conclusion that the S&P 500 outperforms the Lehman Aggregate by 183 bps a year. Mean–variance will undoubtedly skew model weightings toward higher returns. But we are actually in the relative-return business. A football team that scores 30 points could lose the game. And a team that scores 3 points could win the game. It is all relative to the opponent. On close observation, the S&P 500 has underperformed relative to liabilities. An investor could have bought a 20-year Treasury zero that outperformed the S&P 500 by 267 bps a year for the past 10 years. Whoever says stocks always beat bonds over 10 years should be asked the question: What bonds?

Has anybody ever heard of an equity manager managing money to liabilities, managing money to the Treasury yield curve? I have not. If a manager beats the S&P 500 but loses the liabilities, did the pension beneficiary win or lose? The beneficiary loses, and the loss is not known until year-end, at best. Typically, the actuary report on liabilities is produced three months after year-end. Most public funds receive it six to nine months after year-end. Imagine playing football and the scoreboard says "I will tell you the score three months after the game is over." It would be hard to play that game. The team that is ahead by 20 points in the fourth quarter certainly behaves differently from the team that is behind by 20 points in the fourth quarter. If there were no scoreboard, how could the game be played? Having a scoreboard regulates how the game is played.

A liability index has been created that indicates the growth of liabilities, the shape of liabilities, and the volatility of liabilities. Pension plans have to match their assets to the liabilities by behavior. But mean–variance models do not have liabilities in them. A black flag should be waving over every pension fund in the United States that says, "Liabilities are missing in action." They cannot be found in anything on the asset side—not in asset allocation, not in asset management, not in performance management. Asset allocation models are all driven by generic market indexes, and Wall Street loves it. Producing generic asset allocation models is a low-cost effort. Customized models, however, require substantial costs. Although more costly, the right approach is to create custom indexes that match and equal the client objective.

Pension Crisis Solutions

To get out of the pension crisis hole, the first step involves creating a liability index customized to client needs. No two liabilities are ever alike—they all have different schedules and shapes—and because of that variability, they will have different growth rates. Given the wrong benchmark, the client receives the wrong risk–reward. The S&P 500 does not represent liabilities, nor does any generic benchmark. So, the first step is creating this customized index.

Second, plan sponsors desire to fund liabilities at the lowest cost and the lowest risk. The lowest cost and the lowest risk will always be the objective, and an index fund that matches the objective usually comes in the form of the lowest fees and the lowest transaction costs.

Consider the following. In 1999, a manager saw the correction coming in the equity market and decided to sell equities, which were 60–65 percent of the portfolio's asset allocation. Where would the manager put the money? The manager would probably put it on the bond side against the Lehman Aggregate. But in 1999, the Lehman Aggregate underperformed the 20-year liabilities, so the manager would have lost. The manager has to fund this area. He or she cannot simply buy the Lehman Aggregate and certainly cannot buy cash. The manager needs a liability index fund for the piece he or she is trying to match. The manager can match all of it or some of it. A liability index fund, one would think, is a natural fit for this challenge.

It is odd that the majority of the index funds in the United States are equity funds, even though more potential alpha exists in equities. The difference between first quartile and median returns on equities is much bigger than on the bond side. On the bond side, it is 30 bps a year. One would think a plethora of index funds would exist on the bond side, where alpha is so small. Liabilities are a bond portfolio that is hard to beat but not hard to match if the manager buys the right bond. It is difficult to believe that in the United States managers have such dramatic problems trying to beat a Treasury yield curve. No one ever hears of a problem with lotteries because lotteries strive to match their liabilities. They use accountants (not investment people), who know that assets must match liabilities. For the new liabilities, they ask for competitive offerings with zeros to match them. It takes about an hour. They do not use professional money managers; they match the liability and go home. But the pension funds hire the finest brains to manage their money and provide alpha, to create a surplus, and now we have the worst economic crisis in U.S. history. This crisis is bigger than the Depression in dollars. If a few big companies go bankrupt because of a pension crisis, Americans might wake up to this problem and to the Social Security problem.

Question and Answer Session

Ronald J. Ryan, CFA

Question: Shouldn't Social Security more accurately be called a Ponzi scheme?

Ryan: Politicians originally thought they would never have to pay Social Security benefits. When they started it, a person's life expectancy was somewhere around 60 years of age. They thought it would be a profit center. It is far from a profit center now.

Question: If interest rates increase from their six-year low, pension plans will be severely overfunded. Would that be a problem?

Ryan: A surplus is never a problem. The issue might be if you have a surplus, what do you do with it? Back in the 1980s, we had merger mania. What happened back then was companies would buy other companies and then find out that the pension assets were the largest assets of the company. These plans had a surplus in those days. So, companies could actually buy a company, terminate the plan, take in that surplus, and end up buying the company for a lot less money, maybe for free—merger mania.

The U.S. government said no more of this. We are going to tax you 50 percent on terminating these plans and taking that surplus. Now, companies are trying to find other ways to use the surplus, if they have one, which I don't think they do. And the obvious thing to do if a company has a surplus is to start funding the medical liabilities, most of which are unfunded. I think you can shift those surplus funds from pension to medical.

Question: Why aren't more pension funds moving to your approach of using a custom liability index?

Ryan: We are all sheep in this business. Here's what happens. If you made a lot of money doing the wrong things, would you call up a client and say "By the way, I want to change the way I do things." Consultants tend to have the keys to the kingdom, and consultants use the mean–variance models. They are the ones who told their clients to be heavily skewed to equities because over every 10-year period they would beat bonds. It is hard for these consultants to turnaround and say, "By the way, that doesn't work."

It is the same issue with actuaries. They tend to know liabilities. They don't know assets, which is why they don't know how to price the present value of liabilities. You have to take a market approach. It is very difficult for people to change their ways, unless there is a crisis. Maybe this crisis is good in that it will force us to do things differently.

Question: Do you see a trend of companies renegotiating the pension promise with a view to reducing benefits and changing from defined-benefit to defined-contribution plans?

Ryan: Companies are trying everything they can think of to reduce this cost. They're trying to come up with new types of plans. They'd love to get rid of the pension. They can't do that. According to law, a company cannot terminate a plan unless it shows that it is fully funded according to GAAP. And GAAP says companies must show their liabilities based on the 30-year Treasury.

The Treasury, in its infinite wisdom, decided to get rid of the 30-year Treasury on Halloween of 2001. Does it have any idea how the 30-year Treasury drives pensions, or for that matter lotteries? That's where the zero-coupon bonds come from.

Because it is hard to change the plan, it is hard to terminate it. One strategy left is to go bankrupt, which 144 companies did last year. I visited the PBGC in Washington recently, and the staff is scared to death that this is a new strategy—get rid of the pension and then come back out of bankruptcy without a pension (or with something that is less costly).

Question: Wasn't the 2000–03 period an issue about pension funds moving too close to the line (i.e., not building a reserve cushion when they could have) rather than accounting per se?

Ryan: Greed is a terrible thing, but that's what drives this business. Back in 1999, plans supposedly had a surplus. What a great time it would have been to match liabilities with bonds, call it immunization, call it liability index funds—match with bonds taking that surplus and say the game is over. I won.

But that didn't happen. Because of the ROA that drives corporations, a 100 percent bond allocation would knock down the ROA to a level that was not permissible. Therein lies the problem in the magic pencil. ROA is driving the asset allocation.

Consultants have to verify this ROA, so it is not really the consultant's fault on the asset allocation. It is the corporation with a gun to the consultant's head saying, "Our ROA is at 9.2 percent; you verify it." If corporations went heavy in bonds at today's interest rates, how would they get the 9.2 percent? They have to fudge the numbers. They have to come up with new asset classes for which nobody knows the historical risk–reward, and that is what is going on. They're going to hedge funds, private equity, alternative investments—things that could justify a 9 percent ROA because there's no history. They can make up any number they want.

See how the game is played? It is greed. And greed usually loses.

Question: Given your liability index approach, what should a typical defined-benefit plan asset mix look like?

Ryan: You should first separate retired from active lives. Retired lives are the most important liability because they're the shortest and they're the most known. That's where bonds go. You should match the retired lives liability with bonds as a liability index fund.

Active lives is where the problems are. You have a dynamic plan, a dynamic labor force, and inflation; these are the longest liabilities and the most volatile. These liabilities require a little more engineering, but you would still buy short assets for the short liabilities (if there is such a thing here), intermediate assets for the intermediate liabilities, long for long, and so on. You want to buy assets you think can outperform the bonds that represent the liabilities. If you think interest rates are going to go up, that shouldn't be hard to do.

Question: Is it appropriate that a pension plan's obligations have a higher rating, AAA generally, than the company's own debt obligations?

Ryan: If a company matches assets to liabilities using Treasury securities, then it could be a AAA portfolio. You can have a situation where the pension fund is a better solvency, a better credit, than the company. So, the company could go under and the pension plan would be fine.

Unfortunately, it is the other way around. General Motors' pension liabilities are more than twice its net worth. That's an industry trend. As the pension goes, so goes the company. It will take you down. That is why it is so critical. It is so big. In 10 years, medical liabilities will most likely be as big.

Question: Because 10-year results are end-period dependent, should longer return averages be used?

Ryan: As I said in my presentation, this is an annual ballgame. We do it daily at Ryan Labs. We send our clients daily reports on liabilities. We manage the money daily. Just like with a scoreboard, you want to know the scoreboard works in real time, right? It is an annual ballgame. It is not a 10-year ballgame. We just used the 10-year numbers because that is the way people normally look at it.

Question: Is the current spot rate relevant in terms of analyzing pension plans?

Ryan: There should be a rule that says, "If you can't buy it, you can't use it." That's the problem with these discount rates. When companies use a discount rate (6.5 percent for corporations and 9 percent for public funds), they use a single discount rate. They price all their liabilities at one rate.

Have you ever seen a horizontal yield curve? Can you imagine trying to buy 6.5 percent one-year instruments or 9 percent one-year instruments? Such instruments do not exist. If you can't buy it, you can't use it. That is why they have to use real spot rates. And be careful about forward rates. They don't work. You have to be able to buy it, or you can't use it. That should be the rule.

Question: Some pension plans, defined-benefit plans, pay benefits based on final pay. And these liabilities are highly influenced by inflation. What are the best investment vehicles to secure protection against inflation?

Ryan: We conduct studies of everything versus inflation. The closest correlation you get is U.S. Treasury Inflation-Indexed Securities (commonly referred to as TIPS), and nothing comes in a close second. A distant second would be the money market. Equities don't correlate with inflation. They have negative correlation. They might beat inflation, but they don't correlate with it.

The truth is the U.S. Consumer Price Index (CPI) is a manipulated number because most of the government's budget is based on it. Mr. Greenspan will go down in history, I think, as a villain. Let's see what he has done. He lowered interest rates, creating part of the pension crisis, because he wants to help the stock market. We now have earnings drag from pensions that's going to be here for the next 12+ years. He may also be hurting lotteries because they can't find a way to fund their liabilities anymore because the Treasury got rid of the 30-year Treasury.

He also got his hands dirty with inflation. The CPI has stuff in it that's hard to believe. It does not have the cost of housing, although it has the cost to rent a house. That's a manipulated number. Gasoline prices went up 50 percent in 2002. The CPI did not move. If the CPI were to go up, the budget, especially the Social Security budget, which is where Greenspan comes in, would get hurt. They don't want that. That is why they are not issuing 30-year bonds and decided to issue TIPS, because they can control the CPI.

Question: Do you think a rising-rate scenario will help solve the problems by reducing the value of liabilities?

Ryan: Yes. If you price your liabilities at the market correctly, then the liability side of the equation can be done correctly. The asset side can't use that ROA nonsense, but the liability side can. If you price liabilities at the market correctly, at least you'll get half the equation right.

If interest rates were to go up, naturally liabilities would go down. So, suppose you have a liability duration of 10 years, every 100 bps that interest rates go up, liabilities go down 10 percent. At a deficit of 30 percent, you need an increase in interest rates of 300 bps. I think deficits are bigger than that, on average. If interest rates go up 300+ bps in the next 3–5 years, it should help a lot. It should give us more than 30 percent recovery.

Question: What if interest rates stay low or even go lower?

Ryan: If interest rates go lower, it is just going to do more damage. Individuals have moved out of their bond accounts and savings accounts because interest rates are so low.

There's no reason for lower rates. None. It didn't help stocks. And we got this earnings drag from the lower rates. When it is finally revealed, people will wonder how equities are going to grow with 15 percent earnings drag for 12 years. I don't see how lower rates help anything.

Question: How is the liability index cushioned for an endowment fund or an affluent investor who has spending needs and growth (i.e., protection of principal goals)?

Ryan: A liability index is always customized. The endowment, by law, has a spending requirement. It has an I owe you (IOU). That IOU looks like a budget, a spending budget. Usually, it goes out 3–5 years and sometimes longer. That becomes the liability event. It is in dollars; it is not a percent. The endowment knows how much it has to spend every year. That should become the index, the objective index. It is a liability schedule.

Individuals are the same way. If you ask individuals what are their objectives in life, they will give you liabilities. They will say retirement, their children's education, and weddings. These liabilities are date sensitive. They know when that child will go to college. They think they know when that child will get married. They think they know when they're going to retire. If you encourage individuals to put it in monetary terms, you have a liability schedule.

Once you see the liability schedule, you can understand the asset allocation. If 12 percent of my liabilities are short, I'm going to put 12 percent of my assets short. If 32 percent of my liabilities are intermediate, I'm going to put 32 percent of my assets intermediate. If 47 percent of my liabilities are long, I'm going to put 47 percent of my assets long. If I didn't know the shape of liabilities, how could I do asset allocations? That is the eternal problem we have in this business. Without a liability index, without knowing the shape of liabilities, how could you do asset allocation?

Developing and Implementing a Risk-Budgeting System

Leo J. de Bever
Senior Vice President, Research and Economics
Ontario Teachers' Pension Plan
Toronto, Ontario

> Sponsors need a better understanding of funding risk because their behavior can completely undo asset/liability management. Safe pension funding strategies are inherently expensive, and actuarial valuation surpluses are not money in the bank. Unless interest rates move up sharply and market indexes beat their mediocre outlook, return to full funding will be some years away. Managers can help by better allocating risk and return across all active and passive strategies.

The Ontario Teachers' Pension Plan (OTPP) is structured as a partnership between the 250,000 Ontario teachers covered by the plan and the Ontario Government. Each partner is legally responsible for 50 percent of any funding deficiency. Plan benefits are indexed to consumer price index (CPI) inflation. OTPP has roughly a 50/50 stock/bond split, and 60 percent of its assets are invested in Canada. Very early in its history, OTPP started using derivatives extensively to modify the asset mix. Like many pension funds, OTPP suffered in the boom/bust cycle of the 1990s, for reasons unrelated to investment policy. The issue was something pension managers rarely worry about: sponsor policy around benefits and contributions. I will begin this presentation by focusing on sponsor behavior because I think it is the biggest risk in any pension fund.

Role of the Sponsor

Sponsors generally lack a good understanding of the volatility of financial markets. They especially need a better understanding of funding risk. Part of the problem is a mismatch between finance and actuarial practice on how to treat liabilities. Actuarial valuations do not incorporate the concept of risk. They tend to price liabilities based on the expected return on the assets and future contributions that are funding those liabilities. That approach is fundamentally wrong. Finance theory says that a riskier way of investing pension contributions implies a pension benefit that is less secure and less valuable than one funded with more-secure assets.

The road back to full funding could be very long unless real interest rates move up sharply, which seems unlikely. I also do not think equity markets will be very helpful in the next 10 years. As a result, a lot of pension funds are aiming for unattainable returns through high-yield and alternative investment strategies. These funds may be underestimating the risk involved with these strategies.

Managers must simultaneously assess risks and returns across all active and passive strategies. The typical active/passive risk management split is suboptimal.

The Pension Funding Crisis

Half a century ago, pension plans collected contributions from members for 40 years to fund a retirement that would last 10 years. Then, because of longevity, 40-year careers started to be followed by 20 years of retirement. In many cases, people are now aspiring to work for 30 years and then be retired for 30 years. That situation has consequences for the cost of retirement and the trade-off between what has to be contributed out of current wages and what has to be earned on contributions to fund these three types of pensions. **Table 1** shows these three types of pensions for two scenarios. At OTPP, we are concerned about the first one—the real returns required to fund a pension indexed to the CPI. As the table shows, for people who wish to work 30 years and be retired for 30 years, it now takes 25 percent of current pay to fund what is currently a risk-free real rate in Canada (3.1 percent). Most pension funds, however, contribute only 15

Table 1. Required Returns to Fund Benefits for Three Combinations of Years of Work/Years in Retirement

	Work Years/Retirement Years		
Pension contribution[a]	40/10	40/20	30/30
Real return required to fund CPI-indexed benefit			
10%	1.7%	3.7%	6.4%
15	0.0	2.4	4.9
20	−1.2	1.4	3.9
25	−2.2	0.7	3.1
Real return required to fund nominal benefit			
10%	1.3%	3.1%	5.5%
15	−0.4	1.7	4.0
20	−1.7	0.7	2.9
25	−2.8	−0.1	2.0

[a]Contribution as a percentage of wages.

Note: Assumes a five-year final average, 1.5 percent annual productivity growth, and CPI inflation of 2.5 percent.

---

percent of current pay. They fund their plans with a combination of equities and bonds and then hope that the equity risk premium will elevate returns to rise sufficiently to cover expected retirement benefits.

For pension funds that do not index their benefits to inflation, the bottom panel shows what their contribution figures would be assuming 2.5 percent inflation. These plans will see their real pension liability erode if inflation rises. When times are good, they may be doing an ad hoc indexation adjustment, but when times are bad, that indexing is not mandatory. A pension eroding at 2.5 percent a year for 30 years will buy half of what it buys today. If the goal is real purchasing power, this type of plan does not make the real cost of real pensions explicit, although it may mitigate funding risk.

The real cost of retirement is inherently higher than most people think. No investment strategy can eliminate that problem, which was masked by the fact that during the 1980s and 1990s, the return from taking risk appeared relatively high.

Pension Risk

After about seven years at OTPP, I realized that focusing on risk management as just an investment issue was wrong. Risk management is also very much a sponsor issue. If a plan's sponsor behaves inconsistently with the plan's investment and risk management strategy, things are going to go wrong. Sponsors rely on actuarial valuations. If an actuarial valuation estimates one dollar more in assets than in estimated liabilities, the sponsor assumes incorrectly that that dollar is available for spending. In reality, an actuarial valuation is based on a ton of assumptions, and any of those assumptions could be wrong.

Policy Risk. Sponsors typically consider pension costs and benefits only in a short-term wage-bargaining context (i.e., as a human resources problem, not a finance issue) and generally without proper costing.

The second problem is that sponsors are eternally optimistic. They believe in the long-term equity premium but ignore its short-term volatility and the fact that counting on the extra return is very risky. They are encouraged by valuations that assume there is no basis to use expected returns that differ from the long-term historical averages. That logic is debatable. Based on history, investors back in 1999 should have known that the bubble was going to burst soon. Robert Shiller has shown that expected rates of return in future time periods vary based on the starting point.[1]

The disconnect between managers and sponsors is that managers consider plan surplus as the reserve needed to make sure good times balance bad times. To a sponsor, the reserve is something that is as certain and ready to be spent as a cash balance.

Surplus Risk. As mentioned earlier, OTPP got into trouble in the 1990s (as did so many plans). I will explain how that happened. **Figure 1** compares the fund as initially planned versus actual plan results. The solid line shows what would have happened to the plan if the benefits had been kept as they were when the plan was set up in 1991 and privatized. The dotted line is what actually happened. The difference between the two is the result of sponsor spending of the surplus. At OTPP, we have banished the word "surplus" from our vocabulary because surplus, as actuaries define it, is not extra money that can be spent. Instead, the actuarial surplus just measures the midpoint of a wide range of possible estimates of a plan's funding status.

Figure 2 shows a stylized market cycle. If market cycles were as simple as the one shown in the figure, investors would be able to anticipate market cycle upswings and downswings. Managers would simply save the surplus during the fat years and have it available in the lean years. The OTPP plan was calibrated in 1991 to require a real return of 4 percent. The assumption was that with our asset mix, we could make CPI plus 5 percent, giving us a cushion. Our biggest problem, we were told, was that the plan would have too much money in the long run. I have not heard that said recently.

---

[1] For more on this topic, see Robert J. Shiller and John Y. Campbell, "Valuation Ratios and the Long-Run Stock Market Outlook," *Journal of Portfolio Management* (Winter 1998):11–26.

Figure 1. Funding Ratio at Market Prices for Actual Plan and Plan without "Surplus" Distribution

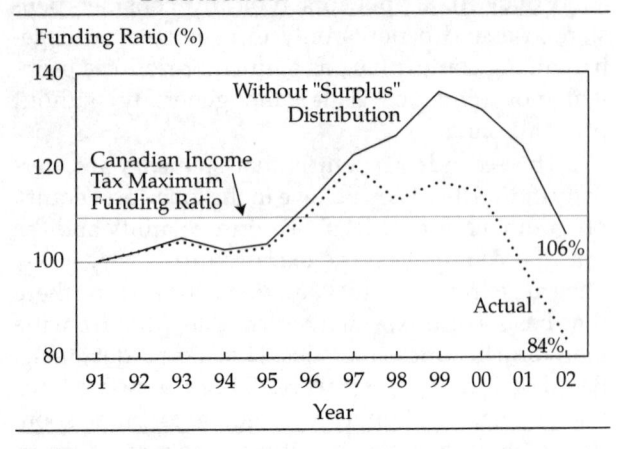

Figure 2. Market Cycle with Upward Trend

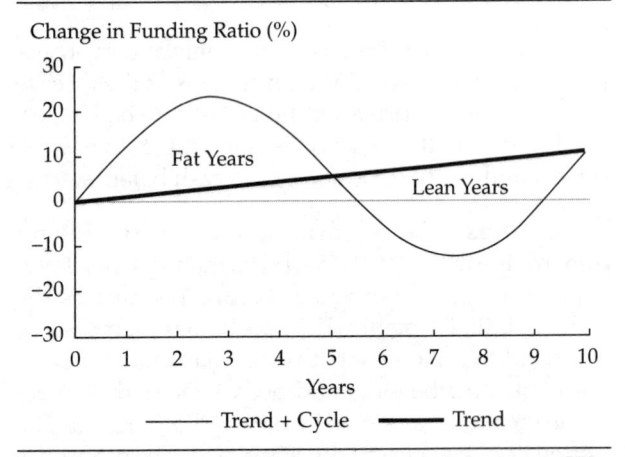

Note: Required return is CPI plus 4 percent; policy return is CPI plus 5 percent.

Figure 3. Relationship between Contribution Rate and Real Return Assumption

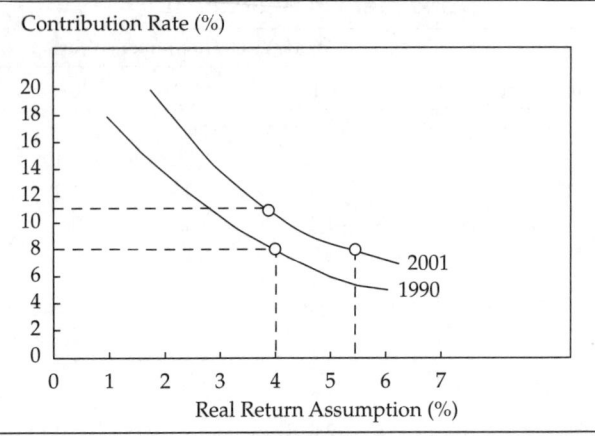

Note: Contribution rate is calculated as a percentage of wages.

the inverse relationship between contribution rates and rates of return on plan assets. In our case, the benefits were substantially improved around the year 2000, so the curve shifted up. Instead of having the teachers and the government each contribute 8 percent and assuming a real 4 percent rate of return (as we did in 1990), we now have to earn a real rate of 5.4 percent or receive an 11 percent contribution from the government and the teachers.

Changes in OTPP Policies

Following the decline in our funding position through the combined effects of sponsor decisions and market drops, we set new policies and goals.

Funding Policy. To prevent a future surplus problem, we reached an agreement with the teachers and the government to build a reserve beyond the 100 percent funding point. We have agreed on a funding zone, which acknowledges the uncertainties surrounding actuarial valuations. So, we now recognize that the world does not end the moment the plan falls below 100 percent, but we also recognize that the plan may need to be significantly above 100 percent funding before the sponsor can assume reasonably that it has more money than it needs. This funding agreement allows for any surplus generated in good years to offset any deficit generated in bad years.

Future Prospects. Our plan is currently 80 percent funded. To get a sense of how that funding level may change over the next 10 years, I graphed all 10-year histories for our current investment policy since 1927 in **Figure 4**. As the figure shows, the plan could

True, if we had saved the money in the fat years to have it available in the lean years and if interest rates had not changed and if the markets had not dropped, then at the end of 10 years, we would have ended up with a surplus. But we spent the money during the fat years, markets did drop, real interest rates did fall, and we now do not have a reserve for lean years. Chances are we will still be underfunded in 10 years.

Part of our problem arose from the notion that surplus can be spent. When the actuary estimates that a benefit improvement can be financed out of surplus, that actuary takes into account only current plan members. But the reality is that these improved benefits are also promised to future plan members, typically without changing contributions. This action acts as a ratchet on required returns: Over time, the plan has to earn a higher rate of return to fund obligations to these future members. **Figure 3** shows

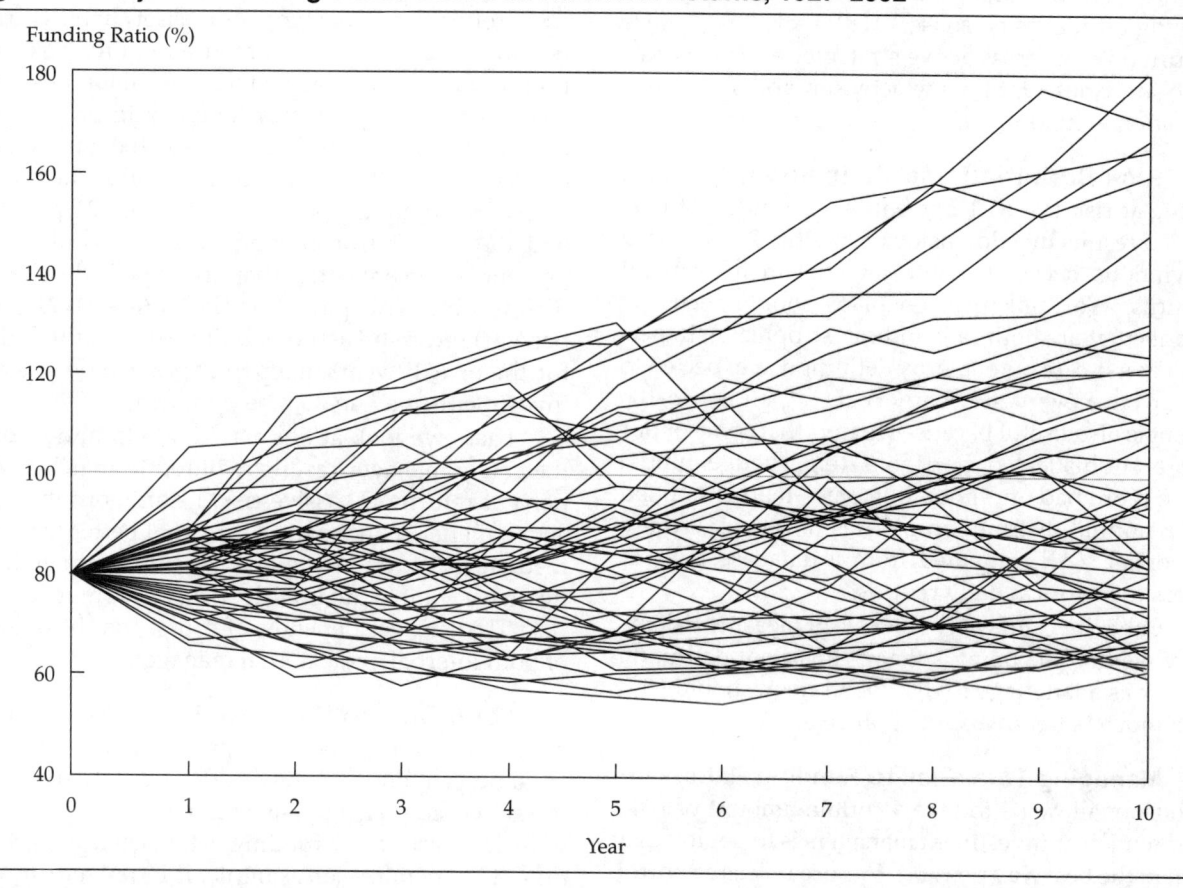

Figure 4. Projected Funding Status Based on Historical Returns, 1927–2002

go to 60 percent funding based on these historical scenarios, but it could also end up with 180 percent funding. So, all may not be lost.

Most of the good scenarios shown in Figure 4, however, started with market P/Es of less than 10. Unfortunately, the current market P/E is 22, and **Figure 5** shows the results for plan funding status when the market P/E was greater than 20 at the start of the 10-year period. This figure suggests that if a plan is counting on the stock market to bail it out in the next 10 years, that bet has a fair chance of not paying off.

Pension Management Goal. If markets are not likely to help us out, we need to go back to first principles as investment managers. At OTPP, we continuously evaluate the risk in our assets relative to the liabilities. We do not look at funding risk relative to a T-bill or a long bond but relative to the risk in our liabilities. In our case, the liabilities have a 20-year duration. The yield of real return bonds (RRBs), which is the Canadian equivalent of U.S. Treasury Inflation-Indexed Securities (commonly referred to as TIPS), is about 3.1 percent. For current members, we need to generate a real return on assets equal to the RRB yield plus 1 percent. For new members, however, a real return on assets of the RRB yield plus 2.3 percent is required. The gap between new members

Figure 5. Projected Funding Status Based on Historical Returns from 1927–2002 for Starting P/E Greater than 20

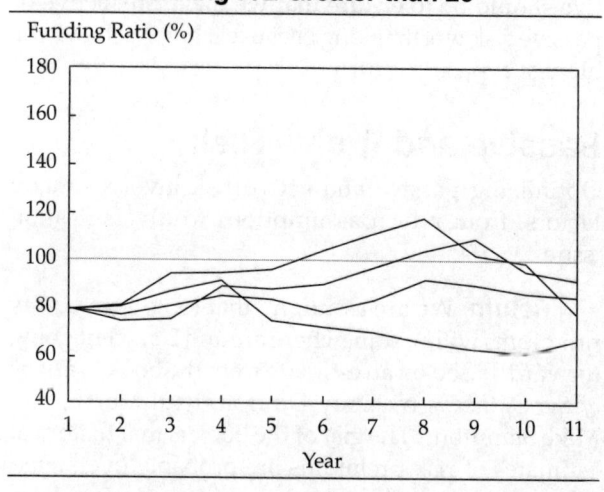

and current members is large and growing. And as the plan goes forward, that 2.3 percent is going to be a bigger part of the average return we need to generate. So, in the future, we are going to need higher contributions or assets with a higher rate of return.

Pension plan risk comes from pursuing incremental return over the risk-free liability match. Where can risk be taken most efficiently to get the highest return? Taking risk that has little chance of paying off makes no sense. OTPP seeks to optimize return on risk across active strategies as well as passive strategies. Optimizing active and passive risk in isolation is suboptimal.

Risk Definition and Estimation. We use a value at risk (VAR) 1 percent tail definition of risk, which results in a downside of roughly 2.6 standard deviations because of the fat tails in investment returns. We think pension plans should focus on events that are both rare and catastrophic. A 16 percent worst-case outcome, by definition, is expected to occur once every six years. Focusing on a 1-in-100 event is also useful because we find that some of our more sophisticated portfolios (e.g., hedge funds) have more bad and good outcomes than is implied by a normal distribution of rates of return. We use historical VAR estimated from a database with 16 years of historical daily returns.

Other investors may not scale or measure risk the way we do. The point is that a consistent definition of risk as a language to discuss strategy should lead to a much better investment process.

Managing Total Risk to Funding Ratio. Our sponsors allow us to take a certain amount of risk, and our job as investment managers is to deploy that risk in the best way possible. We use risk as a control tool, but it is primarily a way to discuss strategy. Risk is a resource. Our clients really do not care whether our potential losses are active or passive. The objective should be to ensure that we make any active or passive risk worth taking because it helps achieve the highest expected return.

Passive and Active Risk

Optimizing passive and active risk involves many factors, from return assumptions to diversification issues.

Return. We are assuming that long-term equity premiums will be somewhere around 2 percent going forward, based on an estimate from the book *Triumph of the Optimists* by Elroy Dimson, Paul Marsh, and Mike Staunton.[2] The gist of the book is that historical estimates of risk premiums are probably overstated because the statistics contain a strong survival bias. Moreover, the U.S. stock market in the past 100 years may not be representative of a normal stock market. The authors illustrate this finding by looking at other markets where the returns have not been as good as those in the United States.

[2]Elroy Dimson, Paul Marsh, and Mike Staunton, *Triumph of the Optimists* (Princeton, NJ: Princeton University Press, 2002).

If we financed all our liabilities at the risk-free RRB return of 3 percent, our asset/liability risk would be zero. If we assumed an equity risk premium of 2 percent and financed our liabilities with 100 percent equity, the portfolio would provide a 5 percent real return and have a 1-in-100 annual risk of a 42 percent drop in the funding ratio. The risk in a 50 percent equity portfolio would be 21 percent, and the payoff from taking that risk would be 4 percent, 1 percent better than the expected risk-free RRB returns. This payoff implies a $(4 - 3)/21$ (or 5 percent) return on asset/liability risk. We think that for the next 10 years, a 5 percent return on passive investments may, in fact, be optimistic.

Then, we look at our active side to understand the active manager results required to match that 5 percent return on passive risk. It turns out that our active managers have to be 5 percent better than the median manager. Finally, we have to evaluate how much we want to put in each pocket in terms of active risk. That answer depends, of course, on the quality of both internal and external managers.

Total Risk to Funding Ratio. We currently have a distribution between passive and active risk of 20 percent on the passive side and 6.5 percent on the active side. That passive number reflects the risk of losing part of our funding ratio because markets do not cooperate—for example, if index returns are less than what we need on the liability side. On the active side, the 6.5 percent is the stand-alone risk of managers not meeting their passive benchmark returns. Adding the active and passive risks together, the total funding risk to the portfolio is 21 percent, which assumes zero correlation between the active and passive risk. In reality, the correlation between our active program and our passive mix is negative.

Active/Passive Management. If the goal is to maximize total return subject to total risk, some people may wonder why we do not judge our managers on that criterion. The answer is that in the long run, doing so would make sense but that on an annual basis, asset and liability market volatility dominates anything a manager can do to mitigate its negative effects.

Therefore, most pension plans use an active/passive split. They construct an asset mix and hope to outperform their liability requirements by a certain amount. In our case, we take 20 percent passive risk to earn an incremental 1 percent over our liability growth. We then overlay that program (like most plans) with an active program.

We are aiming to be first-quartile managers, which means having a 25 percent return on active risk (or a Sharpe ratio of 0.65). If we are successful, active risk will contribute 1.6 percent (25 percent × 6.5 percent) to total fund return. If that is the case, our combined return (active and passive) over RRBs will be 2.6 percent. Unfortunately, being a first-quartile manager year after year after year is difficult.

Note that our assumptions about the required return on active risk (25 percent) are much more stringent than they are on passive risk (5 percent). Most pension funds seem to be willing to rely mostly on market volatility instead of active management returns.

Risk Optimization. If our managers can be 5 percent better than the market indexes, the optimal split to maintain 21 percent total risk is 15 percent passive and 15 percent active. The technical problem is that active programs often are not scaleable; plans may not have the proper controls and the proper staffing in place to expand their active programs.

But an even more fundamental problem exists. In obtaining board approval for our total risk system, we suggested that we aim for a higher, more stable rate of return on total risk. The consequence is that our fund will, at times, look very different from other funds. If the market is rising, chances are we will underperform because we have diversified our risk between the market and the active program and the active program will most likely be uncorrelated with the market. Thus, our active program probably will not keep pace when the market has a high return. The payoff will be in years such as 2001 and 2002. If the market is down, our plan will be down a lot less. The problem with this strategy is that it requires a true long-term focus. If the market ever recovers and we lag somewhat, which is likely to be the case, it will be interesting to see whether people remember what they signed up for.

Active Risk Allocation. In the beginning of our risk management approach, we created a methodology to control active risk through annual risk budget negotiations. In other words, we determined acceptable risk levels in various programs by analyzing the best overall fund opportunities and examining available internal and external manager resources. Many pension funds do not take advantage of what I perceive to be their comparative advantage: Pension funds can mobilize a lot of cash, and they can afford to wait a long time. So, they can pursue illiquidity premiums in inefficient markets.

Our manager performance incentives are tied to return on risk. Each manager is expected to make a contribution to the total active investment return target. To do so, each manager is given a risk budget as a resource. We encourage managers to think of investing as a team sport; that is, risks diversify, so they should not be looked at individually but be judged on how they fit together. Managers tend to have the view, "I am okay, but I am not so sure about you." Managing as a team takes effort. Because of the way our fund is run, however, we need that team aspect to make the whole program work.

Controls on Active Risk. We give our managers a lot of freedom within a predefined risk budget. Each of our five senior vice presidents (SVPs) supervises the risk budgets of the managers. Each SVP is allocated a risk budget, and he or she can allocate that risk budget down to individual portfolios. Most anything legal and ethical is allowed as long as the SVPs stay within that risk budget. To go beyond it, they must obtain permission from the next level up—the executive vice president. They are stopped out at 33 percent beyond their risk budget. It is an effective control mechanism that replaced a system that relied extensively on a lot of "thou shalt" and "thou shalt nots," which managers found very cumbersome.

Active Risk Use and Diversification. The good news is that our strategy does work; we get the diversification out of our active program that we expect to get. What we have found is that we get very close to the theoretically expected diversification of 2.5:1 between the sum of the active risks at the asset class level and the diversified total fund active risk. When I originally put the system in place, I assumed that active programs were uncorrelated, which is mostly true. Only in a few cases are active programs correlated. If we had nine equally sized active programs and they were truly uncorrelated, then active risk would diversify 3:1 (i.e., as the square root of the number of programs). But the risks allocated to each program are not the same, and because we only have eight programs, diversification is somewhere between two and three times.

The object of the game is to be a first-quartile manager in the long run, and to do so we must have consistency both over time and across programs. I have omitted the names of the programs in **Exhibit 1**, but it shows their performance relative to their benchmarks since 1995. The up arrows indicate positive relative performance, and the dots indicate that the program produced negative returns relative to its benchmark. In most years, two or three programs did not add value. But a good program will add value in most years. That consistency both across programs and across time is needed to make sure that the plan delivers consistency over time.

We watch these numbers quite closely, but we cannot be too hard on managers who have a bad year. We need to analyze why the manager had a bad year; the randomness in markets means that

Improving the Investment Process through Risk Management

Exhibit 1. Relative Value Added by Various Programs, 1995–2002

Program	1995	1996	1997	1998	1999	2000	2001	2002
Program #1	↑	↑	↑	↑	↑	↑	↑	•
Program #2	↑	↑	↑	•	↑	↑	↑	↑
Program #3	•	•	↑	•	↑	↑	↑	↑
Program #4	↑	•	•	•	↑	↑	↑	↑
Program #5	•	↑	↑	↑	•	•	↑	
Program #6	↑	↑	↑	↑	•	↑	↑	↑
Program #7	↑	↑	↑	•	↑	↑	↑	↑
Program #8	↑	↑	•	↑	•	↑	↑	↑

Note: Up arrows represent value added; dots represent no value added.

good strategies do not always pay off. Then again, a sober second thought may reveal that either the logic or the implementation was deficient.

Alternative Investments

We have examined alternative programs as a way to enhance our asset mix and found that some caveats do exist. There is nothing wrong with real estate, private capital, or hedge funds—in principle. The problem is that in practice, investors do not always have good management in place, so they may fool themselves about the amount of embedded risk.

Hedge funds, in particular, suffer from that problem. I see hedge fund proposals indicating ridiculously high Sharpe ratios, say of 3 or higher. That number can usually be reduced to 1 by doing a little bit more work on how these numbers were calculated. Sharpe ratios are easy to "game" (e.g., by introducing optionality or ignoring correlated returns between successive periods). Hedge funds should not claim they can walk on water. It is good enough to be good. If a hedge fund can deliver a Sharpe ratio of 0.4 or 0.5, which is good and credible to most clients, it should not try and fool investors with something that cannot be sustained.

We have also become involved in timberland and infrastructure projects. These investments are difficult to acquire and labor intensive to manage. One has to have good people looking after these assets to make sure the plan sponsor truly understands the underlying holdings.

Asset Mix and Total Risk

As I mentioned previously, the active/passive split that most funds use is not optimal. Plans often calculate the rate of return between those two components and balance the composition. That approach is not good enough because asset mix is not a proxy for fixed risk, which is why we have started to deemphasize asset mix as a control tool. The change in the volatility of a passive asset mix can be bigger than the incremental risk from the active management that we do. So, if a plan takes asset mix as a given and focuses all its attention on controlling active risk, it is just managing noise.

Figure 6 illustrates this problem. The solid line is our policy risk relative to liabilities. The dotted line is our actual total risk relative to liabilities. As the figure shows, most of the time, our active program subtracts risk, and even when the two track closely, the difference is mostly noise. Another interesting point is that with the exception of the grey vertical bars, the asset mix was fixed in the fund. So, theory would say that the solid line should be a flat line outside those gray bars. It certainly was not. The reason is that indexes do not have constant volatility. Their volatility goes up and down, particularly in a momentum market, because indexes are capitalization weighted. The more overvalued a stock becomes, the bigger a component of the index it becomes and the more volatility it contributes to the index. Asset mix is not a proxy for risk. Therefore, there really is no point in managing asset mix. Instead, plans should manage the risk within their asset mix.

The agreement with our board is that we operate within a 21 percent total risk limit, which has (like most asset mix controls) a range around it. Our "green" zone is 20–22 percent risk. If we go outside that green zone, either on the upside or the downside, we have to notify the board. If we get to either the 19 percent or the 23 percent level, we need to get board approval.

Some people wonder why we have a downside limit on risk. The answer is that if we think we are taking risk because it has a return, then taking too little risk is as much of a problem as taking too much risk. It is a two-sided distribution.

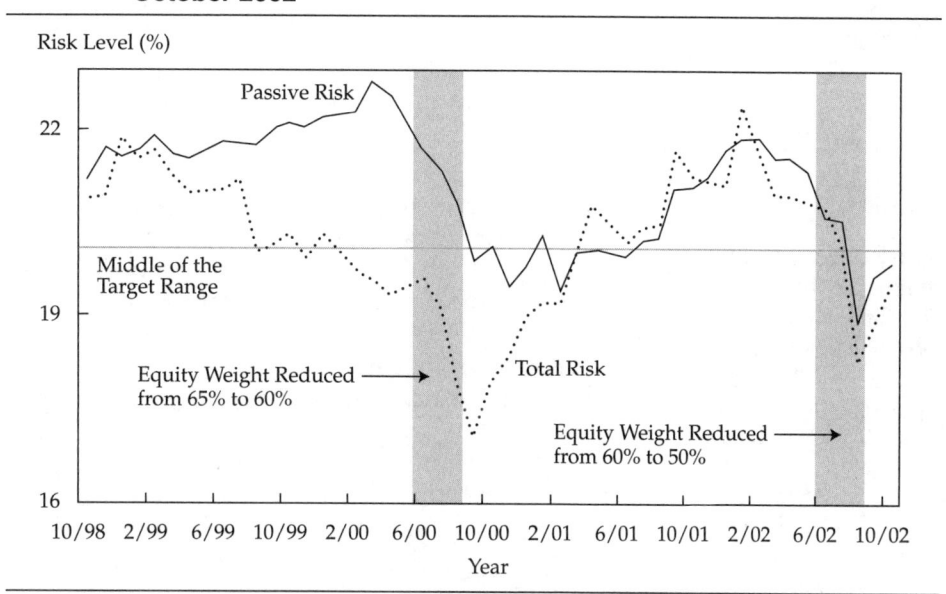

Figure 6. Passive and Total Risk Relative to Liabilities, October 1998–October 2002

Conclusion

We are still in the process of implementing this approach. We have just received approval to run the funds by attempting to maximize the total return on the total 22 percent risk. We are trying to come to terms with the maverick risk that this approach implies. We are also doing a lot of work to get a data fix on the 1 percent tail, representing a worst outcome. The VAR of any of these methodologies basically says, "What is the 1 percent worst thing that can happen to this portfolio?" It does not say anything about the structure of that tail which, by definition, is very difficult to get a handle on because so very few observations exist. This issue is important, however, because a plan can have not only correlation between asset classes or between strategies but also correlation in the fat tails of certain strategies. It is an issue, but it is not a big one for us because our strategies are aggregated.

The final issue, which in most risk systems is fairly significant, is that credit risk is not measured properly by most market risk systems. Basically, credit risk is an extreme event; default does not happen very often. If a plan is trying to measure risk by observing the volatility of bonds, it is unlikely to capture that 1-in-200 event that prompts a credit default.

Question and Answer Session

Leo J. de Bever

Question: Why is it costly for pension funds to match liabilities with RRBs, and what duration do you use for your RRBs?

De Bever: The RRB real duration is around 16, so it is short of the 20-year real duration of our liabilities. It is expensive to use RRBs because they yield only 3 percent plus inflation. Our liabilities are growing faster than 3 percent plus inflation.

Question: Exhibit 1 shows four programs that weren't doing well in 1998 and two programs that weren't doing well in 1999, and in the three years following, only one program had not done well. Is that by luck, or is it the changes in the way you've managed your overall mix?

De Bever: The past three years were particularly good to us because our value orientation worked well, but as a manager, you always should assume that luck also played a sizeable role. There is some evidence that our methodology has made people smarter about taking risk, which is something I hoped would happen. People will try and game systems. They'll try and optimize risk, but basically what the system encourages you to do is to squeeze the most return out of risk—to minimize the amount of risk used to get a certain return.

I think the answer to the question is that a year like 1998 shows that a value style did not work. What has happened since 2000, in particular, shows that it did work well. So far, 2003 looks like a decent year. But one should never assume that you have a fix on the problem and that any improvement is a result of just skill.

The difficulty of generating persistent positive performance because of random variation is a hard point to grasp. I once asked "Do you realize if we aim to be a first-quartile manager and that if it turns out *ex post* to be the fact that we are a first-quartile manager over some period, we should expect to underperform our benchmarks one year in four?" I was proud that I seemed to have explained the point, but then came the comment: "But if you picked the right manager, you should be able to avoid that one year in four."

Question: What have been the really big changes in your thinking over the past two or three years?

De Bever: I no longer believe that diversifying bets within an asset class active strategy is always a good thing to do for efficient total risk diversification. We probably spend too much time on individual portfolio diversification and not enough on efficient total risk diversification. Fewer, more concentrated, and better managed strategies may be more efficient in aggregate.

We are also observing that after an initial reluctance to take risk when we put the system in place in 1996, managers have started to take more risk. But they've done it in a different way. In some sense, we look like an index fund with a hedge fund on top. It is that focus on what you really like and what you really don't like that I think has sharpened in the past three or four years.

Question: Do you still have problems getting managers to take enough risk?

De Bever: Yes. Again, it tends to be a problem when you've had a few good years. We are measured on a four-year cycle. People naturally tend to protect their winnings. With a few exceptions, managers rarely go to the limit of their risk budget, despite my argument that "If you really believe in your program, you should be able to expand your positions and get more return by using up all of your risk budget."

There is a tendency to pull back to avoid large absolute losses. That is a problem because risk of loss goes with opportunity for return. Anything you do in a big pension fund has a lot of zeros behind it, both when you lose money and win money. That is why it is very important that you stand behind a manager who has had a bad year. If you don't do that, that manager will pull back and take no risk whatsoever.

Question: How do you monitor or measure the risk of your alternative programs when there is insufficient historical return data, especially with respect to the VAR methodology that you use?

De Bever: You need to use risk proxies, and it is the quality of the proxies that becomes important. This is true for all illiquid or non-transparent alternative investments, but hedge funds are our big problem, although the pension industry is slowly winning the battle for transparency.

Hedge funds keep telling me that their risk systems are so sophisticated that I wouldn't know what to do with their risk information. I keep telling them to try me. We have transparency right now of less than 40 percent. The only data that most of them currently provide are *ex post* monthly rates of return. Andrew Lo and a number of other people have written on how that systematically understates the risk that these funds run.[1] So, we currently allocate these funds 2.0–2.5 times more risk than they estimate themselves. It is the protection for the credibility of your risk system.

Question: How do you go about modeling tail risk?

De Bever: It is an underdeveloped science, again because of the paucity of data. We've looked at a number of approaches to squeeze more information out of the historical data. But the general problem in risk management is that there is only one history and that history is not long enough to make statistically valid conclusions.

Inevitably, there comes a point where you realize that you can torture the data only so much and make an assessment as to whether history is likely to be a valid indicator of the future. What we often do is communicate that view through our proxies. In essence, you have to be a Bayesian on risk to protect the guilty because there is not enough statistically valid information to do it any other way.

Question: How does a pension fund's comparative advantage of being able to invest in illiquid markets get impaired by radical funding requirements as a result of highly variable mark-to-market episodes?

De Bever: We have about C$65 billion in assets. The pension payroll is C$3 billion a year. Most pension funds act as if they may have to cough up all their assets next year. I think that's silly; you can afford to take some liquidity risk with probably 80 percent of your assets. In our fund, contributions coming in used to match money going out. Now, outflows are bigger by a few billion dollars a year, but that is more than covered by investment income. Changes in market value of assets matter little as long as income from bonds and stocks is sufficient to fund the pension payroll.

Question: When you have reasonably large changes in market valuations, how do you deal with the rebalancing issue in your public and liquid market instruments as opposed to your private market instruments?

De Bever: When we started looking at this issue, we quickly concluded that the gain from a lot of our rebalancing was far outweighed by the transaction cost. A related issue is the value and efficiency of rebalancing to specific benchmark indexes. In Canada, we have something called the ScotiaMcLeod Bond Universe. The index provides an independent measure of the relative performance of a bond manager. But it has a lot of bonds in it, and mirroring the index perfectly is of no particular benefit to the fund's objective of achieving a certain interest rate exposure. Passive indexes should achieve the fund's objective without the need for costly fine-tuning.

Question: To what extent do you use OTC and exchange-traded derivatives in your portfolio?

De Bever: We started out in 1991 with 100 percent nonnegotiable Ontario debentures. To get a better asset mix over a reasonable amount of time, we started to use a lot of fixed income and equity swaps. Now, we have about C$20 billion of these instruments on our books.

We have extensive control on counterparty risk. We have mark-to-markets and exchanges of collateral on an average of 3–6 months. It has become a well-oiled machine. I don't think there are any serious issues. Occasionally, a counterparty starts to get into trouble, and we wind down our exposure.

Question: How do you monitor credit risk within the portfolio?

De Bever: We have some very old-fashion limits. "Thou shalt not have more exposure than X to a company of credit Y." We think that's totally inadequate, and we are trying to integrate market and credit risk, but the industry isn't there yet.

Some risk software companies have developed fairly sophisticated credit analogs to the market risk models, but market and credit risk still live in different universes. Within the next one or two years, we may get to my ideal of integrated risk measurement (i.e., being able to look at an enterprise and decompose the total risk in an enterprise between its credit and market risk).

Question: Does your strategy distinguish between short- and long-term return potential?

De Bever: When I joined the fund, we used only long-term expected returns. Then, we started to apply the Shiller and Tobin's q argument that starting points matter and that 10-year returns (or longer-term returns) are, to some extent, predictable. From today's starting point, we are shading our strategies in the direction of being very selective about equity risk. At one point, we had 75 percent exposure to equities. Currently, it is more like 45 percent. That drop reflects this assessment of expected returns.

Question: Investors generally have a true long-term horizon when markets are strong, but they become much more short term as the markets become difficult. How have you found your sponsors to be?

De Bever: Our sponsors were naive, but our board has a lot of financial expertise. Still, boards are probably not too different from people in general. When markets are strong and you suggest pulling back on equities, they are hesitant to leave the party too early. We started to reduce equities at OTPP

---

[1] Andrew W. Lo, "Risk Management for Hedge Funds: Introduction and Overview," *Financial Analysts Journal* (November/December 2001):16–33.

at the end of 1999. The summer of 2000 was very uncomfortable because that did not look like a bright move. Two or three years of weak markets later, it has given us some credibility.

That credibility is very sensitive to recent history, and scrutiny is asymmetric. Boards should be skeptical from a risk perspective whether returns are exceptionally good or exceptionally bad. A program that gives returns way beyond anybody's expectations should stimulate as much scrutiny as one with exceptionally bad returns.

Techniques for Controlling Embedded Short Option Risk in Credit Securities

Jeffrey A. Rosenberg, CFA
Managing Director
Head of Fixed-Income Credit Strategy Research Group
Banc of America Securities
New York City

> Investment managers need better tools for understanding credit risk. The standard approach of using rating agency credit ratings to gauge credit risk is no longer sufficient. Equity-market-based credit models provide investment managers with a more robust framework for analyzing and understanding credit risk. Furthermore, modern credit risk management allows credit risk at the issuer level to be rolled up to the portfolio level, thus providing an enhanced view of portfolio credit risk over standard approaches.

Credit risk is special because it is asymmetrical, and recent market events have highlighted the limited upside and virtually unlimited downside of credit risk. The leading question becomes: Why invest in an instrument with an upside of approximately 5–7 percent gain and a downside of 100 percent loss? Understanding and managing the asymmetrical nature of credit risk is the focus of this presentation.

I will examine some of the factors that drove the recent dramatic increase in corporate bond defaults and the implications for creating a model for credit risk. Finally, I will discuss how best to view credit risk in the portfolio context. Credit risk has many unique characteristics that make it a challenge at the portfolio level.

The Recent Default Wave

In January 2002, U.S. speculative-grade default rates hit a cyclical peak of slightly less than 11 percent, which was roughly the same order of magnitude as the previous cyclical wave of defaults in February 1991, as shown in **Figure 1**. Of course, the default cycle mirrors the business cycle, but a critical difference is not reflected in this figure. The most recent credit market erosion was much more dramatic than in virtually any previous cycle. Figure 1 shows issuer-weighted defaults (that is, the number of issuers that defaulted relative to the number of issuers rated as speculative grade). Thus, this figure fails to capture the portfolio impact, or dollar volume, of the defaults.

On a dollar-volume-weighted basis, the 2002 default rate was nearly twice as high—almost 20 percent—making this a much more severe wave of speculative-grade defaults than the 1991 default wave.

Another interesting phenomenon of the most recent wave is the erosion of credit quality in the investment-grade universe, even among the highest-quality credits. As shown in **Figure 2**, in 2002, the U.S. investment-grade default rate hit 1.07 percent on an issuer-weighted basis. Of course, it is uncommon and unexpected for investment-grade companies to default. "Investment-grade default rate" means issuers who had an investment-grade rating within one year of their default, which is notably different from what happens with speculative-grade default. On a dollar-volume-weighted basis, the investment-grade default rate hit 2.95 percent. Historically, this default rate has been virtually zero. In fact, the average default rate for the past 30 years of investment-grade default experience was about 25 bps, which represents long periods of zero-default rate with a few blips in 1977, 1982, and 1986. Clearly, investment-grade defaults are not supposed to happen. Something has changed in the credit market to produce a level of default that is four times the historical rate on an issuer-weighted basis and more than 100 times the historical dollar-weighted rate. Obviously, the dollar-weighted rate reflects some extraordinarily large defaults, such as Enron, WorldCom, and the California utility companies. Nevertheless, this

Figure 1. U.S. Speculative-Grade Issuer-Weighted Default Rate, February 1970–June 2003

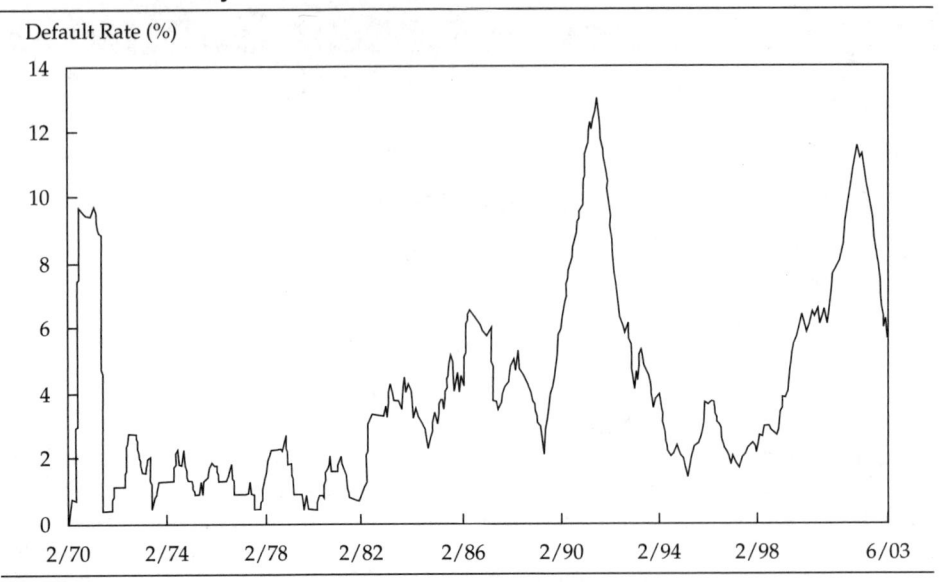

Source: Based on data from Moody's Investors Service.

Figure 2. U.S. Investment-Grade Issuer-Weighted Default Rate, November 1998–December 2002

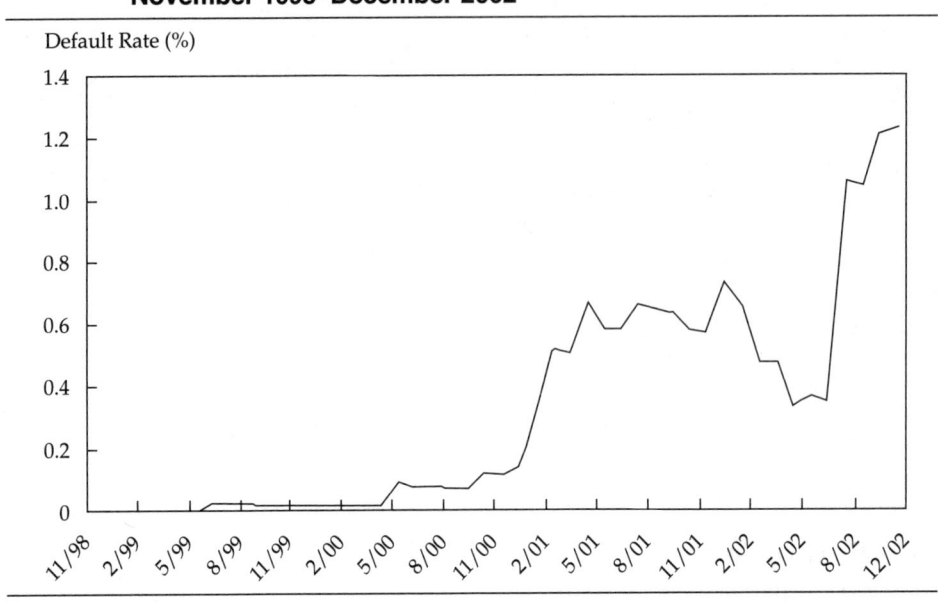

historic rate of default has motivated renewed focus on risk management in the credit spectrum.

In the mid-1990s, aligning the interests of management and shareholders was a key focus of the consultant community. The attempted solution was to give management equity—not equity that affected the bottom line but equity in the form of stock options. One of the unintended consequences of focusing management's attention on equity was a dramatic increase in net corporate debt issuance beginning in the mid-1990s and continuing through early 2001, as shown in **Figure 3**. Nearly half of all the corporate debt issued since 1995 went to fund stock buybacks. By issuing debt to buy back equity, corporations were leveraging their capital structures, sowing the seeds of the recent credit disaster in both the high-grade and speculative-grade markets.

The value of a long equity call option increases when the likelihood of large gains in the underlying stock price increases. Of course, the likelihood of large declines in the stock price also increases, but the long call optionholder benefits greatly on the way up and loses relatively little on the way down. The result in the 1990s was greater stock-price volatility. The best

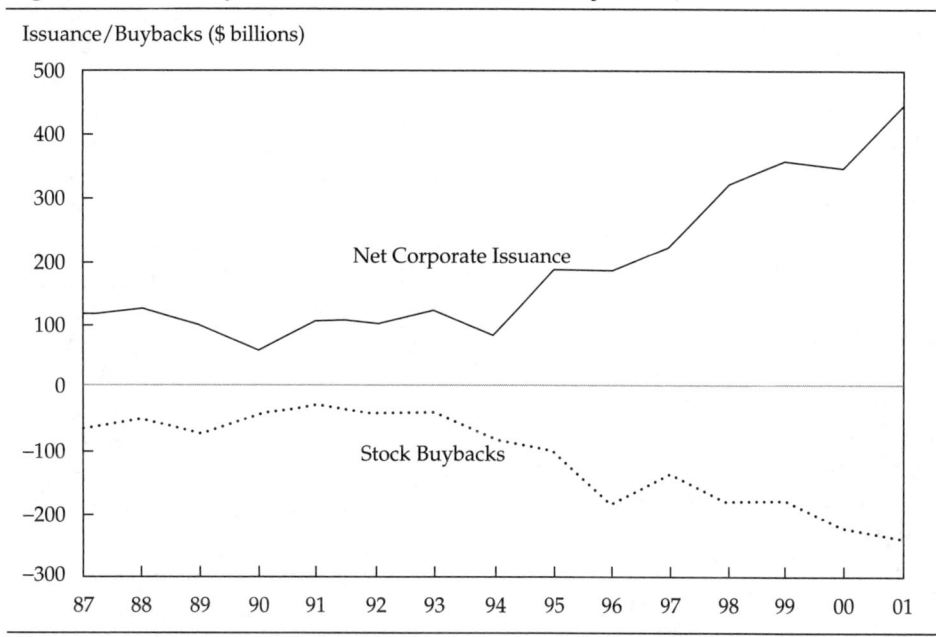

Figure 3. Net Corporate Issuance and Stock Buybacks, 1987–2001

measure of aggregate large-cap volatility, shown in **Figure 4**, is the "VIX" Index. Published by the Chicago Board Options Exchange, VIX (the name comes from its ticker symbol) is a weighted average of the implied volatility from eight calls and puts on the S&P 100 Index. By this measure, the volatility in the large-cap market went from about 10–15 percent in the mid-1990s to 50 percent on 10 October 2002, a quintupling of the level of volatility. For owners of equity call options, this increased volatility was good because it meant that their options were vastly more valuable.

This is where the credit angle comes into play. A creditor provides, in effect, call options to equityholders and to managers, so the increase in volatility that was good for management and good for long equityholders was bad for the creditholders. If the average corporate issuer was engaging in such activity, something even more devious must have been

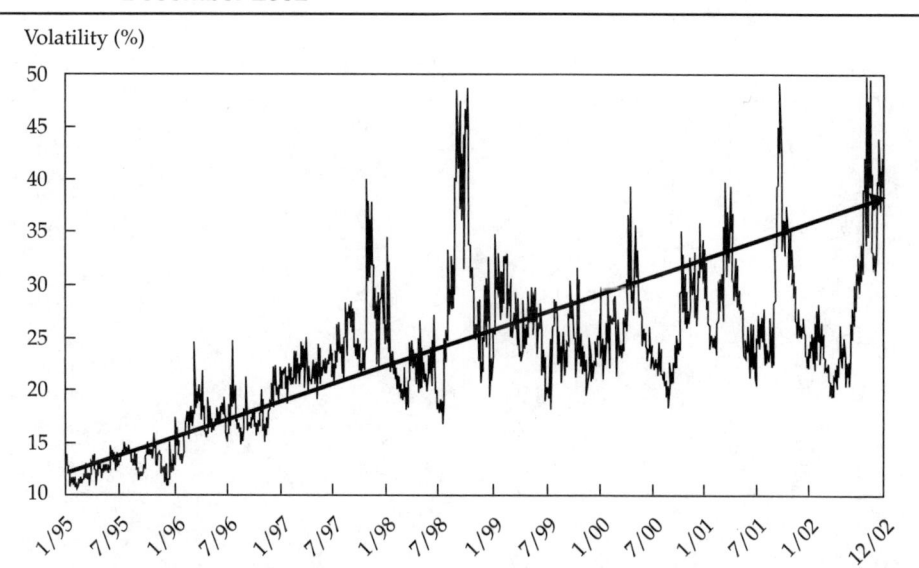

Figure 4. Option-Implied Volatility for the S&P 100, January 1995– December 2002

Note: Since producing this graph, the Chicago Board Options Exchange has reworked its VIX Index. The data presented in this figure represent the "old" VIX Index, which is now published under the ticker "VXO."

occurring at the extremes of the distribution. That something was the erosion of the standards of corporate governance, which led to the failures of Enron and WorldCom, among others, and it was mirrored in the leveraging of the balance sheet. At the extreme, corporate managers levered their balance sheets to the detriment of bondholders for their own personal gain. Thus, the recovery currently under way needs to include the unwinding of corporate governance problems, and this seems to be happening.

Market-Based Credit Models

Most credit models fall into one of two classes. One approach is based purely on financial data. The other approach is the market-based model, and this model is the subject of the rest of this presentation. Most market-based models start with credit spreads (such as spreads to risk-free T-bills) or the quality spread (the difference in the price of credit risk between high- and low-quality credit instruments) versus return on the S&P 500, as shown in **Figure 5**. Notice that in 1987 and 1991, stock prices and credit spreads had the typical and intuitively expected inverse relationship. That is, as stock prices declined, the price of credit risk rose, reflecting the increase in credit risk. Two other periods are examples of what happens when the expected relationship breaks down. In the 1993–94 credit rally, spreads continued to tighten while stock prices moved sideways. For the 2003 credit rally, two points are of note. On 10 October 2002, the average investment-grade credit spread was 280 bps over Treasury bonds. By the beginning of April 2003, the spread had collapsed to 140 bps over Treasuries. During the same time period, the S&P 500 was at 880 on 15 October and near 880 at the beginning of April 2003. Stock prices experienced volatility, but the return remained unchanged over this time period. At the same time, credit spreads, reflecting the price of credit risk in the market, narrowed by half.

This observation indicates that another variable is important in assessing credit risk: volatility. In credit risk models, volatility is used in many different areas. In this particular case, the volatility measure that is the most important is the forward-looking volatility measure. The volatility of the option market (that is, implied volatility) is really the price of insurance. The insurance premium that is embedded in that volatility is a reflection of investors' anticipated, or forward-looking, uncertainty, which determines the price they are willing to pay for insurance today. Backward-looking volatility is calculated *ex post* from realized changes in the stock price.

Consider the same two time periods in terms of the relationship between the credit spreads and option-implied volatility, as shown in **Figure 6**. In the 1993–94 rally, banks cleaned up their balance sheets by writing down nonperforming assets, causing volatility to fall. The decline in volatility led to a decline in credit risk. The same thing happened beginning in 2002. Average credit spreads in the investment-grade universe collapsed by half, and option-implied volatility also collapsed by about half, from 50 percent on 10 October to about 25 percent at the beginning of

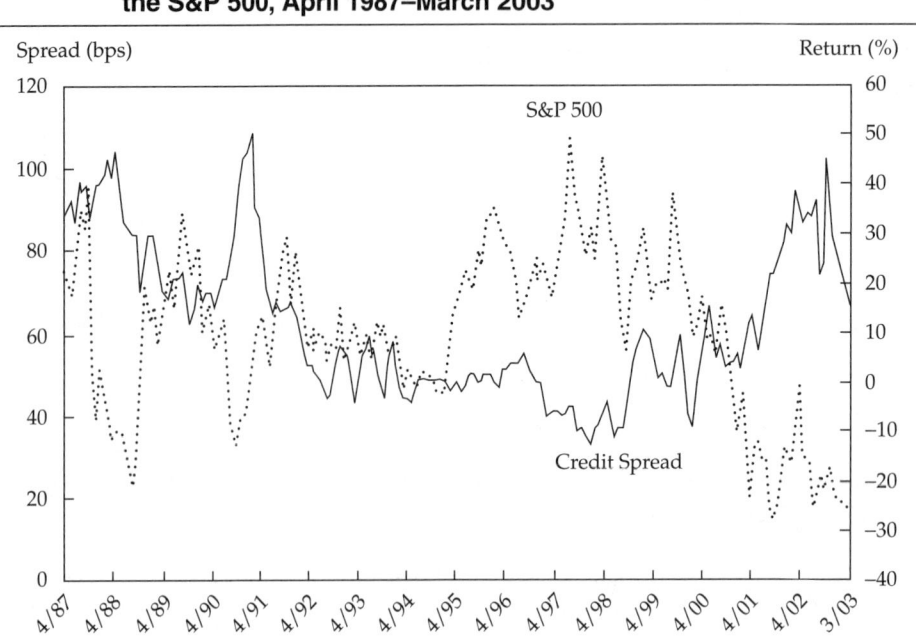

Figure 5. Spread between Baa and Aa Credits versus Year-on-Year Return for the S&P 500, April 1987–March 2003

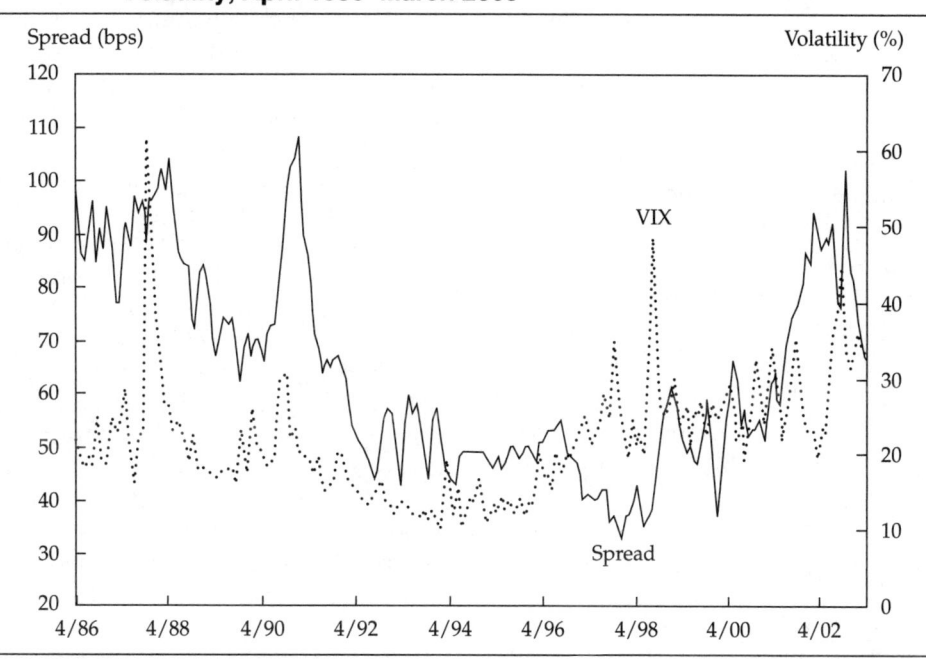

Figure 6. Relationship between the Baa–Aa Spread and Option-Implied Volatility, April 1986–March 2003

April (not shown in Figure 6). So, the decline in volatility was a critical signal for the decline in credit risk.

Figure 7 illustrates the same type of observation for the relationship between the average stock price for investment-grade corporate issuers and the average option-implied volatility for the same issuers. Typically, stock prices and implied volatilities tell the same story, reflecting risk aversion in the option markets. When stock prices are falling, demand for insurance portfolio protection increases, and volatility, which is simply the price of insurance, increases. The result is the observed strong inverse relationship between implied volatility and stock prices. The most important time periods are the exceptions, the periods when stock price and implied volatility tell different stories, which is what happened from October 2002 to January 2003. Notice the change from October 2002, when the average investment-grade option-implied volatility was at 60 percent, to January 2003, when volatility dropped to 40 percent. During this time,

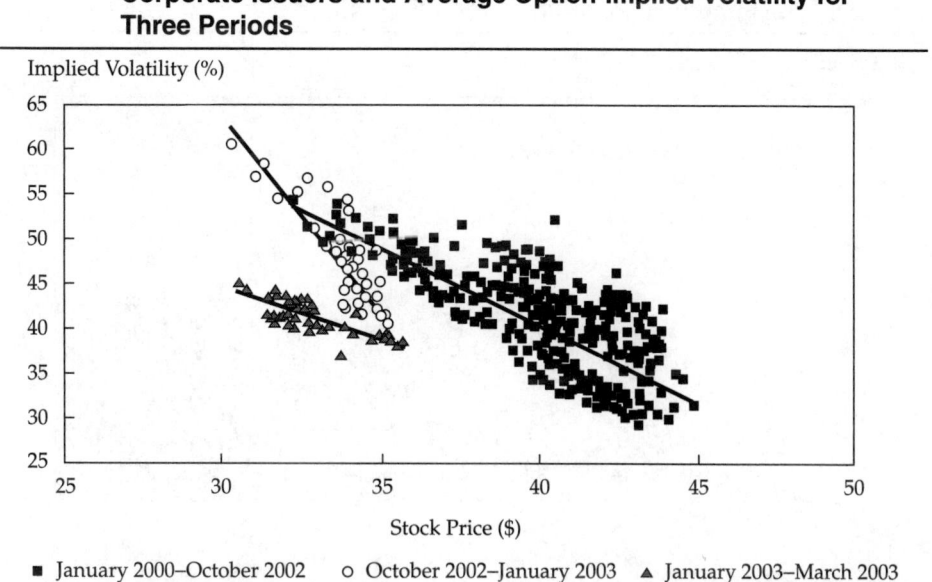

Figure 7. Relationship between Average Stock Price of Investment-Grade Corporate Issuers and Average Option-Implied Volatility for Three Periods

implied volatility in the credit markets repriced lower. Why would implied volatility decline by 20 bps over such a short time period? The answer is that corporate managers were deleveraging their balance sheets, selling off assets, issuing equity, and keeping cash for the debtholders, as opposed to using the cash to buy back stock. This period was the first time in at least 10 years that such deleveraging had been seen. The change in corporate behavior was reflected in the decline in implied volatility, which was subsequently reflected in the decline in credit risk in the credit markets.

So, this observation provides an important link between equity analysis and credit analysis. Not only are stock prices important, but the uncertainty of stock prices is also important. Furthermore, an objective, market-based measure of this uncertainty is provided by option-implied volatility.

The Nature of Credit Risk

In 1974, Robert Merton published a paper applying his option valuation methodology to corporate debt.[1] This paper provided the fundamental theoretical background for most of the market-based risk models. Merton's critical observation was that the purchase of corporate debt resembles the writing or short selling of a put option.

Models applying this theory differ in their implementation, but the fundamental theory is the same. In this presentation, I will describe one approach based on the Merton model. It is certainly not the only approach, and various approaches have different advantages and disadvantages.

Consider the illustration of credit risk in **Figure 8**. If a creditor lends, say, $5 and the assets of the company are worth $5 at maturity, the creditor will get $5. But if the assets are worth less than $5, the creditor will be left holding the bag and must claim the assets to get the recovery value. The vertical line represents the default point. Note that the payoff looks like the payoff to a short put position.

A good example of this phenomenon for an investment-grade bond is Ford Motor Company, as shown in **Figure 9**. Because of the asymmetrical payoff profile, with limited upside and unlimited downside, when a credit begins to become distressed, the market becomes concerned about the value of the assets relative to the ability to pay off debt. The price of the bond can be represented by the bond's spread to the risk-free rate, as represented by the yield on a comparable-duration U.S. T-bond. The relationship can become highly nonlinear, especially as stock price falls. For example, for a small decline in Ford's stock price, the credit spread widens dramatically. This phenomenon is called the "credit cliff." All the major investment-grade blowups—Georgia-Pacific, Owens-Illinois, Owens Corning, Rite Aid, WorldCom, and Enron, to name only a few—followed the general pattern shown in Figure 9.

Figure 9 is an important illustration for understanding the link between equity markets and credit markets. Failure to appreciate the significance of this link can lead to erroneous interpretations. Note that the observed correlation between a company's equity price and its credit spread is extremely low for the flat area of the curve—in Ford's case, between $14 and

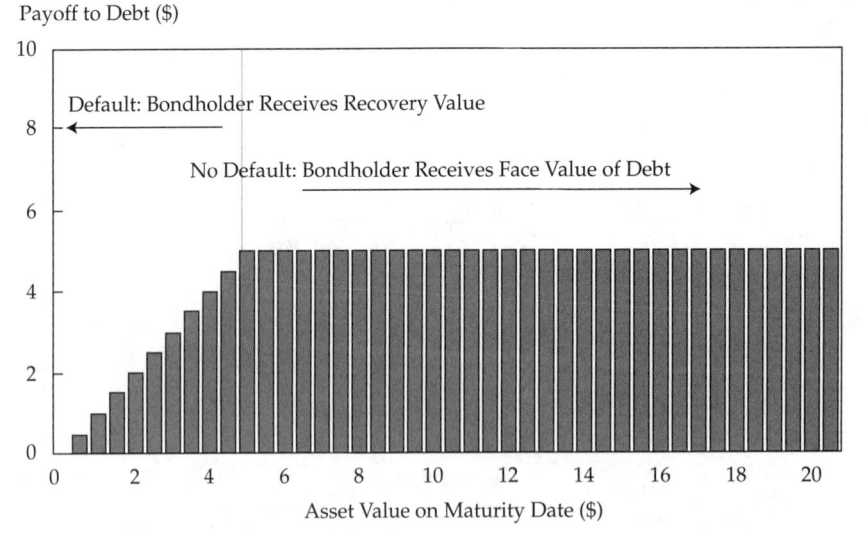

---

[1] Robert Merton, "On the Pricing of Corporate Debt: The Risk Structure of Interest Rates," *Journal of Finance* (May 1974):449–470.

Figure 8. Asymmetrical Payoff for Credit Risk

Figure 9. Nonlinear Relationship between Ford Stock Price and Spread to T-Bills for Ford Corporate Debt 2002
(weekly data)

Figure 10. The Generalized Credit Cliff: Relationship between Company Leverage and Projected Spread Change

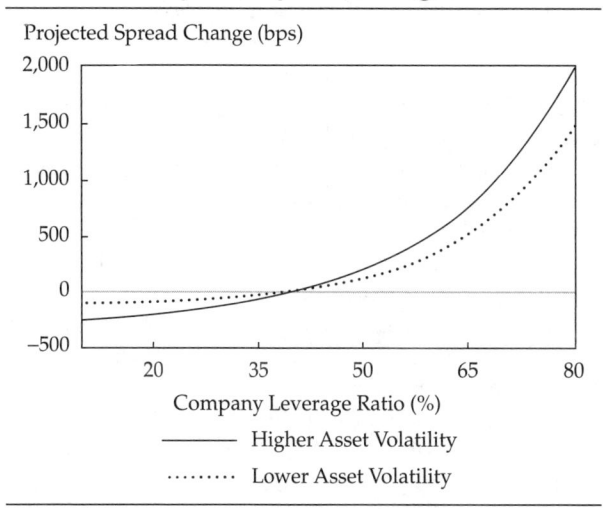

Note: Company leverage is the ratio of debt to the sum of debt plus equity market cap.

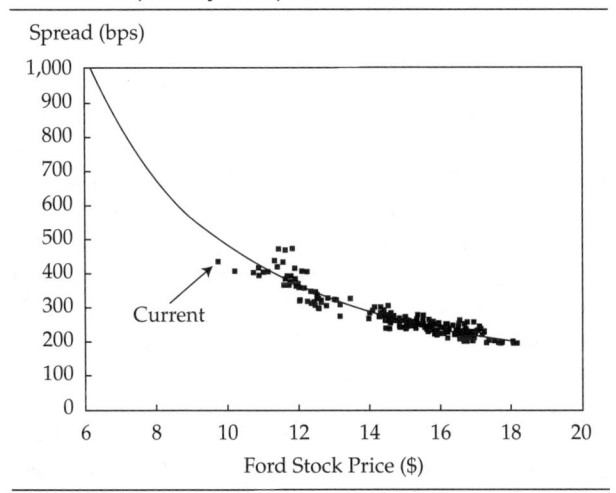

$18—because spread volatility has little to do with changes in the observed stock price. The same pattern shown in this portion of the curve would be reflected in correlations between equity and investment-grade credit spreads in the mid-1990s, for example. In fact, some suggest that using equity prices in assessing credit risk is meaningless. This conclusion, however, misses the forest for the trees. Although the correlation may be low in the narrow view, it can be considerable in the grand view.

So, for investment-grade credits of high quality (I will define "high quality" shortly), low realized correlations are observed between equity prices and credit spreads. When the credit spread falls off the credit cliff, however, the correlation rises significantly. For Ford, when the stock price is in the $9 to $12 price range, the correlation with the credit spread is extremely high, about 92 percent. This strong correlation pattern means that equity-based techniques for measuring and monitoring the potential credit risk can work quite well, but two more inputs are needed.

First, stock price cannot be used as an absolute value to assess credit risk. What is needed is a more generalized model. The Merton model suggests the theoretical shape of the credit cliff for different issuers. **Figure 10** is based on a normalized measure of leverage as expressed by debt as a percentage of total firm capitalization (the ratio of debt to the sum of debt plus equity market capitalization). As the stock price falls toward zero, the leverage ratio rises to 100 percent. In such a case, the orientation of the credit cliff flips. The flat part of the curve is around the 20 percent leverage ratios, the leverage ratios of high A rated credits. At this point of the curve, high-quality credits will have low correlation between spread change and stock price.

Now, consider the 60–65 percent range of leverage ratios in Figure 10, an area typical for speculative-grade credits. Credits with high leverage have a high correlation between spread and equity price. The greater a company's leverage, the greater the sensitivity of debt to the equity price. For example, at the extreme of zero equity value (i.e., default), the debt value is the equity value. In the middle are the credits from the lower end of the investment-grade market—A, BBB—which have the greatest potential to move from a region of low credit risk and low equity sensitivity to a region of high credit risk and high equity sensitivity. Which line a credit is on depends on the underlying business risk or asset volatility. Higher-risk companies have greater uncertainty of future cash flows (i.e. higher asset volatility) and thus should show greater spread sensitivity to increasing leverage. Thus, the Merton-model-based equity approach helps to assess the location and shape of the credit cliff.

This analysis demonstrates that the expected distribution for returns to corporate debt is skewed. Consider the hypothetical spread change of a corporate issuer with a leverage ratio of 40 percent. At 40 percent, the change in the spread is zero bps. As the equity price falls, the spread widens. As the equity price increases, the spread tightens, but notice the asymmetry. For equal movements of the price down or up, the widening of the spread is much greater than the tightening of the spread. Limited upside plus unlimited downside equals a return distribution that is heavily skewed toward the downside.

Examining the leverage ratio as defined previously offers a better understanding of the credit cliff mentioned earlier. The credit cliff is specific to each issuer; that is, each credit has an individual credit cliff. So, for each issuer, one can determine where the cliff lies relative to a 40 percent leverage ratio and so on. The important point is that no one ratio of leverage is the right measure for where the credit cliff begins. The credit cliff depends on the riskiness of the underlying issuer. The higher the risk of the issuer, the lower the level at which the credit cliff begins, as shown by the two lines in Figure 10. (I will return to this theme later in the presentation when I discuss portfolio risk and the need for granularity of credit risk in measuring portfolio risk.)

The best historical determinant of credit risk has been the VIX measure of volatility, as shown in **Figure 11**. This graph relates the VIX to the spread of BBB versus Treasury bonds. Although stock prices and volatility typically provide the same information, as I have already mentioned, unusual periods can have superior explanatory power. During periods of high credit risk—for example, the 1987–91 and 1998–2003 periods—the correlation between VIX and BBB credit spread was in the 80–90 percent region. In periods of low credit risk, the correlation fell because the underlying credit risk had little movement. At the macro level, this observation indicates that implied volatility is a good measure of forward-looking credit risk, a point that can be incorporated into a credit risk model.

Combining forward-looking risk with the model shown in Figure 10 results in **Figure 12**. The dotted line represents the credit cliff. The spread begins to slope up to the cliff at a leverage ratio of 40 percent. Also, a normal probability distribution for equity return can be overlaid, providing a good proxy for the likelihood of the extreme outcomes in the tails of the distribution—and most important, the likelihood of suffering a big decline.

This observation gets back to my leading question. The reason someone should invest in an instrument with 5 percent upside and 100 percent downside is that the probability of the more extreme event is extremely low. The point of constructing a risk–reward credit profile is to assess the probability of a major downside outcome. The best measure of the market's estimate of this probability is the implied volatility of the equity option market. The narrower distribution curve represents an implied volatility of about 40 percent. The wider distribution represents an implied volatility of about 70 percent. The higher the volatility, the higher the probability of suffering outcomes in the tails. Volatility does not indicate direction, but it does provide information about uncertainty. Uncertainty is what credit investors are most concerned about because the mark-to-market cost of being on the downside of the distribution is much greater than the potential gain from being on the upside of the distribution.

I should point out that from the perspective of credit risk management, the credit risk in the investment-grade space is transition risk, or downgrade risk, as opposed to default risk. Remember, a 100 percent leverage ratio means the value of equity falls to zero and the debt is the only thing left. The average investment-grade ratio of debt to market capitalization is 30–40 percent, so Figure 12 is the picture for an investment-grade issuer whose probability of default is extremely small (in fact, close to

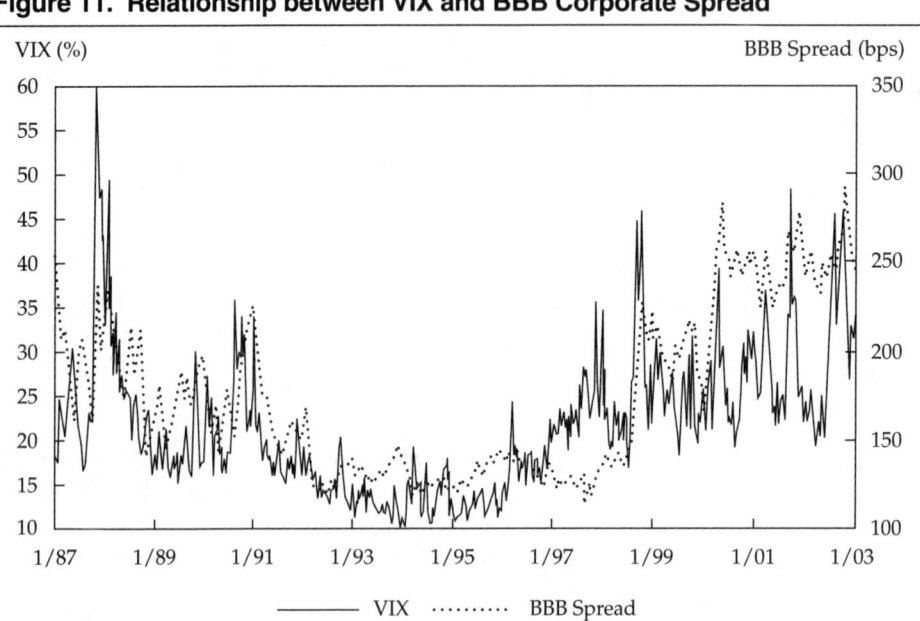

Figure 11. Relationship between VIX and BBB Corporate Spread

Figure 12. Forward-Looking Risk Applied to the Credit-Cliff Model

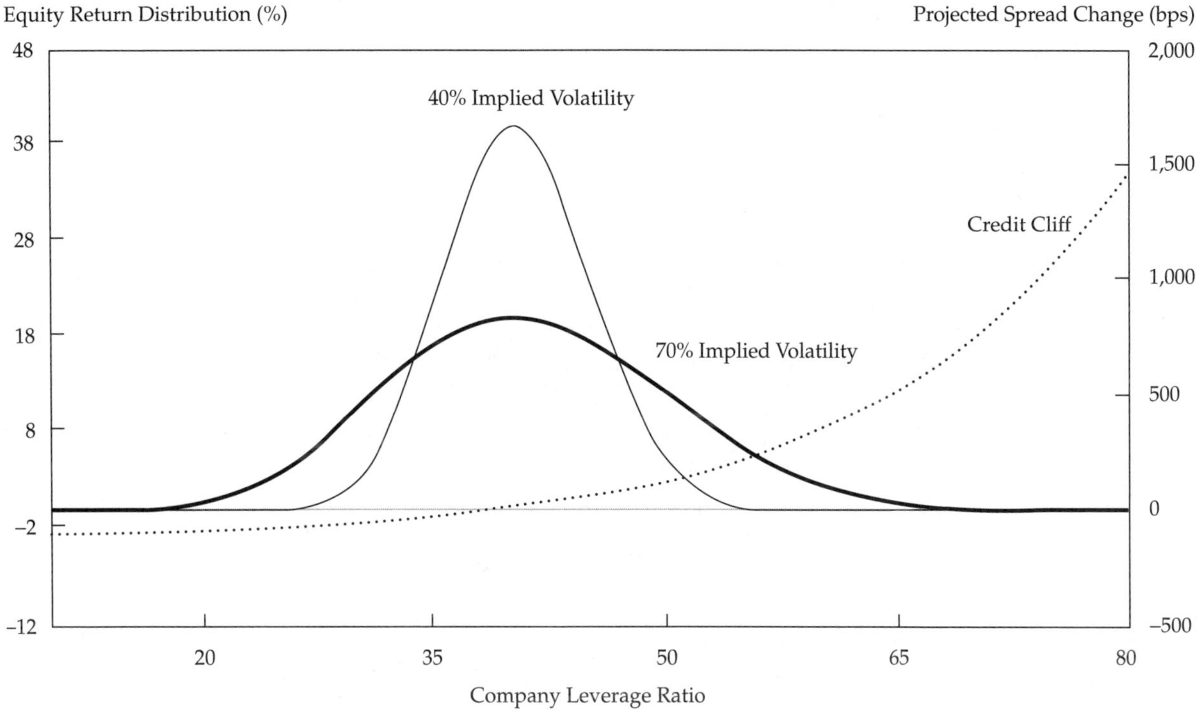

Note: Company leverage is the ratio of debt to the sum of debt plus equity market cap.

zero). Thus, for the purpose of creating a measure of portfolio credit risk (given an investment-grade portfolio), the key is not the risk of default, which is highly unlikely to happen, but the risk of the credit spread widening, which has a greater probability of affecting the portfolio. In reality then, this credit risk model incorporates both the probability of default and the risk of spread widening. For the investment-grade universe, however, the probability of default is usually irrelevant (although it clearly was not irrelevant in 2002).

One can use this information to create a quantitative credit risk model with which one can assess the credit risk objectively using market-based signals without subjective inputs. The point of market-based risk models is to add another tool for credit risk analysis. Since 2002, using agency ratings to manage credit risk in the portfolio has become a minimal requirement. Investors are searching for tools to augment the ratings-based approach in order to assess risk both at the portfolio level and at the issuer level. Using the example of Ford's credit risk, **Figure 13** shows how risk can be tracked over time. Our risk measure is the credit risk line. The goal is to set triggers to alert management of deteriorating credit risk. Most models of this type alert managers to credit risk long before the ratings have eroded, which is why they have been the focus of such tremendous interest. Our particular scheme uses a simple green light/yellow light/red light method. In February 2003, Ford's credit risk passed through the "red light" threshold at 400 bps, indicating increased risk of mark-to-market widening. Subsequently, bond spreads widened more than 70 bps. The risk measures in our model also indicate where risk is decreasing and highlight potential opportunities for total-return active managers. For example, risk peaked at slightly less than 600 bps and then fell dramatically, passing back through the red-light threshold. By the end of the sample period, Ford's credit spreads had tightened by about 150 bps from the mid-March levels.

Similar credit risk tools that provide a market-based, proactive measure to help trigger a credit risk review are currently available from commercial vendors. These tools are designed not to replace people in the management of credit risk but rather to help people better manage credit risk.

Managing Portfolio Credit Risk

The tool I described in the previous section is limited to evaluating individual issuer risk. The next step is a model that can be applied to portfolio risk, which has some unique challenges. **Figure 14** represents hypothetical corporate bond return distributions in different volatility environments. Note that the scale

Improving the Investment Process through Risk Management

Figure 13. Ford Credit Risk

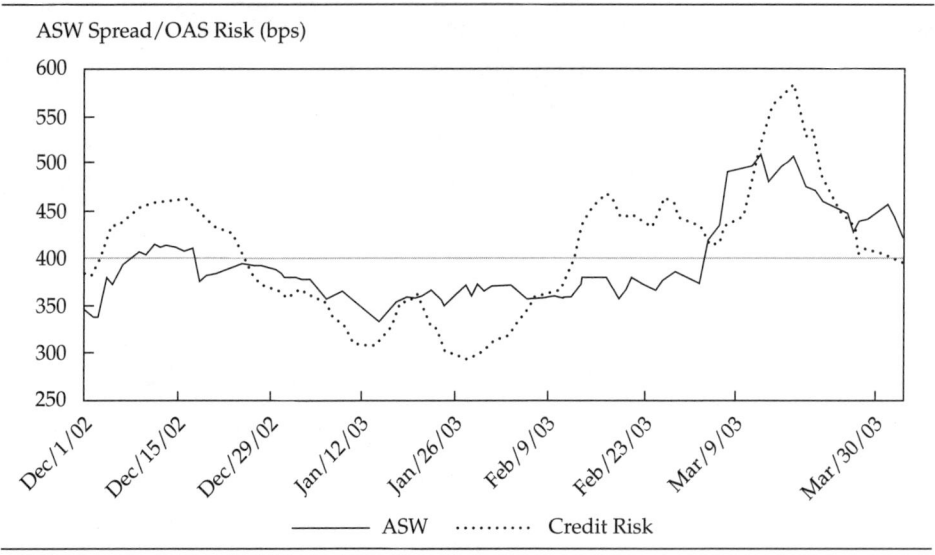

ASW = asset swap spread, OAS = option-adjusted spread.

Figure 14. Hypothetical Corporate Bond Return Distributions under Different Levels of Volatility

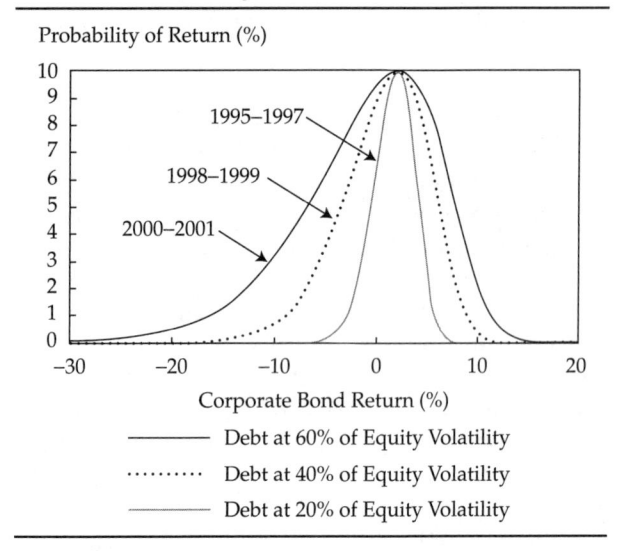

of the probability axis has been altered in order to compare the *shapes* of different distributions. (If the distributions were all drawn to the same scale, they would all have the same area under the curve, so the peak of the 60 percent volatility distribution would be well below the 20 percent volatility distribution.) In the mid-1990s, represented by the innermost distribution, the worst-case return for a corporate bond portfolio was about 5 percent below the mean and the best case return was about 5 percent above the mean, a roughly symmetrical return distribution. As the level of market volatility increases, the distributions become more skewed to the negative side of the distribution.

Consider again the example in Figure 4, in which VIX volatility rose substantially from 10 to 15 percent to 50 percent. When the endemic level of uncertainty increases, some of the credits will suffer significant losses, which will lead to (smaller) portfolio losses. The problem with credit risk is that although credits in a portfolio can lose 100 percent, none of the credits in a portfolio can gain 100 percent. Consequently, in an environment of higher credit risk, the distribution of corporate bond returns will become heavily skewed to the downside, which means that traditional bell-curve approaches to managing credit risk provide inadequate measures of overall portfolio credit risk.

A significant problem that occurs as a consequence of using normally distributed portfolio returns is overstating diversification. We at Banc of America Securities call it credit divers*ifiction*. Consider a simple example of an equity portfolio containing two stocks. The stocks have the same underlying volatility and have assumed negative correlation of 100 percent. In a normally distributed return environment, if one stock goes down by 40 percent, the other will go up 40 percent, so overall portfolio risk will be zero. Now, consider an example of a portfolio that contains two corporate bonds with the same assumption of 100 percent negative correlation. If one bond declines 40 percent, the other bond will not gain 40 percent because the upside is limited to par, plus perhaps a little total return. The portfolio is left holding a lot of credit risk. The extreme negative correlation does not lead to a large reduction in overall portfolio risk because of the skewed downside risk.

Figure 15 illustrates the diversi*fiction* concept. As correlation falls, diversification increases. As the portfolio moves from 100 percent correlation to zero percent correlation, the risk of a worst-case portfolio loss decreases, but the credit line, driven by the asymmetrical return distribution, descends more slowly than the equity line. Failure to assume skewed downside for a credit portfolio results in portfolio risk models that *over*state the level of diversification and *under*state the level of credit risk.

Figure 15. Credit Diversi*fiction*

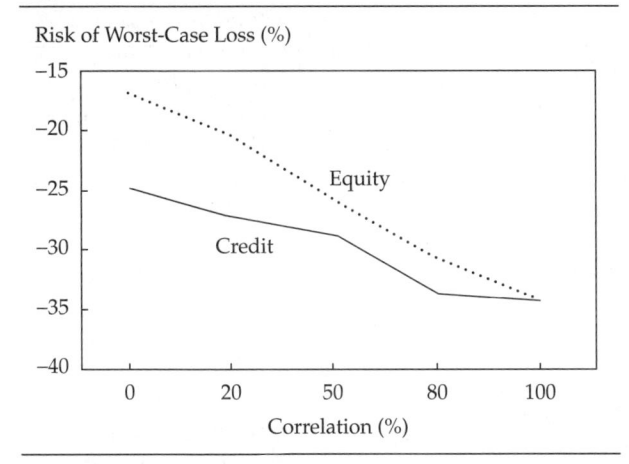

Problems with the Standard Approach

Using volatility in credit modeling leads to the assumption that upside and downside risk are equal and thus creates a diversi*fiction* problem. Using historical volatility measures fails to capture potential risk—that is, the credit cliff. Historical volatility will not capture the potential large change in portfolio or credit risk for high-quality credits.

Risk attribution is about granularity. On a portfolio level, portfolio risk models have difficulty treating portfolio diversification. Standard models lead to a residual diversification value, and it is unclear where this belongs. Newer techniques allow the manager to create an attribution of risk at the issuer level in such a way that all the issuer risks add up to the total portfolio risk, which results in risk assessment at both the portfolio and the issuer level. For modern credit portfolio risk management, the ability to measure exposure at a granular, issuer-by-issuer level is extremely important.

Conclusion

The primary task of all market-based credit analysis tools is to measure credit risk. Managers need to augment the standard credit-rating system. Knowing that the average portfolio credit rating is A or that BBB credits account for 30 percent of the portfolio no longer suffices as a way of assessing or measuring the total credit risk in a portfolio. Market-based approaches provide another way of quantifying portfolio credit risk. If it can be measured, it can be monitored, and measuring and monitoring credit risk are the first two steps in managing it.

The other purpose of market-based models, as I demonstrated with the Ford example, is to provide early warning indicators, and this is particularly important because the rating agencies failed to provide early warnings in such recent cases as WorldCom and Enron. With early warning indicators, managers now have many more tools available to manage credit risk—credit default swaps, derivatives, and so forth. Thus, managers can reduce or add credit exposure with greater precision. One of the latest trends is to use the equity approach I described to create equity hedges, or equity option-based hedges, as another strategy for hedging portfolio credit risk.

Question and Answer Session

Jeffrey A. Rosenberg

Question: Is equity option volatility an indicator for spread movements, and if so, what sort of lead time is provided?

Rosenberg: The statistical evidence indicates that equity options provide, at worst, a coincident indicator of spreads and, at best, a leading indicator of spreads. So, some evidence supports the idea that looking at option volatility can provide a leading indication; furthermore, we at Banc of America Securities have experienced it in our own modeling approach. Now, the next question should be: Why should such a relationship exist? What distinguishes option markets from every other market is the ability to get leverage quickly. Bond investors can get leverage by buying bonds on repo. It is a little bit less than one-to-one leverage. We can do it in our margin accounts, buying equities or selling equities without up-front cash. The leverage amount, however, is limited, whereas options provide a much higher degree of leverage. Thus, the ability to change equity exposure quickly means that new information should be reflected first in the option market. This leading behavior probably will not last. Arbitrage funds have been established to exploit this type of dislocation, which should eventually lead to the collapsing of the leading behavior. Nevertheless, the approach still has value, which comes from the objective ability to measure credit risk at the issuer level and the portfolio level.

Question: Do you look at the relationship between spreads and volatility with a nominal spread or with spread as a percentage of rates?

Rosenberg: The approach depends on the time frame. For long-term measures of spread, we use nominal spread values. Obviously, if we're looking at spreads in a 12–14 percent yield environment, as was the case in the early and mid-1980s, nominal spread values versus volatility can be very deceptive. Sometimes, we use two approaches: relative spread and an implied default rate calculated from the spread. This dual approach can adjust for differences in the yield levels. Over shorter time periods for which the yield levels are relatively constant, or at least not significantly different, we can use nominal spreads.

Question: If the franchise or underlying asset value—not simply the stock value—of the average company is also lower in 2003, what is the implication for credit spreads tightening as much as they have in 2003 to date?

Rosenberg: The credit cliff model can help answer this question: How close am I to the cliff and how quickly am I approaching it? The speed at which I am approaching the cliff is the most important variable in the pricing of credit risk over short periods. In looking at the volatility, you are also looking at how close you are to the cliff. To understand what I mean, go back to Figure 7, which showed the shift downward of implied volatility. The shifting downward of implied volatility reflects the pricing in of expected deleveraging. Leverage is a major influence on the level of volatility, so the big downward shift in volatility is the market telling investors it expects deleveraging to occur, which is why credit spreads have tightened. Aggregate measures of leverage, which are backward looking (and complete data are available only through fourth-quarter 2002 and a little bit through first-quarter 2003) don't show a huge amount of deleveraging. Deleveraging is occurring in the telecommunications and utility sectors, but overall, the level of leverage has not declined. What has changed, and what has led to the justifiable decline of credit spreads in investment-grade markets as well as in high-yield markets has been this expectation of lower forward-looking risk, which means that the price of credit risk can go lower. If expectations are not met, the result will be an increase in volatility and in credit spreads. But we at Banc of America Securities do not think this failure is the most likely scenario. The change in corporate behavior was driven not by corporate managers suddenly discovering that supporting bondholders was in their own best interest but rather by having a gun to the back of their heads while standing on a plank over an ocean full of sharks. In other words, the capital markets withdrew liquidity, and the lenders of last resort provided liquidity at a cost. The cost was a demand for them to change their behavior and deleverage their capital structures. Thus, in our view, downshift in implied volatility is the right measure and credit spreads have tightened appropriately.

Question: Would you add the lower level of interest rates to stock-implied volatilities and stocks' rates of returns as explanatory variables for credit spreads?

Rosenberg: You could, but you'd get the direction wrong. Usually, rates and spreads are inversely related, but in this cycle, the effect has been "double blood pressure." In the Marx Brothers movie "Day at the Races," Dr. Hackenbush (Groucho Marx, impersonating a doctor) tells a patient, Mrs. Upjohn (played by Margaret Dumont), "You have double blood pressure. You have high blood pressure on one side of your body and low blood pressure on the other." Two recent headlines that occurred on the same day are an example of double blood pressure in the financial markets: "Greenspan says inflation not a risk and interest rates rally" and "Greenspan says economy to recover and stock prices rally." Which one is it? Typically, interest rates and equity markets go in opposite directions, but in the recent market rally, they are moving together. A decline in interest rates is usually associated with a weakening economy and, hence, a widening of credit spreads. In this market, the direction has been the opposite. The most important driver of credit spreads has been the stock-price increases. The decrease in volatility and decline in interest rates are a reflection of the Federal Reserve's engineering a recovery by keeping short-term rates extremely low.

A Simplified Alternative to Monte Carlo Simulation

Damian Handzy
Co-Founder, Chairman, and Managing Director
Investor Analytics LLC
New York City

> Monte Carlo simulation techniques provide a powerful analytical tool for modeling problems with complex underlying probability distributions. The technique is often so complex, however, that only the model developer may fully understand the model's implications, resulting in Monte Carlo techniques often being termed "black boxes." An alternative technique may offer results even more robust than Monte Carlo simulation while avoiding many of the hidden assumptions.

The nonlinear properties of options result in them having expected return distributions with fat tails. Thus, they are the quintessential example of why one might use Monte Carlo simulation techniques; they provide the best tool for the particular problem of fat tails. I will discuss a Monte Carlo simulation example using a simple hypothetical portfolio. I will then discuss how the inherent complexities of Monte Carlo techniques often lead to the creation of black-box models. As a result, many of the model's underlying assumptions are known only to those who create the model, not the end users, with the result that end users frequently are not able to make the best possible use of them. To this end, I will suggest an alternative analytical method that is easy to implement yet provides equally robust results.

Options Are Nonlinear

Consider a simple two-part portfolio: The first part consists of $1,000 invested in an S&P 500 Index fund with an assumed average annualized return of 20 percent and an annualized volatility of 24 percent. The one-day Monte Carlo simulation in Panel A of **Figure 1** shows the range of expected prices for the S&P 500. The other part of the portfolio is a short put on IBM Corporation stock. The strike price is $70, and the current share price of IBM stock is $79. Panel B of Figure 1 shows a one-day Monte Carlo simulation for IBM. The correlation between IBM and the S&P 500 is 0.80.

The normal distribution, or normal curve, is one way to look at the expected values of these two securities. The equation for the normal distribution has only two parameters (mean and standard deviation), but it is remarkably powerful in modeling an enormous number of phenomena in fields as diverse as biology, engineering, and finance.

Unfortunately, applying the normal distribution to options valuation is difficult because options have distributions with much fatter tails. A good example is the Black–Scholes option pricing model, which is extremely complicated. In fact, because it is so complicated, people tend not to use it. Instead, they use the delta approximation, in which the value of an option tomorrow is approximated by the value today plus a correction term. To refine it further, one can add the delta gamma correction. Further refinement is possible by adding theta, rho, and vega. But all of these refinements rely on using the same set of equations as the Black–Scholes model, and all use a version of the Gaussian curve:

$$f(x) = \frac{1}{\sigma\sqrt{2\pi}} e^{-\frac{(x-\mu)^2}{2\sigma^2}}.$$

Monte Carlo simulations often involve some use of Gaussian curve mathematics, even if not used explicitly.

No matter what method is used, the goal is to find the relationship between underlying prices and option values. **Figure 2** elaborates on the curve shown for the short put position in Panel B of Figure 1 by relating expected IBM prices to their respective expected option values. IBM's current price is about $80. Clearly, this price is right on the cliff of the option

Figure 1. Expected Value for S&P 500 Long Position and IBM Short Put

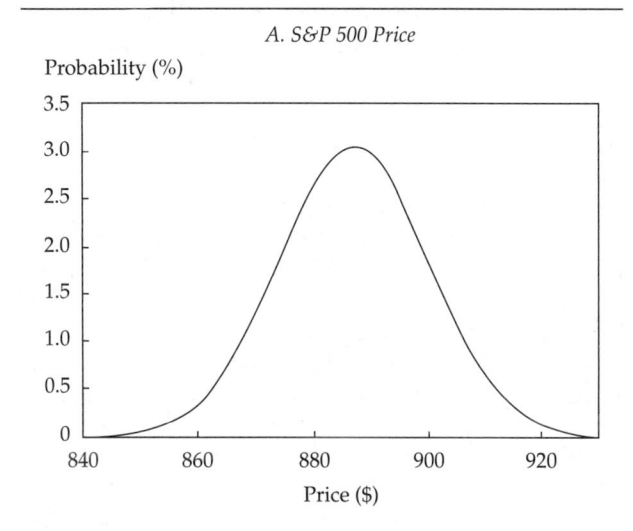

A. S&P 500 Price

B. IBM Stock Price

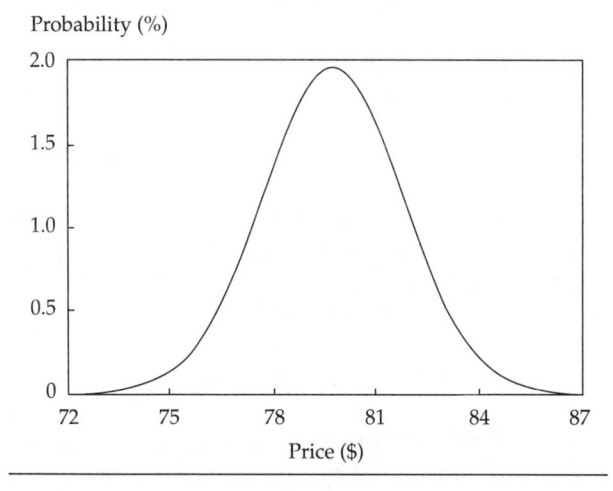

Figure 2. Nonlinear Aspects of Relationship between Price of Underlying Asset (IBM Stock) and Option Value

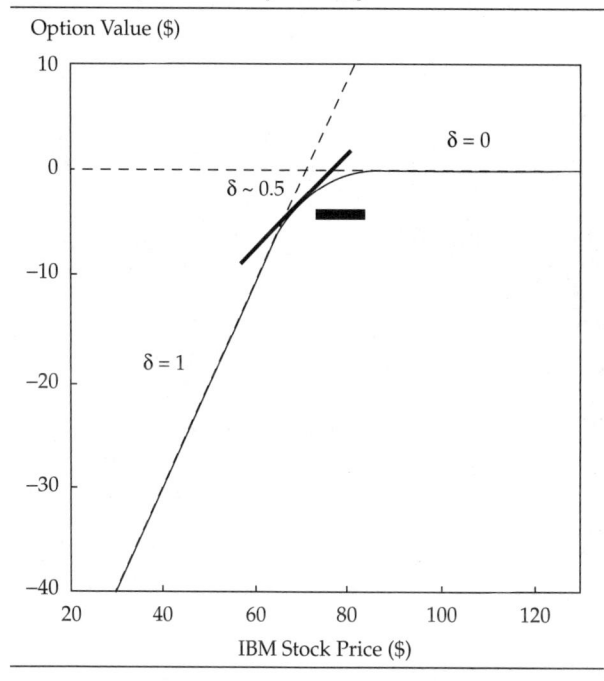

and represents the most likely range of values of the actual IBM price.

The part of the curve near this bar is the focus of **Figure 3**. By combining Figure 1 and Figure 2, Figure 3 helps explain the underlying fat-tail distributions of

Figure 3. Why Options Distributions Have Fat Tails

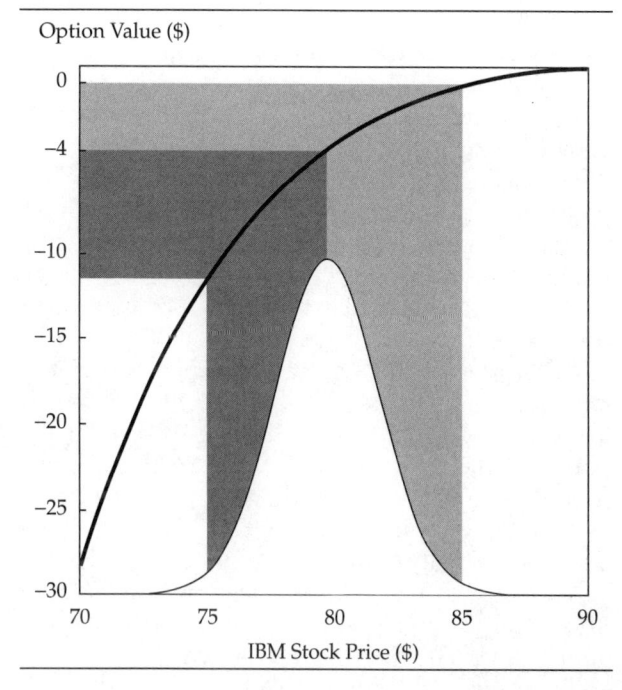

valuation. It is well known that options are nonlinear, and Figure 2 suggests that they are extremely nonlinear but in two different places. If the strike price was $100, the delta value would be near zero and the option value also would be near zero. If the strike price was $40, however, the option value would fall dramatically to around –$30, with a delta approaching 1. The challenge is properly addressing the strike price. Obviously, sudden price changes often lead to severe option value changes. (For example, mergers often cause large quick movements in underlying prices.) In such circumstances, investors often find that they have undergone an abrupt transition and that their approximation of option value is grossly inaccurate. The two examples just described, with deltas of 0 and 1, demonstrate the well-known idea that deltas represent the slope, or the first derivative, of the option valuation curve. The fat solid bar corresponds to the point at which delta equals about 0.5

options. Even if IBM is assumed to have a nice symmetrical shape to its distribution of expected prices, with no fat tails per se, the distribution of option values naturally will have a fat tail. To explain this situation more fully, consider the following illustration using Figure 3. The most likely price of IBM is approximately $80, which means that the most likely value of the option is –$4. At one extreme, as the expected IBM price rises to $85, the expected option value rises very slowly in a compressed fashion, as shown by the light shaded area of the figure between –$4 and zero. At the other extreme, as the expected IBM price declines to $75, the expected option value falls significantly, translating into a much wider band of possible option values, as shown by the dark area between –$11 and –$4. One extreme stock price is as likely as the other, but the lower stock price translates into a much wider area of option values. Clearly, the option value will have a large tail, including more negative numbers. Even if the distribution of the underlying asset is skewed in some way, the option will still be nonlinear and will have a fat tail because of the curved nature of the option valuation line.

Note that if option valuations were linear—for example, at the extremes of the option valuation curve, or where delta equals +1 or 0—the option curve would be a straight line. In this case, the fat-tail problem would not exist for the distribution underlying the option valuation curve.

Applying Monte Carlo Techniques to Options

Monte Carlo simulation techniques handle the problem of nonlinearity and, hence, fat tails. The Monte Carlo method is named for the city famous for its roulette wheels, which were found to be excellent random number generators. At one time, the casinos in Monte Carlo actually published volumes of random numbers for use by mathematicians. Thus, this particular technique is called "Monte Carlo" because it is based on picking random numbers and using the random numbers in further calculations. The Monte Carlo technique is used extensively in finance, engineering, physics, biology, and medicine.

Consider the following example of how to determine the option value probability curve. Step one is to determine the option value for IBM only; the impact of the dynamic price of the S&P 500 on the portfolio comes later. Accordingly, the first step is to pick the option value at random from the underlying asset's expected price distribution. The second step is to compute the option value from the random price. The third step is to remember, or store, the option value. The entire process is then repeated until sufficient iterations are achieved.

Note that picking a number "at random" typically means that any number in the distribution has an equal probability of being chosen. The challenge in our case is: How can one choose a number at random so that $79 is chosen most often and $72 and $87 are chosen rarely? Many mathematical techniques exist for addressing this problem. The simplest one, the brute force method, works regardless of the shape of the distribution. In effect, it is a dartboard approach. The distribution is the dartboard. If a dart lands inside the curve, the number the dart hits is kept. For a dart that lands outside the curve, that throw is ignored. Note that in order to get $75, the dart must hit precisely $75 (not $74.9 or $75.1) so that numbers are selected in proportion to their likelihood according to the distribution. No special importance is attached to using a Gaussian, or normal, distribution. This simple technique can be used with any distribution. Although better methods are available for a normal curve, this simple but inefficient method works.

Now apply this method to the IBM case. The IBM price curve is well represented by a three-sigma curve. In other words, because the IBM stock price is well modeled by a normal distribution, the price falls within plus or minus three standard deviations 99.8 percent of the time. For this short put, the option value should neither fall below –$20 nor rise above zero. Panel A of **Figure 4** shows a thousand-run Monte Carlo simulation. Only once in a thousand runs did the option value selected fall below –$20. Statistically, perhaps such a result should not happen as often as once in a thousand times, but unexpected events do indeed happen. Panel B shows the results for 100,000 runs. Clearly, as the number of simulations increases, the distribution gets smoother; it is approaching a theoretical limit. For 10 million simulations, the distribution would be even smoother.

The next consideration is to perform this analysis for a portfolio of securities—in this case, the S&P 500 index fund and the IBM put option. First, pick the S&P 500 price from its distribution. Then, pick IBM's price from its distribution, and from that price determine the option's value (using the Black–Scholes model or delta or other similar technique). Add the value of the S&P 500 to the value of the option, store the result, and repeat the process. Remember, however, that IBM and the S&P 500 are correlated. Picking a random number from the IBM distribution and a random number from the S&P 500 distribution independently would mean that they had a correlation of zero. Establishing a correlation for two random variables is tricky, but a solution exists.

A simple way to force IBM to be correlated with the S&P 500 is as follows. Assume that the expected prices for the variables are normally distributed, then

Figure 4. Example Monte Carlo Simulations

A. 1,000 Runs

B. 100,000 Runs

Figure 5. Monte Carlo Simulations for Total Portfolio

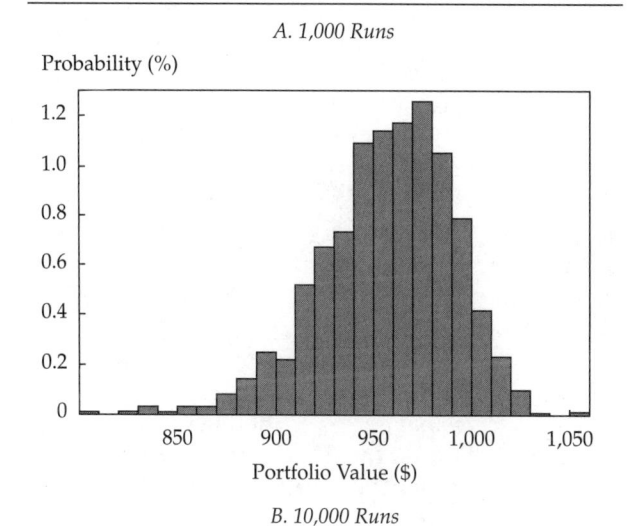

A. 1,000 Runs

B. 10,000 Runs

C. 100,000 Runs

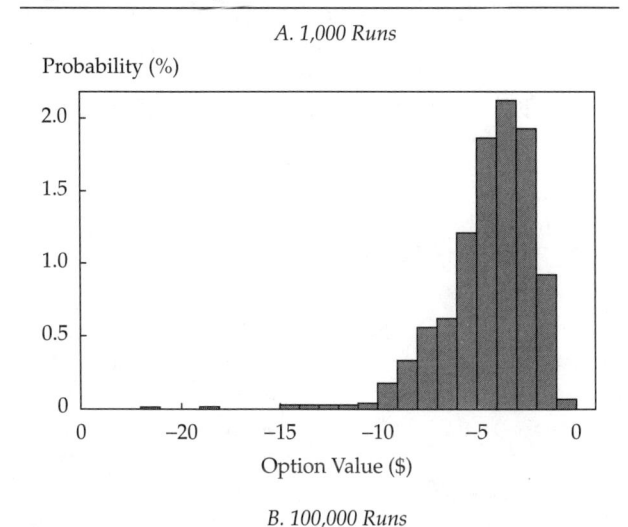

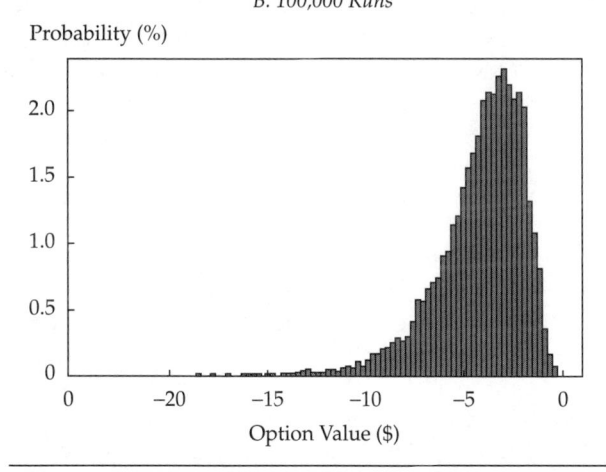

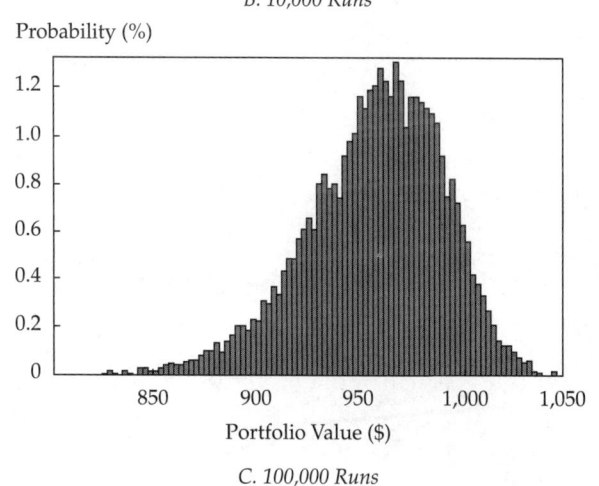

pick each one from its own distribution—x for the S&P 500 and y for IBM. These variables are transformed using a specific methodology into the variables x' and y' in a process called the Cholesky decomposition. For this example, instead of using the selected x and y, one would use x' and y', which are the correlated variables. So, x becomes x'. The S&P 500 price, x, actually does not change in this case ($x = x'$). But the IBM price, y, does change into y' (y' does not equal y) in a way that not only leaves the variables x' and y' representative of their distributions but also has them correlated in the appropriate way (in this case with a correlation of 0.8).

Repeating this process 1,000, 10,000, or 100,000 times, as shown in Panels A, B, and C of **Figure 5**, results in several total portfolio return distributions. In this case, the optionality is explicit. The tail to the right is obviously fatter than the tail to the left. As the simulation is refined (panels A through C), the distributions become less digitized and appear to get increasingly closer to a smooth curve limit.

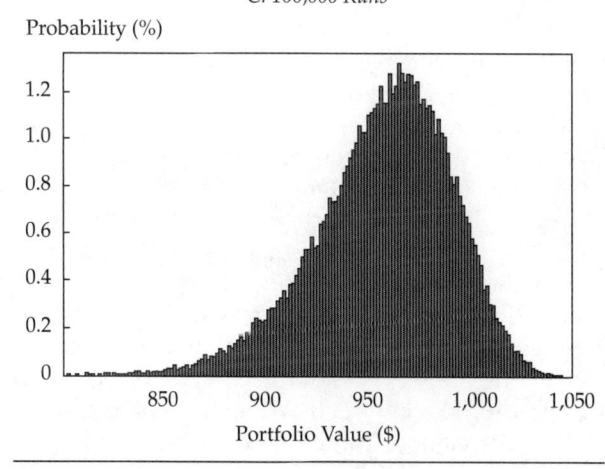

Monte Carlo Assumptions

Many assumptions underpin the Monte Carlo simulation framework, but five are quite important. First, the simulation driver variable(s) must be chosen. In my example, the random variables are the market prices of IBM and the S&P 500. The returns, volatilities, or other factors, although considered important, are not the key drivers in this case.

Second, an assumption about the shape of the distribution is embedded in any Monte Carlo model. In my experience, most Monte Carlo models tend to use the Gaussian, or normal, distribution because it is the simplest one to use and some extremely fast algorithms are available for selecting the random data points. Using any other distribution is more complex. Moreover, as noted previously, the normal curve is already embedded in the Black–Scholes valuation model.

The third assumption involves ensuring the selection of truly random numbers. Many Monte Carlo programs have been written using algorithms that have a little known but extremely significant problem. After selecting a certain quantity of random numbers, the program begins selecting the same numbers again. Thus, the numbers selected are not random. Ensuring the selection of random numbers is a topic beyond the scope of this presentation, but suffice it to say that it is important to have truly random numbers. In choosing how many "runs" to perform, consider that if only a thousand iterations are run, the curves of the distribution will not be smooth, even for simple portfolios. In some cases, millions of iterations are necessary, especially in applications such as credit analysis, for which the tails of distributions are important (i.e., risk numbers beyond 99 percent confidence). Without great care, users can be easily fooled into believing their simulation is much more accurate than it truly is simply because the numbers are not really random.

Fourth, because portfolios contain multiple securities and securities generally are correlated, the issue becomes one of generating *correlated* expected portfolio returns. There are several ways to accomplish this task under the assumption of normally distributed expected returns. One can try using a spreadsheet, in which a simple correlation equation can be found, but because Monte Carlo simulations often involve hundreds of thousands of iterations, spreadsheets are often overwhelmed by the volume of data. Besides using the traditional equation for correlation (which, by the way, assumes a normal or Gaussian distribution), other methods exist. For example, ranked correlations can be used, but the builder of the Monte Carlo simulation must obviously be familiar with this more complex approach. Market data also can be used to establish a correlation relationship between two securities.

Finally, one must determine the number of iterations to run to complete the Monte Carlo simulation. This issue involves the trade-off between the potentially high cost of computer technology versus the number of iterations desired. Examples include users purchasing more than a quarter of a million dollars worth of computer hardware in order to generate millions of simulations overnight. Often, however, many of the simulations are rejected for one reason or another by the simulation engine, resulting in far fewer effective simulation runs.

An Alternative to Monte Carlo Simulation

Typically, one corporate team builds the Monte Carlo simulation and a different team actually uses the simulation. The builders are usually programmers; the users are usually portfolio managers or risk managers. Only the builders know how the simulation actually works; the users know how it ought to work, given their needs. Hence, Monte Carlo engines tend to be black boxes. Users could make much better use of the model if they could see the steps behind the black box.

A notion seems to exist that Monte Carlo engines are better than any other analytical tool. I am often asked whether my firm, Investor Analytics LLC, provides Monte Carlo services as a risk consultancy for all our clients. The answer is no, because Monte Carlo methods are not always appropriate and many other methods offer the same information. Some people find this answer shocking.

As an example, consider the simple two-curve graph discussed earlier in Figure 3. But instead of the IBM stock price driving the option value, consider the option value driving the stock price. Start with an option value of –$7. This value corresponds to an IBM price of about $77. The corresponding probability of this IBM price occurring, as shown in **Table 1**, is about 4.5 percent. **Figure 6** graphically represents the 18 points in Table 1. The panels in **Figure 7** represent the Monte Carlo results for 1,000, 10,000, and 100,000 runs. So, with no more than 18 points, I can generate a result comparable to that of a 100,000-run Monte Carlo simulation.

The analysis for an entire portfolio is more complicated. The first step is to relate S&P 500 values to the corresponding IBM stock-price distribution. With Monte Carlo simulation, if enough numbers are picked at random, the most likely values should be picked in proportion to the least likely values, but this method is extremely time consuming. A much simpler approach involves partitioning, or slicing, the distribution into groups. In this approach, the first step is to choose the likely values of the S&P 500 for a bad day, a mediocre day, and so forth. These values are then used to drive the analysis for the rest of the portfolio. In this case, the rest of the portfolio is IBM. The second step is to relate the corresponding stock-

Table 1. Joint Probability of Certain Option Values and IBM Stock Prices

Probability	IBM Stock Price	Option Value
0.000%	$72.91	–$17
0.028	73.23	–16
0.050	73.56	–15
0.089	73.92	–14
0.157	74.29	–13
0.277	74.68	–12
0.489	75.10	–11
0.862	75.56	–10
1.511	76.05	–9
2.624	76.59	–8
4.484	77.19	–7
7.460	77.87	–6
11.856	78.65	–5
17.397	79.58	–4
22.027	80.74	–3
20.641	82.31	–2
9.440	84.85	–1
0.562	142.20	0

Figure 6. Option Value Probability

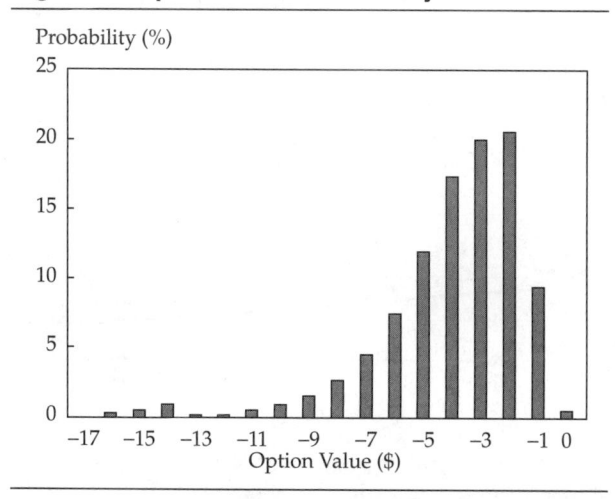

Figure 7. Monte Carlo Simulated Option Values

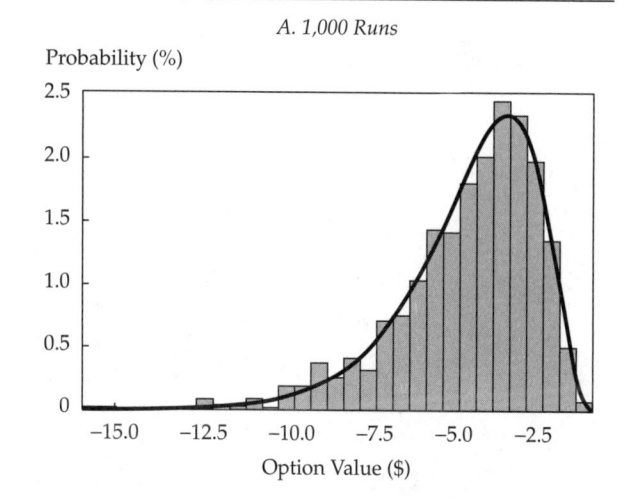

A. 1,000 Runs

B. 10,000 Runs

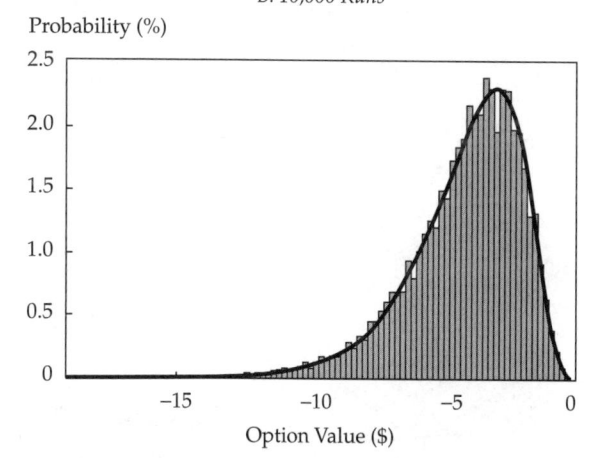

C. 100,000 Runs

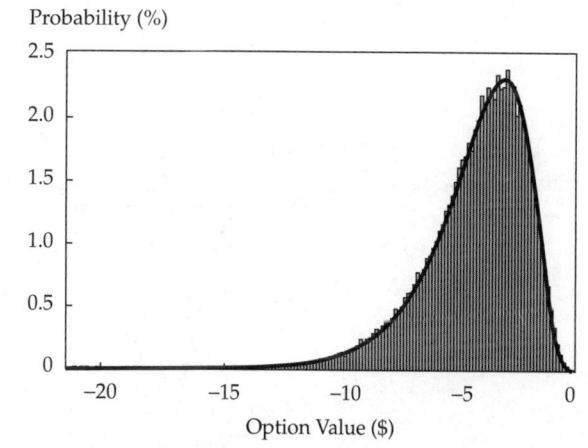

price and option value probabilities. The final step is to create the portfolio probability distribution. In other words, evaluate how combining the option probability curve and the stock-price curve affects the total portfolio curve.

A more sophisticated analysis is to consider all possible paths—that is, what will happen under different circumstances, as shown in the panels of **Figure 8**. First, start with the S&P 500 index fund, as shown in Panel A. Consider what happens to the portfolio as a whole when the S&P 500 price takes on different values. In other words, slice the distribution into several parts (loosely grouped into bad, average, and good days) and then see what happens to the rest of the portfolio. Panel A of Figure 8 shows three slices: bad (around $860), average (about $890), and good (just less than $920). Second (Panel B), determine the *conditional* probability distribution for IBM's price when the S&P 500 has a bad, average, and good day. In other words, what is IBM's probability distribution if the S&P 500 has a bad day? Panel B shows IBM's

Improving the Investment Process through Risk Management

Figure 8. Alternate Analysis for Two-Asset Portfolio: All Possible Paths

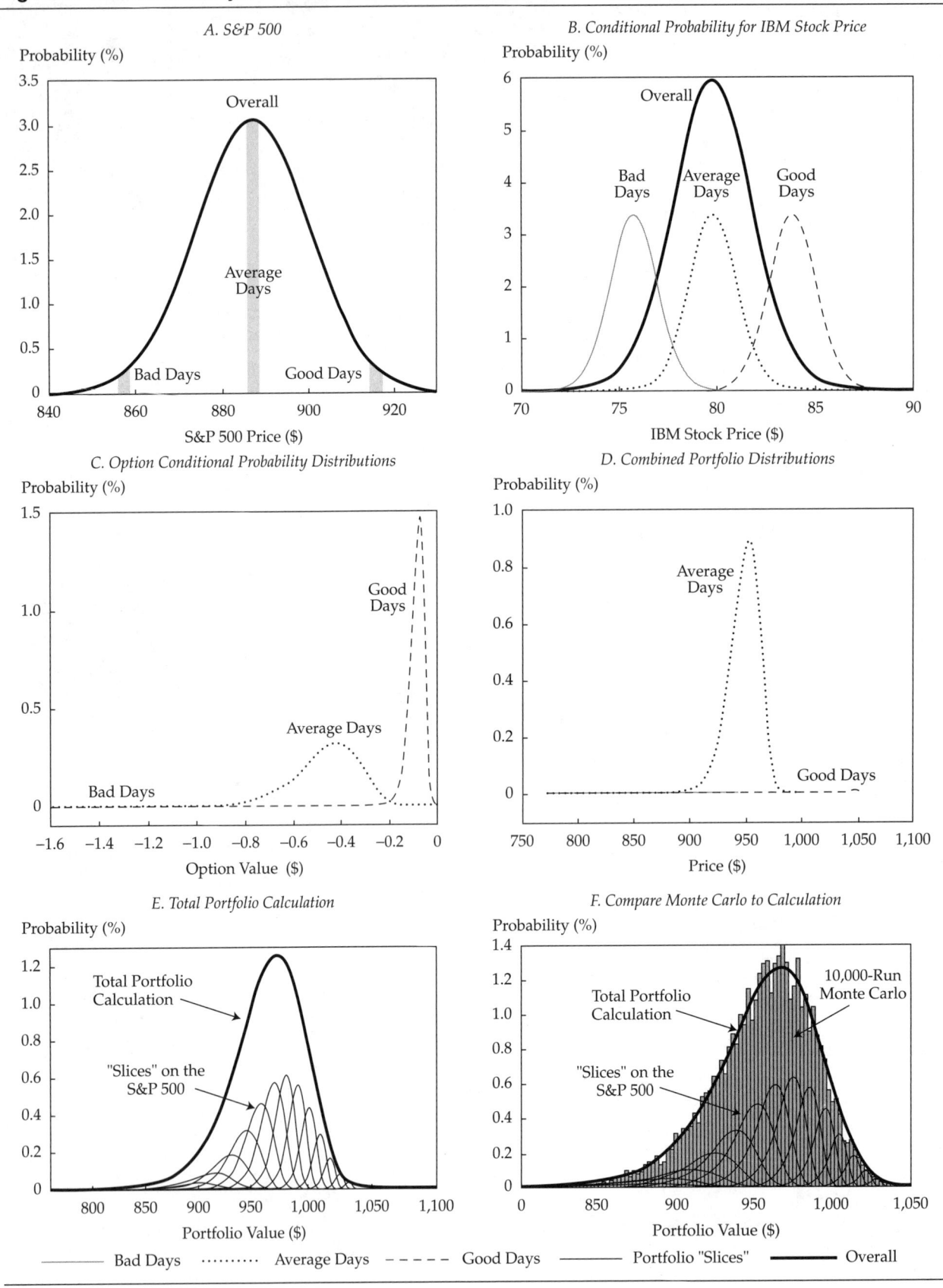

A. S&P 500

B. Conditional Probability for IBM Stock Price

C. Option Conditional Probability Distributions

D. Combined Portfolio Distributions

E. Total Portfolio Calculation

F. Compare Monte Carlo to Calculation

——— Bad Days   ········· Average Days   – – – – Good Days   ——— Portfolio "Slices"   ━━━ Overall total probability curve (large curve shown as the heavy line) corresponding to all possible values regardless of the level of the S&P 500 and three conditional probability curves corresponding to bad days (left curve shown as the light gray line), average days (middle curve shown as the dotted line), and good days (right curve shown as the dashed line). Because the price of IBM is highly correlated with the level of the S&P 500, the third step (Panel C), given the first two steps, is to determine the conditional probability curves of the option (shown in Panel B) by transforming the probabilities of the stock to the option. The results in this case show that the "bad" days do not contribute materially (the option's conditional probability is flat zero) and that the average and good days do contribute, as shown in the graph as the dotted and dashed lines, respectively.

Fourth (Panel D), take the three conditional probability curves for IBM's option and the probabilities for the S&P 500 and combine them into three probability curves for the entire portfolio's value (S&P 500 and option). The curve shown as a dotted line corresponds to the "average" days and the small blip shown as a dashed line corresponds to the "good" days.

The fifth step (Panel E) is to combine all of the portfolio conditional probability curves (as shown in Panel D) into one total portfolio probability curve. In this panel, instead of slicing the S&P 500 into the three hypothetical portions being considered, it is sliced into 20 parts (shown as solid lines), each of which corresponds to one of the smaller curves on Panel E. The large curve (shown as the heavy line) is the total portfolio probability curve, which is the result of combining all the individual curves.

The final panel of Figure 8 (Panel F) compares the Monte Carlo simulations against the results of this calculation method. What it shows is that without using a random number generator or going through hundreds, thousands, or hundreds of thousands of iterations to generate the total portfolio distribution curve, this approach used 18 points from one table and 20 slices of the S&P 500's expected price distribution. An infinite number of Monte Carlo iterations would arrive at the same portfolio distribution.

Summary

Although Monte Carlo techniques have a reputation for great analytical power, they have two significant problems: (1) They involve many embedded assumptions, and (2) they tend to be black boxes because of their complexity and because the users and developers represent distinctly different groups. Consequently, Monte Carlo models are difficult to use and produce results that are not necessarily rigorous.

A simpler analytical solution that can serve the same function as a Monte Carlo simulation is possible. So, why should anyone avoid using a Monte Carlo approach when, after all, in the example used in this presentation, the Monte Carlo solution is arguably easier than the analytical solution? Remember that the example was for a two-instrument portfolio. The Monte Carlo technique gets vastly more complicated when the number of instruments is increased; the analytical solution does not. In addition, the analytical approach can be leveraged for additional information. In my example, "what if" analyses are straightforward. (What happens if the S&P 500 has a bad day? We have the conditional probability curves to address this question.) With the analytical approach, the information for only one part of the portfolio (in my example, the S&P 500 index fund) could be used to generate a theoretical solution for the rest of the portfolio. A similar analysis using the Monte Carlo technique would require additional simulations. Also, most Monte Carlo models do not have the flexibility to zoom in on particular areas, or if they do have the capability, using it means rerunning 1,000, 100,000, 1 million, or 10 million iterations.

In my view, accepting a black-box solution from any computer system, whether the author of the system claims to know Monte Carlo techniques or not, is a mistake. Anyone using Monte Carlo simulations should know how the computer model works, how many assumptions it requires, and so forth.

Question and Answer Session

Damian Handzy

Question: What is the functional form of a distribution that models fat tails better than the "normal" or "Gaussian" distribution?

Handzy: That is the million dollar question. If someone finds an answer, that person will probably win a Nobel prize. The normal distribution is widely used because it is familiar and straightforward. Unfortunately, for different markets and different asset classes over the past 20 years, the tails of the return distributions have been fat, not of the functional form e^{-x^2}, which is the quickly sloping normal curve. The most common fat-tail distribution functional form that's being examined is x^{-3}, which is showing a lot of promise.

A quite readable article in the 15 May 2003 issue of *Nature* provides a very simple model for stock return and trade volume distributions.[1] Based on some simple assumptions, the researchers were able to recreate some broad class return distributions, specifically in the tail region.

Question: The non-Monte Carlo approach works for non-path-dependant options, but what if no closed-form solution exists, as with mortgage-backed securities?

[1] Xavier Gabaix, Parameswaran Gopikrishnan, Vasiliki Plerou, and H. Eugene Stanley, "A Theory of Power-Law Distributions in Financial Market Fluctuations," *Nature* (15 May 2003):267–270.

Handzy: You are absolutely correct, and I do not mean to suggest that my alternative method can replace Monte Carlo simulations for all uses. Monte Carlo techniques certainly have a place. My point is that Monte Carlo methods are used far more often than is necessary and that using them is often inappropriate. It is like using an elephant gun on something less than an elephant. For non-closed-form problems that do not have a good theoretical underpinning—and path dependency is definitely one of those things—Monte Carlo or binary tree simulations are a valuable and completely appropriate tool.

Question: How well does your alternative technique work with a portfolio of 100–200 bonds with embedded path-dependant options?

Handzy: As long as you know the relationship between the underlying asset and the option, you can use the technique I described because you do not need an equation to follow. You simply need a few points. In my example, I used 18 points. I also did not invoke Black–Scholes, except to generate the points. I could have easily used real market numbers instead.

Question: Can your non-Monte Carlo modeling approach incorporate dependencies among three or more assets that aren't embodied in correlations?

Handzy: You can always measure a correlation between dependant assets. The value may be zero, but there will be some correlations between them. When we tested the method to see if it actually works, we did not do it on a trivial two-instrument portfolio. The leap from two to three instruments is huge, but it can be done, and it actually turns out to be less of a problem than we originally thought.

Question: How do you know the complete probability distribution for IBM stock, and how do you know your option formula handles all cases?

Handzy: I don't have such complete knowledge. Assumptions are necessary. IBM presumably has an expected return or expected value distribution. You can use any distribution you want, whether Gaussian or not. Again, the proposed method does not rely on any assumptions of normality or of any particular pricing model. We used 18 points of a price curve to generate these results. Those 18 points can be produced any which way you like.

Question: Can you recommend a book or article that is an introduction to your analytical method?

Handzy: Phillip Zecher, my colleague and co-creator of our analytical method, and I are preparing several forthcoming articles.

U.S. POSTAL SERVICE
STATEMENT OF OWNERSHIP, MANAGEMENT, AND CIRCULATION
(Required by 39 U.S.C. 3685)

1. Title of Publication: *AIMR Conference Proceedings*
2. Publication No.: 013-739
3. Filing Date: October 18, 2003
4. Issue Frequency: Seven Times a Year
5. Number of Issues Published Annually: 7
6. Annual Subscription Price: US$100
7. Complete Mailing Address of Known Office of Publication (Street, City, County, State, and Zip+4) (Not Printer)
    Association for Investment Management and Research
    P.O. Box 3668, Charlottesville, VA 22903-0668
8. Complete Mailing Address of Headquarters or General Business Office of Publisher (Not Printer)
    Association for Investment Management and Research
    P.O. Box 3668, Charlottesville, VA 22903-0668
9. Full Names and Complete Mailing Addresses of Publisher, Editor, and Managing Editor (Do Not Leave Blank)
    Publisher (Name and Complete Mailing Address)
        AIMR, P.O. Box 3668, Charlottesville, VA 22903-0668
    Editor (Name and Complete Mailing Address)
        Kathryn D. Jost, AIMR, P.O. Box 3668, Charlottesville, VA 22903-0668
    Managing Editor (Name and Complete Mailing Address)
        Jaynee M. Dudley, AIMR, P.O. Box 3668, Charlottesville, VA 22903-0668
10. Owner (If owned by a corporation, its name and address must be stated and also immediately thereafter the names and addresses of stockholders owning or holding 1 percent or more of the total amount of stock. If not owned by a corporation, the names and addresses of the individual owners must be given. If owned by a partnership or other unincorporated firm, its name and address as well as that of each individual must be given. If the publication is published by a nonprofit organization, its name and address must be given.) (Do Not Leave Blank)
    Association for Investment Management and Research, P.O. Box 3668, 560 Ray C. Hunt Drive, Charlottesville, VA 22903-0668
11. Known Bondholders, Mortgagees, and Other Security Holders Owning or Holding 1 Percent or More of Total Amount of Bonds, Mortgages or Other Securities. If none, check here. ✔ None.
12. For completion by nonprofit organization authorized to mail at special rates. The purpose, function, and nonprofit status of the organization and the exempt status for Federal income tax purposes: (Check one.)

    ✔ Has Not Changed During Preceding 12 Months   Has Changed During Preceding 12 Months (If changed, publisher must submit explanation of change with this statement.)

13. Publication Name: *AIMR Conference Proceedings*
14. Issue Date for Circulation Data Below: September 2003

15. Extent and Nature of Circulation	Average No. Copies Each Issue During Preceding 12 Months	Actual No. of Copies of Single Issue Published Nearest to Filing Date
a. Total No. Copies (Net Press Run)	36,274	2,200
b. Paid and/or Requested Circulation		
1. Sales Through Dealers and Carriers, Street Vendors, and Counter Sales		
2. Paid or Requested Mail Subscriptions	30,778	0
c. Total Paid and/or Requested Circulation (sum of 15b(1) and 15b(2))	30,778	0
d. Free Distribution by Mail, Samples, Complimentary, and Other Free		
e. Free Distribution Outside the Mail	200	200
f. Total Distribution (sum of 15d and 15e)	200	200
g. Total Distribution (sum of 15c and 15f)	30,978	200
h. Copies Not Distributed		
1. Office Use, Leftovers, Spoiled	5,296	2,000
2. Returns from News Agents		
i. Total (sum of 15g, 15h(1), and 15h(2))	36,274	2,200
Percent Paid and/or Requested Circulation (15c/15g × 100)	99	

16. This Statement of Ownership will be printed in the 2003, no. 4 issue of this publication.
17. I certify that all information furnished on this form is true and complete. I understand that anyone who furnishes false or misleading information on this form or who omits material or information requested on the form may be subject to criminal sanctions (including fines and imprisonment) and/or civil sanctions (including multiple damages and civil penalties).

Signature and Title of Editor, Publisher, Business Manager, or Owner
Jaynee Dudley, Publisher

INVEST in YOURSELF

AIMR's Professional Development Program

- Hundreds of educational opportunities in convenient learning formats
- PD Diary keeps track of your educational activities online
- Self-tests available for selected AIMR publications
- Protects your most important asset — yourself

In your business, you know that learning doesn't end when you earn the CFA charter or an MBA... learning is a career-long commitment that guides you through an ever-changing profession.

Take the time to invest in yourself. Find out more at **www.aimr.org/pdprogram**.

AIMR PD
QUALIFIED ACTIVITY

Institutional Investor

AIMR
Setting a Higher Standard for Investment Professionals Worldwide™

INTRODUCING THE NEW PLUS PACKAGES
FROM INSTITUTIONAL INVESTOR AND AIMR

II and AIMR are pleased to announce the following suite of packages for AIMR members. The "Plus Packages" allow AIMR members to purchase these products at a specially negotiated rate, exclusively for AIMR members.

Fixed-Income Plus

▶ *The Journal of Fixed Income* and *The Journal of Portfolio Management*

Equity Plus

▶ *The Journal of Private Equity* and *The Journal of Portfolio Management*

Hedge Funds Plus

▶ *The Journal of Alternative Investments* and *The Journal of Portfolio Management*

Wealth Management Plus

▶ *The Journal of Wealth Management* and *The Journal of Portfolio Management* and *Integrated Wealth Management: The New Direction for Portfolio Managers*

SER Plus

▶ *The Journal of Compliance* and *The Journal of Portfolio Management*

Firm Management Plus

▶ *The Journal of Compliance* and *The Journal of Portfolio Management*

To subscribe to any of the products in the Plus Packages please visit **www.aimr.org/memservices/plus**. More information is available at this link or you may contact Institutional Investor at 212-224-3173.

AIMR Education Central

Strengthening the profession. Enhancing your career.

AIMR Education Central is your connection to the latest developments in investment management.

A Topic for Every Investment Professional

At Education Central, you'll find offerings in the following categories:

- Equity
- Fixed Income
- Private Wealth
- Hedge Funds
- Firm Management
- Standards, Ethics, and Regulation

A Program for Every Learning Style

How you want to learn is up to you. You can choose to attend a conference, view a webcast from your computer, or read a print copy or online version of an AIMR publication.

Visit **www.aimr.org/featuring/ed_central** to browse current and archived content arranged by topic and to register for, subscribe to, or purchase educational offerings.